J. Abbink (ed.)

Fractures and Reconnections: Civic Action and the Redefinition of African Political and Economic Spaces

A publication of the
African Studies Centre
(Leiden, The Netherlands)

LIT

Fractures and Reconnections: Civic Action and the Redefinition of African Political and Economic Spaces

Studies in Honor of Piet J.J. Konings

edited by

J. Abbink

LIT

Cover Picture: Cameroon's contested 'Monument of Reunification',
on Ngoa-Ekelle hill in the capital Yaoundé
Courtesy of: http://files.cameroonwebnews.com

∞

Gedruckt auf alterungsbeständigem Werkdruckpapier entsprechend
ANSI Z3948 DIN ISO 9706

Bibliographic information published by the Deutsche Nationalbibliothek
The Deutsche Nationalbibliothek lists this publication in the Deutsche Nationalbibliografie; detailed bibliographic data are available in the Internet at http://dnb.d-nb.de.

ISBN 978-3-643-90256-6

A catalogue record for this book is available from the British Library

Klosbachstr. 107
CH-8032 Zürich
Tel. +41 (0) 44-251 75 05
Fax +41 (0) 44-251 75 06
e-Mail: zuerich@lit-verlag.ch
http://www.lit-verlag.ch

LIT VERLAG Dr. W. Hopf
Berlin 2012
Fresnostr. 2
D-48159 Münster
Tel. +49 (0) 2 51-620 320
Fax +49 (0) 2 51-23 19 72
e-Mail: lit@lit-verlag.de
http://www.lit-verlag.de

Distribution:
In Germany: LIT Verlag Fresnostr. 2, D-48159 Münster
Tel. +49 (0) 2 51-620 32 22, Fax +49 (0) 2 51-922 60 99, e-mail: vertrieb@lit-verlag.de

In Austria: Medienlogistik Pichler-ÖBZ, e-mail: mlo@medien-logistik.at

In Switzerland: B + M Buch- und Medienvertrieb, e-mail: order@buch-medien.ch

In the UK: Global Book Marketing, e-mail: mo@centralbooks.com

In North America: International Specialized Book Services, e-mail: orders@isbs.com

Contents

Introduction: Piet Konings's contributions to African Studies

J. Abbink

The book

This book pays tribute to Dr. Piet J.J. Konings and his scholarship in African Studies, highlighting his track record as a researcher producing wide-ranging and often path-breaking contributions to the sociology of African societies. Piet's work, especially during his 30-year career at the African Studies Centre in Leiden, has shown a number of constant themes that currently have a renewed relevance in the study of developing Africa today, such as labour relations, ethnic and identity politics, rapid socioeconomic developments and class formation, and the changing global connections of Africa.

Africa and African Studies today: some notes

In the 2010s Africa has gradually been taking its economic role in the world by becoming a major target of external and domestic economic investments. Africa is the 'last frontier' of global economic development, and with growing populations and market integration worldwide it is prime territory for more international competition, fuelled by the rise of 'new' players like India, China, Malaysia, South Korea, Saudi Arabia or Brazil. Not only Africa's minerals and oil are in demand but also land, an allegedly under-used and widely available natural resource in many countries on the continent. It is leased in huge chunks for commercial land investments either by foreign parties and members of the state elites or the emerging domestic business classes, often under weak preconditions and bypassing existing social and agro-ecological contexts. Economic growth figures in many Sub-Saharan African countries since the global downturn in 2008 have remained among the highest in the world, albeit primarily on the basis of growing exports of oil and raw materials, continued donor aid flows, or migrant communities' remittances, and still little based on autonomous industrial, productive growth. There are also expanding middle classes with more money to spend, fuelling domestic markets as well as imports and developing new consumptive and socio-cultural profiles, gradually moving away from poverty and 'tradition'. The high speed of ICT expansion via cell phone telephony and information media in general is one major indication of this, impacting in a 'feedback loop' on the nature and levels of economic growth.

However, the impact of these material and geo-political processes on socio-political and civic spheres, i.e. the way in which they reshape the civic spaces and social organizational forms of African citizens, is not without problems. If only to pursue the subject of the ICT revolution: some state authorities purposely slow down the rates of growth of Internet use, cell phone use, etc. below technical and economic capacity, and do this for reasons of political and economic control. Especially countries like Rwanda, Ethiopia and Eritrea are always mentioned as notably restrictive, thereby subverting socio-economic dynamics and the civic order. They seem to be creating new ultra-surveillance states that intimidate citizens and aim to prescribe (and proscribe) their behaviour and access to information in detail. In these countries, for instance, there is only one Internet provider (the state).

In general, rapid change is challenging the position, identity and agency of social actors, groups and institutions in Africa, and politico-economic elites are exerting themselves to confirm their dominant position, and to inventively adapt and neutralize challenges to their power, notably from younger and better educated generations, opposition political parties or from labour organizations, which have remained relatively weak throughout the continent.

The economic upsurge in Africa has thus been proceeding despite the persistence of autocratic regimes, deep social inequalities and significant class differences, and without solutions to border disputes and ongoing ethnic and religiously inspired conflicts. Examples again are not difficult to mention: among the politically divided countries experiencing severe internal conflict we have the DR Congo, Chad, Mali, Sudan and South Sudan, Nigeria, and the Central African Republic. Among the strongly autocratic surveillance states we have, e.g., Eritrea, Rwanda, Angola, Equatorial Guinea, Sudan, and Ethiopia. And in many countries, also among the more democratic ones like Ghana, Zambia, Tanzania, or Kenya, corruption and bribing have permeated public life, inhibiting economic progress, environmental governance as well as secure public law, independent justice or equal opportunity structures. Ethno-regionalist resistance or secessionist revolts are still in progress in Senegal (Casamance), Ethiopia (Ogaden, Gambela, parts of Oromiya), Uganda, Chad (North vs. South), Sudan (Darfur, Nuba Mountains),

Mali (divided in two since early 2012) and Angola (Cabinda). Few of these conflicts show signs of a negotiated solution, reflecting the still highly problematic political-juridical order in many parts of Africa. This situation will also inhibit equitable growth and redistributive effects when not addressed in national policy and international relations.

A crucial issue for social research in Africa in the coming years will therefore be if and how new political orders and inclusive policies will be developed or negotiated that meet the socio-political demands, new aspirations and changing consumptive habits of ordinary Africans. It is likely that rising economic activities, higher overall incomes and a gradual reduction in poverty in many areas will evoke social and political responses that will translate into new forms of civic action, demands for representation, and contestation. This not primarily applies to (local) NGOs that are usually 'donor darlings' and often embedded in a discourse of international cooperation and project implementation, but also – if not more – to resistance and autonomy movements that make clear claims for change in the socio-political order (see Konings' book of 2009 on 'neoliberal bandwagonism'). And even in areas marred by internal contradictions and violent conflict this rising tide of political claim-making will be exerting pressure, as economic and media developments will produce countervailing forces in society. In this process, the powers-that-be will try (and are already trying) to further co-opt and incorporate the emerging new social groups and forces by all means into the existing power structures, so as to neutralize the challenges to their (often minority-based) power. These processes are most evident in, for instance, Cameroon, Ethiopia, Rwanda, Sudan or Angola, dominated by long-established, power-monopolizing parties, but are also visible in countries with nominal democratic structures and periodic 'free and fair' elections, such as Kenya, Nigeria, or Mozambique.

In all these contexts, studies focused on changing and emerging forms of civic and political action of the masses of African citizens will be most fascinating and profitable to carry out. As in the early 1990s, when Africans were in the forefront of the wave of global demands for democratization and political liberalization, there will likely be a continued groundswell of pressure towards inclusive economic development and equitable distribution – processes far from guaranteed in the context of the competitive global economy of today which allows incumbent elites a big advantage. Key issues in the comparative study of these issues will be, among others, institutional development, the determination and juridical entrenchment of property rights, land tenure and access to land, and the definition of statutory vs. customary law regarding land and resource issues, set in contexts of contestation and counter-politics. In a broader sociological sense, the issues of youth action, generational change, resistance and rebellion, and also class formation and labour relations, will probably also make a more emphatic come-back (if they ever have been away).

Beyond the more immediate level of economic and political developments, one has to look also at their constitutive interconnectedness with social and cultural repertoires as well as historical continuities that partly condition and constrain these very developments.

The work of Piet Konings

These subjects and more are prominent in the work of Piet Konings, who during a distinguished research career at the African Studies Centre in Leiden (1978-2008) has produced a remarkable corpus of empirical and comparative studies, notably on Ghana and Cameroon. Especially on the latter country he is one of the foremost authorities, and many of his publications are based on carefully executed field research in these countries.

This volume in his honour, belatedly marking his official retirement from the ASC in 2008, contains fresh studies that address various forms of contemporary civic action in the political, economic and social domain in African societies. The book directly or indirectly addresses many of the key themes that were treated by Piet Konings in his own work in the past three decades. Piet called himself a sociologist of development, but he is so in a wide, inter-disciplinary sense because he interpreted 'development' in a comprehensive socio-cultural sense and also made forays in history, anthropology and religious studies, based on a versatile methodological mix of archival study, interviews, participant observation, and the analysis of documents and mass media products. No doubt his background in philosophy and theological studies has contributed to his wider perspective. In fact, he started his career as a lecturer in religious studies at the University of Ghana in Legon-Accra in the years 1969 to 1972.

Although editor of this book I do not claim to be an authority on Piet's work or give an in-depth analysis of it but simply want to underline his significant achievements in Africanist scholarship, more than can be evaluated here, and thereby express the general feelings of deep collegial appreciation and friendship that exist among most of those who know him.

The study of Africa is best advanced by those who maintain high scholarly standards, seek innovative perspectives and subjects, and – not in the least – develop a commitment to the subject, i.e., to Africans and their predicaments and achievements in a globalizing world. Piet Konings has shown evidence of all of this, and over a long period has produced a consistent flow of works that have made their mark in the field of African studies. In conjunction with his many contributions to the study of Ghana and Cameroon he worked on important themes like African development and 'neo-liberalism', trade union activities, labour relations, educational systems and policies, political history, ethno-regionalism and federalism, religious phenomena, and last but not least to civil society and civic action in Africa. His bibliography to date, which is included as an appendix in this volume, testifies to the scope and variety of this work. His titles range from solid socio-economic studies and detailed political analyses to contributions that are more ethnographic or urban-sociological in nature. One of his most fascinating papers in my opinion is his 2006 study of the young 'bendskin' (motorbike taxi) drivers in Douala, Cameroon, while among his most important books is surely his study *The Politics of Neoliberal Reforms in Africa* (2001), presenting many of his previous research results in a broad-ranging synthesis.

Despite the many subjects that Piet has treated, there is an underlying unity of focus and method, inspired by questions of how Africans, in their social and historical situatedness, meet the constant and often very basic challenges of survival and insecurity, achieve agency in social life and try to take charge of their own lives via civic and political action in often very difficult socio-economic circumstances. Piet's work is also geared by a deep humanistic concern and shows an understanding of the issues at hand which is not abstract and unduly generalizing, but based on long-term, carefully performed fieldwork of great quality, and on respect for Africans and the way they face these manifold challenges. His track record and the above-mentioned wide range of his studies on Africa deserve admiration, and many of his publications have inspired the contributors to the present volume. Piet's high reputation in African studies is recognized in many places, and notably in Cameroon and Ghana, even among the powers-that-be on which he wrote critically. His personal relations with Africa and Africans were cordial and collegial, in fieldwork as well as in academic meetings and contacts. His academic standing is also shown in the significant number of co-authored works that he produced, as well as in the tireless efforts he has made to stimulate and supervise (often de facto as main supervisor) African PhD students, many of whom received their doctoral degree in the Netherlands.

As noted above, Piet Konings always called himself a sociologist of development, and his first work was on labour relations, trade unions and developmental issues in Africa. His 1977 doctoral dissertation at the University of Tilburg in the Netherlands was an historical-sociological study on the relation of Ghanaian trade unions and governmental development strategies from 1874 to 1976. This was followed by many other papers on labour relations and labour protests – a subject much in vogue in the political and academic climate of the 1970s. He was then working at the Institute of Social Studies in The Hague (1974) and the University of Brabant (Tilburg) from 1975 to 1978, and in this period he also did a number of reports for the Ministry of Development Cooperation on projects in Ghana. In the 1980s he published a number of studies in social science journals on Ghana's rural society, revolutionary development, and the role of miners, before moving gradually to research on Cameroon in his new job at the African Studies Centre in Leiden. Since 1986 Piet has predominantly published on Cameroon.

As we saw, he has subsequently covered more and more themes in his study of Cameroon society, but not without losing the underlying sense of focus on how people, in their specific circumstances and historical conditions, have strived to take charge of their own lives in contexts of insecurity and state unpredictability, and in surviving and developing in a multidimensional (not only economic) way.

A quick survey of his work since his dissertation of 1977 shows that despite his moving into these other fields Piet has always remained loyal to the study of labour issues, because this often provided a way to get an understanding of wider political problems and of questions of insiders-outsiders in the socio-political domain. This focus on labour relations and has remained evident in his more recent monographs (1988, 1993, 1995 and 1998) on agro-industry, labour resistance, and the Unilever and tea estates in Cameroon.

In his paper of 1996 in the *Journal of Commonwealth and Comparative Politics* Piet focused for the first time on the emerging Anglophone Cameroonian opposition movement, as linked to the privatisation of agro-industrial para-statals. The history and development of the 'Anglophone problem' in Cameroon became a theme richly elaborated in his subsequent work, and yielded authoritative studies. In the years following Piet has thus intensively studied identity politics and the 'allochthone-autochthone' debates in Cameroon, resulting in important books (one with Francis Nyamnjoh in 2003, his monograph of 2009, and many papers and chapters). He also addressed educational issues, developments in the urban transport sector, church-state relations, political parties, and the nature and impact of neo-liberal reform policies. Last but not least, at the African Studies Centre he pioneered the first studies (in 2007) by staff on the (re)emerging relations between China and Africa.

Next to his own academic research, publishing and student supervision, Piet Konings was active in a number of editorial boards, among them at Langaa Publishers in Cameroon and with various Cameroonian social science journals, as well as those of the journals *Africa Development* and *Labor History* and of various book series at Brill Publishers, e.g., African Dynamics.

Another aspect of Piet's career that deserves mentioning is his very frequent advisory work for lawyers, refugee support groups, NGOs and other civil society organizations, e.g., assisting in cases of African asylum seekers in the Netherlands and abroad. He rarely said no to any of these requests and has over the years been of great assistance to numerous people. Many of such community activities were not visible to the wider public.

The chapters ahead

In what follows we see the various themes of Piet work taken up in studies by his former close colleagues, co-authors, and former PhD students co-supervised by him.

Peter Geschiere in his chapter on contends that Piet's consistent focus on labour throughout his academic career enabled him to relate to widely different other aspects of society: to the broader economic context but also to politics, gender relations and religious organization, as well as to struggles over autochthony and citizenship in the South-West Province of Cameroon, where Piet has done major work. The specific labour relations that developed in this area since colonial times have proved to be a crucial factor for understanding the recent explosion of 'autochthony' claims in the region, and this regional trajectory was also to play a key role in national politics, enabling long-incumbent President Paul Biya's (former) one-party (in power since 1982) to maintain its grip over the country despite mounting democratization pressures since the early 1990s. Geschiere follows Konings' approach in focusing on two critical moments in the region's history that showed the interactions between labour relations and tensions over belonging and citizenship: the role of British colonial Nigeria governor Lord Lugard around 1920 in imposing a labour regime on the plantations in the Southwest Cameroonian region (assigned to Britain after WW II) that seemed to his staff and to go against the very principle of British colonial rule, as it condoned some form of forced labour inherited from the German system. A second feature was the introduction by the British (in S.W. Cameroon) of a 'one man, one vote'-based democracy around the 1960 independence period, which created confusion and havoc created in the area (due to its formally extending council representation to newcomers, 'strangers'). The discussion is related to the rising issue of identity politics, of 'autochthons' vs. 'strangers' in today's Cameroon, set against the introduction of the notion of autochthony in Africa by French colonials shortly after

1900, which helps to understand how this notion could become so central in later struggles over labour and citizenship.

Deborah F. Bryceson elaborates on the labour issue – but not in Cameroon – with an insightful discussion on *ganyu* labour, a longstanding form of ad hoc casualized rural labour that came to the fore in recent years in Malawi as the major coping mechanism for the rural poor to combat food insecurity. She explores *ganyu* in the light of long-term trends in the country's local rural economies and the shocks of famine and the HIV/AIDS pandemic experienced at the outset of the 21st century. She argues that *ganyu* evolved from 'balanced' to 'negative reciprocity' over the past hundred years. During Malawi's 2001-02 famine, with many rural families adversely affected and victimized – either directly or indirectly – by HIV/AIDS, *ganyu* labour increasingly altered in character in terms of the growing inequalities of rural asset holdings, labour exchange negotiated under extreme duress, growing labour negotiations between members of the famine-affected rural areas with non-kin from outside of the local community, a diminishing ethical foundation to labour contractual terms and, in the case of women, sometimes the necessity of accepting morally degrading sexual compromises for the sake of securing vital food supplies or cash.

Ineke van Kessel in her chapter presents labour migration as a defining feature of Ghana's history over many centuries. In popular memory and in the academic literature, the Atlantic slave trade is the most prominent example of labour migrations from West Africa. In recent decades, large numbers of Ghanaian migrants have fanned out to Europe, the United States and the Middle East. Less known is an episode in between the age of the slave trade and the contemporary period of voluntary migration. After the abolition of the slave trade, indentured labour became the preferred method of meeting global labour demands. The terminology of indentured labour is usually associated with Asia and the Americas, but certain recruiting practices used in 19th century West Africa fall into the same category. One example is the recruitment of West African soldiers for the Dutch colonial army in the Netherlands East Indies, whose story was the subject of her book *Zwarte Hollanders* (Black Dutchmen), published in 2005. While the book focuses on the history of these more than 3,000 West African men and their Indo-African descendants, in her contribution to the present book Van Kessel interrogates her research material from a fresh perspective, and inspired by the work of Piet Konings she analyses the recruitment of these African troops for the Dutch colonial army from the vantage point of labour studies.

Robert Akoko describes a new category of young Cameroonians that specialize in providing 'traditional medicine' to make a living and often rise to great local fame. The emergence of this group of practitioners has occurred against the background of Cameroon's persistent economic crisis during the last two decades, which resulted in much poverty among the ordinary population. Even though conditions were particularly frustrating to the young generation, the paradox is that many of them increasingly devised alternative strategies to survive, and succeeded in earning a living and even to accumulate capital. With revealing examples drawn from the city of Buea and its environs, Akoko examines the exercise of traditional medical practices, a domain which before the coming of the economic crisis was primarily associated with elderly people and most often with inherited (family) skills, but that has recently been embraced by many young people. The study reveals that many youths have not only inventively taken up this activity and are making their own drugs from plants and barks of trees, but have also shown that they accumulate lots of money through it.

In the next chapter Francis Nyamnjoh addresses one of the challenges facing the South African state and higher education institutions: that of reconciling in the curriculum the competing and often conflicting values that in recent history shaped the different legal perspectives and realities of citizens (the free, recognized, represented and entitled minority white population) and subjects (prominent among whom the unfree, invisible, dispossessed, disenfranchised, and bantustanised majority black population) of the apartheid era. Formerly the white minority of apartheid South Africa prescribed and enforced legally only what was good for them and their interests and imposed on the majority black population legal regimes informed by distorted and frozen colonial inventions of African cultures and traditions. Such traditions, invented to suit the ambitions of dominance of colonial and apartheid South Africa, were of course controversial and perhaps explain current preoccupations with taking Africaness and African law seriously. Post-apartheid transformation necessitates curricular reform and is urgent because the newly enfranchised majority black population is critical of continued subjection by inherited unpopular laws of an era that denied them humanity. Only by recognizing the place of all citizens South Africa and its people can come fully into its potential. To take Africaness and African law seriously, Nyamnjoh argues, two important series of questions regarding the societal context should be addressed; one about what 'African identity' is and what it means for specifically people in post-apartheid South Africa; and the second about what it is to be indigenous? To define indigenous peoples simply as those who were there first and are still there, and so have rights to their lands, or even as those particular groups who were left on the margins of development, or whose cultures and ways of life are subject to discrimination, contempt, and threatened, etc. is to invite inquiry about the reality of internal and external migration and the political, cultural, economic, and historical factors that have configured competing articulations of being indigenous. This rich and complex patchwork appeals to a sort of flexible indigeneity, to which South Africa, like neighbouring Botswana, can attest historically. African communities are historically renowned for their mobility and their flexibility in indigeneity – a reality only enhanced by the arbitrary nature of colonial boundaries and dominant neoliberal approaches. The history of South Africa demonstrates flexible modes of belonging that make it difficult to claim identities in essentialist terms. The challenge for the evolving legal system in South Africa is how to embrace these complexities, and have the law curriculum reflect the depths and diversity of experiences of South Africans. This is especially challenging given the tendency for the law to prefer clarity over ambiguity. Nyamnjoh argues it somehow would be good to include in a 'new' law curriculum the variety of cultural understandings of the meaning of human dignity that can be found in the multiple cultural 'traditions' in the South African 'Rainbow Nation'.

Paul N. Nkwi discusses football in Cameroon and its ramifications into ethnic relations and politics with remarkable insider knowledge. Since Cameroon's first participation in the 1982 World Cup, emerging without a defeat, the growth and popularity of football in the country has been exponential. Cameroon was represented at six World Cups since 1982. Although it failed to appear in 2004, its participation in 2010 in South Africa confirmed its standing as a major football nation. Implanted in Cameroon during the colonial period largely through missionary schools, football did not gain importance until the 1970s when Cameroon for the first time organized the African Nations Cup but failed to win it on its own soil. In this essay, Nkwi discusses the origins of the sport in Cameroon and its societal and 'developmental' impact, assessing the national team and its major achievements, the ethnic background of the principal players, the management of football at the political level, the alleged relation between football and sorcery, football as a professional business, and the sport's future in Cameroon. Nkwi argues that the impact created by the 1982 participation in the World Cup, placing Cameroon on the world football map, dragged politicians into the fray to exploit this to the fullest. Caught up in the euphoria of the popularity of the sport, the government has fully exploited a sport animated by players whose genius is largely nurtured in the shanty towns of the big cities rather than by a government policy of providing a quality football infrastructure. Although the football federation moved football into a professional league, the state is still a major player because the teams still rely on the state to provide the basic sport infrastructure. But often it is the money that the state and state officials are interested in which regularly drives players of the national team to openly disagree with football officials who enrich themselves at the expense of players. Embezzlement of funds is notorious. Funds destined for players have often disappeared into the pockets of officials, and all this is to the detriment of establishing a durable training and stadium infrastructure for the sport in Cameroon and of disentangling it from politics.

Basile Ndjio, in his fascinating chapter, pursues a dominant theme from his PhD thesis of 2006: young successful confidence tricksters and transnational swindlers commonly characterized in Cameroon as *feymen*, active since the early 1990s. They have become emblematic figures of African economic adventurers and subversive 'criminal' entrepreneurs who transcend national boundaries and operate both in Africa and the West. Through what the public opinion Cameroon generally refers to as *feymania* – a practice which involves business fraud, financial deception and confidence tricks – many of these formerly disenfranchised urban youths have managed to gain access to wealth from which they were previously excluded by the corrupt and clientelist regime of President Biya. Basile argues that, unlike what some analysts have maintained about criminal or unlawful business practices in Cameroon, the propagation of *feymania*-related activities in this country is less the result of the growing process of criminalization of the Cameroonian state, than the logical consequence of the pervasiveness in this country of what is called 'sagacity spirit' and 'ghetto ethos'. By these expressions, he means a way of life which makes an apology for a culture of resourcefulness and inventiveness, although they promote what are basically unethical values and immoral principles. It is this philosophy of the poor which provides ideological and moral support to young Cameroonians who are involved in the practice of *feymania* and other forms of unlawful activities encouraging the propagation of new modes of African entrepreneurship. Moreover, Ndjio maintains that without the prevalence of this underlying ethos in Cameroon, the practice of *feymania* would not have flourished in the country to the point of now having invaded all spheres of life in Cameroonian society.

Ben Nantang Jua, in one of the best recent analyses of Cameroon's surrealist politics that I know, discusses the perennial problems of this country's 'democratization' process. He contends that the promise of Cameroon's initial transition to democracy in the 1990s, a result of elite pacting at the time, was not consolidated. Instead, it mutated into electoral authoritarianism which allowed for only limited forms of pluralism in civil society and multiparty elections. Though elections under transitional regimes are consistently flawed and manipulated, democratization is still a possible outcome in countries where they have been sufficiently institutionalized. This has not been true in the case of Cameroon, and it is argued by Jua that this is partially attributable to the absence of a stable and numerically viable opposition that can cooperate effectively with 'civil society' and mobilize voters. Not even Cameroon's high linkage with Western hegemonic states, notably France and the United States, has helped to promote democracy. The country's (re)presentation by donors as an 'island of peace' in an unstable region, and thus the need to insulate it from the negative 'neighborhood effect', has posed some policy dilemmas and analytical challenges for power elites that have captured policy making in the two states and effectively consolidated autocracy.

Ibrahim Mouiche pursues the analysis of Cameroon's political system and highlights a few lesser known factors in the process in a very insightful manner. With the restoration of multipartyism at the end of 1990, Cameroon entered an era of political turbulence in the form of so-called 'ghost town' and 'civil disobedience' campaigns that almost brought down President Paul Biya's regime. Biya had consistently rejected the idea of a 'National Sovereign Conference' called for by the opposition forces but finally accepted the 'Tripartite formula' (a 'deal' between government, opposition and civil society), which calmed down the political atmosphere. It was a package deal that would pave the way for an eventual democratic alternation in Cameroon, if only by the acceptance by all parties of the formula of limiting the presidential mandate to two terms. Since then, eleven rounds of elections have been held in Cameroon. In each of them, the Cameroon Peoples' Democratic Movement (CPDM), the former single party, has been the winner. This series of repetitive victories has brought many people to conclude that this is simply 'big man democracy', resulting from the consistent pattern of 'manoeuvring' in favour of the dominant party and its president, supported by all powers made available by the state apparatus. In 2008 the CPDM regime even banned the constitutional clause of the limitation of presidential mandates, thus taking away all the chances of political alternation in Cameroon and thereby, for many Cameroonians, putting the country indefinitely on hold and on the way to an 'anocracy', as often ethnic-based elite groups continue competing with each other and cannot agree on forming an effective coalition or make deals to share power.

Envoi

I am grateful to the African Studies Centre, Leiden, for facilitating work on the preparation and production of this volume. Gratitude is also expressed to the authors for their patience and tolerance of my repeated rounds of editorial remarks and suggestions on the texts gathered here. Their original contributions have made this volume a very readable and stimulating one and I am pleased – albeit somewhat embarrassed due to the significant delay – that this collective effort in honour of Piet Konings and his achievements in African Studies has finally seen the light of day. He is a fine colleague and an exemplary scholar whose work deserves to be read for a long time to come – because of its historical sensitivity, its critical acumen and originality of social analysis, and its committed, human approach. We hope that more inspiring work may flow from Piet's pen, and we wish him and his partner Lenie all the best for the coming years.

The political economy of autochthony: labour migration and citizenship in Southwest Cameroon

Peter Geschiere

One of the strengths of Piet Konings' work is that his consequent focus on labour throughout his academic career enabled him to relate in seminal ways to widely different aspects of society – not only the broader economic context but also to politics, gender relations or religious organizations. In this text I want to link to his growing interest in struggles over autochthony and citizenship in the South-West Province of Cameroon. His historical work showed most convincingly how the specific labour relations that developed in this area since colonial times are crucial for understanding the recent explosion of autochthony in the region. The specifics of this regional trajectory were, moreover, to play a key role in national politics, re-affirming the hold of President Biya's former one-party over the country despite a promising onset of democratization in the early 1990s. In line with Konings' approach I want to focus on two moments in the region's history that were critical to the interaction between labour relations and tensions over belonging and citizenship: firstly, the surprising role of Lord Lugard around 1920 in imposing a labour regime on the region that seemed to his subalterns to go against the very principle of British colonial rule; secondly the first introduction of democracy around Independence (1960) and the havoc created in the area by British insistence on the 'one man, one vote' rule. A first, more general section will deal with the introduction of the notion of autochthony in Africa by French colonials, shortly after 1900, that may help to understand how this notion could become so central in struggles over labour and citizenship.

Introduction

Piet Konings' work is marked by a constant focus on labour. With him, this was never a limitation. On the contrary his work shows in most evocative ways that labour is a theme at the crossroads of crucial aspects of society and history. It made him study relations among workers and their efforts at organizing themselves, but also their relations with their bosses – in practice often the management at the working place –, with politicians at the local or national level, and even broader, workers' position in changing religious or gender contexts.

An important transition in his research career was his move from Ghana to Cameroon.[1] I am not sure whether this was a completely agreeable switch for him personally. In 1987 when we worked together in Buea (SW Cameroon) he seemed overjoyed when we met a Ghanaian teacher on the road. At this occasion Piet solemnly declared that Ghana was his second home country. I doubt whether, even after more than 20 years of fieldwork in Cameroon, he will say the same about this country. Indeed, shortly after Piet's first visit to Cameroon in 1985 things in this country went downhill under the rule of the country's second President Paul Biya, whose regime became ever more marked as an outstanding example of the criminalization of the state in the continent (see Bayart and others 1997). When in 1990, Biya was forced – under direct pressure of his close ally President François Mitterand – to half-heartedly accept the democratisation of the political system, this finally seemed to announce a real *Renouveau* (the President's own favourite notion). However, this soon got bogged down in conflicts over autochthony and the exclusion of 'strangers' that helped the former one-party regime to hang on to power up till this day due to its tactical successes in dividing the opposition. Moreover, it was precisely the Southwest Province, where Piet did his main research, which was to play a key role in the regime's political manipulations. For many years now, observers have predicted that things 'cannot get worse' in the country; yet, the everyday economic and political realities tend to get ever more desperate for the large majority of the population – in sharp contrast to the growth figures of the World Bank for the national economy, especially recently quite optimistic. So, I cannot help wondering whether Piet ever regretted to have made this move to Cameroon – there might, indeed, be a note of nostalgia when he speaks nowadays of Ghana.

Yet, in scientific respect his choice to adopt a new country was most enriching. The move may have been inspired by practical motives – in the early 1980's the African Studies Centre decided to concentrate its research on two countries,

[1] The Center's choice for Cameroon was inspired by Jan Verhoeven, at the time the chairperson of the African Studies Centre, and by promising possibilities for close collaboration with the newly founded Institute of Human Sciences in Cameroon. My contacts at the time with the Ministry of Scientific Research in Cameroon may also have helped in substantiating this collaboration – so maybe I owe an apology to Piet for playing some role in pulling him away from his dear Ghana.

Cameroon and Kenya.[2] But in view of Piet's research interests there were also good analytical reasons for him to go and work in the Southwest Province of Cameroon. This was an area were, ever since the German period (1885-1914), an exceptionally large concentration of migrant workers had developed due to the creation of a large-scale plantation complex on the volcanic slopes of Mt. Cameroon – a situation unique for West Africa. Already under German rule the demand for workers on these plantations became so pressing that draconic measures were deemed necessary to force people from all over the new colony of *Kamerun* to come and work there. Under British rule (1914-1961) and since Independence, the influx continued, so that the local population became a minority in what they saw as their homeland. A consequence was that the workers whom Piet studied were at the very heart of the emerging 'autochthony' conflicts encouraged by the government in its struggle to contain the effects of democratisation and multi-partyism in the 1990s. These *came-no-goes* – as these immigrant workers are called in local Pidgin – came increasingly from the Grassfields in the Northwest Province, the other half of that part of the former British colony that after the plebiscite of 1961 joined the independent state of Cameroon.[3] The position of these workers and the threat they seemed to pose to the local groups (who increasingly came to style themselves as 'autochthons') became crucial in the efforts by the Biya regime to drive a wedge in the precarious unity of the Anglophones. This was all the more important since especially in the early 1990s the most dangerous political opposition seemed to come from these Anglophones.

A recurrent trend in the political developments over the last 20 years has been the regime's success in winning over 'autochthonous' groups.[4] In the crucial presidential elections in 1992, Paul Biya may have 'beaten' the main opposition candidate John Fru Ndi (from the Anglophone Northwest Province) only due to large-scale rigging – at the time many observers concluded that in reality the latter had won – but during the 2006 and 2011 elections hardly any rigging was necessary anymore to give Biya landslide victories over the same Fru Ndi. In the Southwest Province, it were especially the increasingly vociferous Bakweri who profited from this political configuration: to the great jealousy of other

2 The choice for Cameroon was inspired by Jan Verhoeven, at the time the chairperson of the African Studies Centre, and by promising possibilities for close collaboration with the newly founded Institute of Human Sciences in Cameroon. My contacts at the time with the Ministry of Scientific Research in Cameroon may also have helped in substantiating this collaboration.

3 One year earlier, the part of German Kamerun that in 1914 had been occupied by the French had already received independence under the name Cameroun.

4 See Nyamnjoh 1999; Nyamnjoh and Rowlands 1998; and Konings and Nyamnjoh 2003; and for Cameroon in general Geschiere and Nyamnjoh 2000 and Socpa 2003.

'autochthonous' groups – like the neighbouring Douala – the president chose two successive Prime Ministers from among this small group.[5] How directly these political dealings affected relations between immigrant workers and locals in the area is most eloquently illustrated by the famous 'back scratching' speeches by the first of these Bakweri PM's, Peter Mafani Musonge, at his appointment in 1996.

Typically for autochthony discourse, the theme of the speeches was 'gratitude', which Musonge developed in two ways. On the one hand, the Southwest's gratitude to President Biya for appointing their son to this high position; as Musonge put it most graphically: 'President Biya has scratched our back, and we shall certainly scratch the Head of State's back thoroughly when the time comes'.[6] But, on the other hand – and most relevant to our theme – the gratitude the immigrants owed in Musonge's view to the Southwestern autochthons for allowing them to come and live with them. He reminded them '... even if you have a long hand you cannot scratch your own back. You need someone to do it for you... ' The latter phrase was apparently supposed to mean that out of gratitude these immigrants should go along with the political choices of their 'hosts' if they did not want to be treated as 'ungrateful' *came-no-goes*.[7] The message was clear: if the Southwest wanted to retain the unexpected blessing of special access to the summit of the state – a Southwesterner as Prime Minister – not only the locals had to vote for Biya's CPDM, but also their 'guests' had to be forced to do the same, one way or another. These were hardly the kind of future trends we had in mind, when in the

5 The front stage role of the Bakweri group, both in the region and at the national level, is all the more surprising since into the 1980's observers feared for a final eclipse of the group as such. Not only did they seem unable to retain their lands – immigrants succeeding in appropriating, in all sorts of ways, ever more plots – but also Bakweri marriage became a constant worry for the colonizers who noted an increasing tendency among Bakweri women to leave their marriage in order to live in some sort of concubinage with immigrant workers (cf. Ardener 1962). Thus George Courade characterized the group, still in 1982, as beset by *une marginalité volontaire* and *une conduite volonaire à l'échec*. Such older stereotypes suggest that the combination of autochthony and democratization *à la camerounaise* gave, indeed, a powerful boast to Bakweri identity.

6 *Cameroon Post* 12-18 November 1996, p. 1; quoted in Konings & Nyamnjoh 2003: 119; the latter quote also *The Herald* 6-8 June 1997, p. 1 for a remarkable statement by South-West governor Oben Peter Ashu (another SWELA/CPDM diehard) during the campaign for the 1997 elections: 'We are ready to fight to the last man to maintain our son as Prime Minister. This is the time for all South-Westerners to be ready to die or survive ... We have the Prime Minister and what we need now is satisfaction and social amenities ... '

7 *The Herald,* 13-14 December 1996; with thanks to Francis Nyamnjoh.

1970s labour studies were seen as the cutting edge of African studies.[8] Yet, developments in the Southwest Province are certainly not exceptional. They fit in – be it as an especially blatant example – with the 'global conjuncture of belonging' that marks developments all over the world. The current celebration of globalisation as a world wide process often overlooks the fact that this process encourages not only growing cosmopolitanism and ever wider global flows, but also a strong preoccupation with cultural difference and the stressing of boundaries, whether old or new. Indeed, recently many authors highlighted – be it in different terms – the 'global conjuncture of belonging' as some sort of flip side to globalisation.[9]

Viewed in this broader context, the developments in Southwest Cameroon pose a challenge that might be crucial to labour studies in general: how to deal with processes which do not contribute to a further crystallization of class contradictions, but on the contrary seem to overlay them with communal oppositions of a quite different purport? Piet Konings' books and articles from the 1990s on the vicissitudes of labour relations on various plantations in Southwest Cameroon deal with this challenge in very concrete and insightful ways. Thus his detailed overview of the origins of the workers on the plantations in the Mt. Cameroon area – from British times to the present – indicates the highly changing origins of the plantation workers (Konings 1993). The present-day autochthony discourse in the area may suggest that the opposition between the locals and the *came-no-goes* from the Northwestern Grassfields is self-evident and even 'traditional.' Yet, Konings' research shows how 'the Other' for the Southwestern autochthons is constantly changing: from the Nigerians in colonial times to the Francophones in the first decades after Independence to the Northwesterners more recently. His subsequent studies (notably Konings 1998) of the highly complicated Pamol affair regarding the former Unilever plantations in another part of the Southwest highlights again the changing politico-economic background to the concerted 'autochthonous' struggle to block alienation of their lands by a tycoon from elsewhere in Cameroon. And his perspicacious study – together with Francis Nyamnjoh (2003) – of the implosion of an Anglophone identity over the last decades confronts this challenge from the other side: starting from a precarious experience

8 Prominent pioneers of labour studies in Africa were, for instance, Giovanni Arrighi 1973 (on the role of 'labour aristocrats'); or Peter Waterman 1978 (on labour unions).

9 The term 'conjuncture of belonging' comes from the Canadian anthropologist Tania Murray Li (2000), who uses it in her analysis of struggles over 'indigeneity' (and 'ethnic cleansing *by* [and not of] indigenous peoples) in South East Asia. See for an elaboration of the notion for the African continent, Geschiere 2009. Cf. also Clifford Geertz' powerful statement: 'Cosmopolitanism and parochialism are no longer opposed; they are linked and reinforcing. As the one increases, so does the other' (Geertz 2000: 246).

of identity, this study shows how its vicissitudes have to be related to a continuous struggle over labour relations and their political implications in various parts of the Anglophone part of Cameroon. These studies highlight how vital the notion of autochthony has become for re-defining citizenship and excluding *allogènes*, relegating to the rank of some sort of secondary citizens. There is a sharp contrast with the first decades after independence (1960) when both the regime and many local politicians at least formally heavily emphasized the unity of Cameroon and the entitlement of all Cameroonian citizens. However, as we shall see, the autochthony notion has a longer history – and a quite twisted one at that – in the region.

The major lesson of Konings' thorough studies of recent developments in Cameroon might be to show in detail how illuminating it is to relate struggles over identity and belonging to changing politico-economic circumstances. The fervour of autochthony discourse in the Southwest – for instance, the frenzy of funeral rituals turned into celebrations of belonging or the resentment with which the 'ungratefulness' of *came-no-goes* and their mendacity are exposed – may seem to speak for themselves. Yet, Konings' studies masterfully show – especially because of their powerful empirical nature – how enlightening it remains to relate all this excitement to changing *economic* parameters. The aim of Konings' work is certainly not to try and reduce the strong emotional charge of recent tensions in an area like the Southwest to a politico-economic 'infrastructure.' Yet, he most convincingly outlines how a detailed analysis of the political economy of such identities can help to highlight their volatility and proneness to rapid re-definitions under a seemingly self-evident, 'traditional' appearance.

In the remainder of this contribution I propose to elaborate on these lines in Konings' research by following the historical trajectory of notions of belonging and autochthony in this area.[10] Three moments might be of specific interest:

- The introduction of the term autochthony to the African continent by French empire-builders in the Sudan around 1900. This moment can highlight the crucial importance of what could be called 'the colonial paradox' for present-day conflicts of autochthony: the recurrent contrast between the official effort to fix

[10] See for the uneasy relation (in Cameroon as elsewhere) of discourses on autochthony with history: Geschiere 2009, ch. 1; the main aim of that chapter is to try and show how important it is 'to give back' autochthony to history – precisely because autochthony discourse boils down to a straightforward denial of history and movement. The French classical historian Nicole Loraux (1996) offers a brilliant analysis of this impossibility with reference to the very cradle of autochthony thinking, Athens of the days of Pericles and Plato.

and territorialize the population, on the one hand, and, on the other, the practice of most colonial rulers to consequently favouring migrants.

- The somewhat surprising role of none other than Lord Lugard in the Southwest area and his interventions around 1920 in developing a new labour regime for the plantations, which similarly created an explosive mix of building on 'the real natives', while stimulating immigration.
- The turbulent years around independence, which introduced for the first time the idea of 'one man, one vote' to the area, and the desperate opposition of the Native Councils to this change.

Especially the last moment is of direct relevance to the renewed introduction of free elections – but how free in practice? – in the 1990s.

The introduction of 'autochthony' in Africa – the colonial paradox of fixing and moving

A brief overview of the historical trajectory of the autochthony notion that was to play such a crucial role in the confrontations between locals and immigrants in Southwest Cameroon in the 1990s can be helpful for understanding these confrontations in a broader context. In itself, it is quite striking that this term became important in an Anglophone area like the Southwest; after all, it was introduced on the African continent by the French – notably by the first generation of French empire-builders in the West-African Sudan – in relation to quite specific policy choices. The term is ancient: it is a classical Greek notion (*autos* = self; *chtonos* = soil) and it played a special role in the celebration by the Athenians of Pericles' and Plato's time of their city as the cradle of democracy; this may also explain why this notion had such a highly variegated presence in the work of prominent modern thinkers.[11]

For the purpose of the present chapter, it is more important to dwell briefly on the specific reasons why French colonials adopted this particular term when, around 1900, they were confronted with the question as to how they were to administer the vast territories in West Africa that they had conquered in a few decades. Certain inconsistencies in the use of the term 'autochthony' in those early days remain of direct consequence to present-day tensions, also in Cameroon.

In the French colonial conceptions that marked the effort towards a 'pacification' of West and later Equatorial Africa, *autochtonie* was to become the very

[11] For instance, in the work of such different mandarins as Lévi-Strauss, Heidegger and Derrida who all of have their version of the autochthony notion, directly inspired by the classical example of Athens (see further Geschiere 2009).

first criterion for bringing some order into the confusing proliferation of all sorts of diffuse groupings – some more or less integrated in larger state-formations, others constantly splitting up in segments – that confronted the new conquerors.[12] Indeed, *autochtonie* was a basic principle for *la politique des races*, elaborated by the well-known Governor-General of French West Africa William Ponty around 1900, which to the French was, at least in the first decades of colonization, their alternative to British Indirect Rule.[13] While to the British it seemed increasingly vital to discover the 'real' chiefs in order to base the native administration on them, the French were initially rather bent on circumventing at least the higher chiefs, who in some parts of the Sudan had offered determined resistance.[14] Instead, homogeneous *cantons* had to be formed, populated by the same *race* (here used in the sense of what today is called an ethnic group) and administered by local power-holders who would constitute the building blocks for *le commandement indigène*. Therefore, it was urgent for the administrators to discover – within the confusing medley of groups and sub-groups, more or less related but constantly segmenting – the 'real *autochtones*', who were so central in this conception of the *politique des races*.

A typical example is provided by the huge, three-volume book *Haut-Sénégal-Niger* (from 1912 – but based on research done in the 1890s) by the French ethnographer-administrator Maurice Delafosse, who was to become very influential in the building of a French colonial empire. Indeed, a recurrent principle in the book was that '... some *indigènes* are autochthons, whereas others are definitely not... ' (see Delafosse 1912: 280; cf. also Arnaut 2004: 207). And thus the first question in his encyclopaedic description of the various groupings in this area

12 In adopting the notion of *autochtone* the French colonizers in the Sudan may have been inspired by earlier French policies in Algeria, where the notion was used to refer to the Berber culture in order to construe a split within the local populations between Arabs and Berbers – I thank Baz Lecocq for pointing out this direction for further research.

13 Recent authors emphasize that all the binary oppositions that have been used to contrast French vs. British colonial rule are highly tenuous: *politique des races* against Indirect Rule, as much as *assimilation* versus association. Especially during the first decades of colonial rule French officers had often a free hand in imposing highly variable arrangements at the local or regional level. And, as military men, many of them were as impressed as the British protagonists of Indirect Rule by African chiefs and their often theatrical display of power. Still, it is also true that French governors – may be more than their British colleagues – learned to be distrustful of the powerful chiefs, like Samory (or earlier Omar Tall) who opposed them so fiercely in the Sahelian region (see Geschiere 1993; also Cohen 1971, Lombard 1967 and Crowder 1964).

14 In practice, however, the French also soon saw themselves obliged to give chiefs – even if these were somewhat condescendingly qualified as *auxiliaires indirects* – a central role in the their colonial administration (see Crowder 1964, Lombard 1967 and Geschiere 1993).

was whether a certain group was or was not autochthonous Striking in this context is that, despite his determined search for autochthony, Delafosse was clearly much more interested in the migrating groups. Invariably, once he finally found an autochthonous group, it received only a short description in a somewhat condescending language (they are qualified as *malheureux*, poor and backward – see Delafosse 1912: 238; cp. also Triaud 1998). In contrast, Delafosse devoted more than forty pages to, for instance, the Peul / Dyoula ethnic conglomerate, since he was clearly fascinated by their peregrinations throughout West Africa and their reputation as empire builders.

This makes his book a striking example of a widespread colonial paradox, of crucial importance to the vagaries of autochthony and belonging in post-colonial times: on the one hand, there was a heavy emphasis on the urgent need to 'fix' the local populations: only thus would it be possible to administer them – and more specifically levy taxes and recruit labour.[15] The *politique des races* and the principle that the new administration should be built upon autochthon groups, the 'true locals', fitted in with this localizing accent. Yet, on the other hand, most colonial governments in reality showed a clear preference for *migrants*, qualified as more energetic and entrepreneurial – and therefore much more interesting for launching economic projects. In practice, the *politique des races* seems, indeed, to have foundered rapidly on this penchant for privileging migrants among the new colonial authorities, who tended – just like Delafosse – to oppose the latter's dynamics to the locals' 'indolence' and 'resistance to change'. In many areas the French officials soon became inclined to appoint chiefs from such more 'enterprising' groupings over 'backward' locals.[16] Yet, ephemeral as the *politique des races* may have turned out to be, it did introduce the term *autochtones* and its counterpoint *allogènes* as some sort of primal criterion in the French colonial context – initially notably in the West Sudan.

One of the reasons that the term flourished in this new setting was that it easily articulated with already existing local distinctions, be it that these had often a quite different tenor. Indeed, the varying trajectories of the autochthony notion, also inside Africa, offer another example of the ways in which colonial terms were appropriated locally, acquiring a dynamic of their own. Especially in the interior of the West African Sudan, local patterns of organization turned around some sort of complementary opposition between 'people of the land' and 'rulers'; the latter were (and are) often proud to have come from elsewhere, and refer to their ex-

15 See Janet Roitman's seminal interpretations of the notion of *la population flottante* that used to haunt the reports of the first French administrators in the Chad basin (Roitman 2005).

16 See Crowder 1964, Lombard 1967, Suret-Canale 1964.

ternal origin as their justification to rule. Yet, the 'chief of the land' formed, and still forms, a ritual counterpoint to the chief of the ruling dynasty. To the French ethnologists, 'autochthony' was an obvious term to describe this counterpoint position.

A good example is the vast literature on the Mossi, the largest group in present-day Burkina Faso. For generations of researchers, the opposition in Mossi society between what they termed *autochtones* and 'rulers' became the central issue inspiring highly sophisticated, structuralist studies (Zahan 1961; Izard 1985; Luning 1997; see also Gruénais 1985). In this context, the notion of autochthony took on somewhat primitivist overtones. Luning (1997: 11), for instance, points out how in the prevailing discourse of the Mossi Maana, the *tengabiise* (a term now currently translated, also among the people themselves, as *les autochtones)*, were characterized as some sort of 'pre-social,' 'terrestrial' beings, who were only fully humanized – that is, included into a society – by the coming of the *naam*, their foreign rulers. In practice *naam* power was limited in all sorts of ways by the *tengabiise*. Nonetheless, the *naam*, as foreign rulers, were formally at the apex of the prestige scale dominating *les autochtones*. Here, this latter term had a strong chtonic, more or less primitivizing meaning.[17]

This was certainly not the meaning Delafosse had in mind in his search for *autochtones* in *la politique des races*. It was also not the meaning that emerged with such force in the 1990s in the wake of democratisation processes in this part of Africa. One of the main targets of the upsurge of autochthony in neighbouring Ivory Coast, under Houphouët-Boigny's successors – first H.K. Bedié and later L. Gbagbo – were precisely these Mossi immigrants, who were supposed to have taken the land of the 'autochthons' of the rich cocoa belt in southern Ivory Coast. In this version of the term – as in the version propagated by Delafosse and *la politique des races* - an autochthon is certainly not a subordinate; on the contrary the notion implies a claim to priority and the right to exclude strangers. Clearly the notion of autochthony – despite its self-evident appearance – can take on very different meanings depending on the time and the context.

The same ambiguity that marked Delafosse's attitude towards the autochthonous groups – when he finally had identified a group as such – marked the colonials' attitude towards the local population of the Southwest, the *Bakweri*. Already quite soon after their first penetration into this area (early 1890s) the Germans became very disappointed about the Bakweri because of their 'apathy',

[17] Cf. Malkki 1995 on the role this pejorative aspect of the notion plays in the tragic opposition between Hutu and Tutsi in Rwanda and Burundi.

which seemed to make them utterly unfit to provide a reliable work-force for the newly created plantations.[18] At the time, a strong argument for *Strafexpeditionen* (punitive expeditions) into the interior was that thus new labour reservoirs could be opened up of people more fit for productive labour. And, indeed, such expeditions invariable ended with the levying of *Strafarbeiter* (forced labourers), to be deported to the coast (Rüger 1960, Mandeng 1973). As noted before, this stereotype of indolence and a somewhat tragic *conduite volontaire à l'échec* (Courade 1982) was to stick to the Bakweri throughout the colonial times and up to the present day. For the British as well, after they had conquered the area, it seemed evident that they had to appeal to more industrious immigrant workers if the impressive plantation complex had to be maintained. As in so many present-day hotbeds of autochthony strife on the African continent, the colonial intermezzo – and notably the colonial paradox of officially building on the locals while in practice favouring immigration – was to be vital in setting the stage for present-day confrontations.

Lord Lugard and the 'betrayal' of British policy principles in the Southwest

One of the more surprising discoveries when working in the Buea archives – a little treasury, created by Edwin and Shirley Ardener, where Piet has *chopped file* for so many months – was to stumble upon the towering figure of Lord Lugard, the great architect of Indirect Rule in British Africa. Working my way through a huge pile of documents on the taking over of the German plantations by the new British authorities during the First World War, I discovered how directly Lugard himself, at the time Governor of Nigeria, had intervened in this area – then seen as a far-away and minor addition to the proud colony of Nigeria. Moreover, his intervention had been quite unorthodox – to the British officials on the spot it seemed even to go against the very principles of British colonial rule, in a way that was to be of heavy consequence for present-day relations in the area.

18 Most Germans hardly related such apathy to the fact that large parts of Bakweri land had been expropriated for the creation of plantations. Striking is, moreover, that at the very beginning of the 1890's for a short time a completely different stereotype of the Bakweri prevailed when the Buea people, higher up Mt. Cameroun, succeeded in defeating a panicky German expedition force (see Geschiere 2004). Then, at least the Bakweri on the mountain were seen as utterly savage, fierce and dangerous. The recent upsurge of autochthony in this area (see above) and the concomitant high profile of the Bakweri in regional and national politics brought again a rapid change in their ethnic stereotype.

The first District Officers (DOs) on the spot saw the huge plantations that the British had conquered so easily as a major challenge. Their reactions were quite mixed. On the one hand, they were clearly impressed by the whole complex, its infrastructure and the concomitant provisions for the settlers. Yet, on the other, they soon began to fear that this was some sort of poisoned gift, foreseeing that especially the question of how to mobilize all the labour needed for the maintenance of these extensive plantations would became an overriding problem. Indeed, *die Arbeiterfrage* (the labour problem) had been a central issue also prior to 1914 under German rule, when it had led to fierce and constant clashes between the government and the planters (see Rudin 1938, Wirz 1972, Geschiere 2006). However, as said, to the Germans the solution had been self-evident: coercion – the constant levying of forced labour – was the only way to deal with the *Arbeiterfrage*.

To the first British officials after 1914 it was self-evident that this was against the very principles of British colonial policy. To them it was unthinkable that the brutal coercive labour policies of the Germans would be continued under British rule. However, this made the question all the more urgent of how then sufficient labour could be mobilized. Several officials referred to the Gold Coast example of cash-crop production by local peasants as the obvious alternative. This implied that the plantations would have to be divided into small holdings 'to be leased to the natives of the country.'[19]

However, they were in for a surprise. In 1917, Lugard intervened himself, in his capacity of Governor of Nigeria. After he had made a site visit, he was clearly so impressed by the whole outlay of the German plantation complex that for him there was no more question of splitting it up. Moreover, he apparently felt that the DOs on the spot were too sensitive in their objections to forced labour. Lugard's careful formulations are a masterpiece of combining the keeping up of appearances (the British could not condone forced labour) and being practical (the German plantations had to be maintained at all costs):

> I do not quite grasp why the European plantations have been a curse. There was, I understand, ample land, mostly forest and unoccupied.... I am not wholly in agreement with the Resident re genuine voluntary labour and I think greater encouragement to labourers to go in voluntarily would probably have done a good deal. It must be remembered that the transition stage from being forced to go in and their going voluntarily must take some time and I am not in any way in favour of relaxing all at once the strict hand of German rule.... We want to get to British methods, but to relax suddenly would be apt to encourage the natives in their naturally lazy ways. I would therefore encourage by every

[19] See, for instance, Buea National Archives (henceforth BNA), CF 1913, report Stobart, April/May 1916, under 'Plantations.'

> means in my power the native to labour. He has learnt under iron discipline what labour means and I should like him to come to realize gradually that we are entirely in favour of his working though we do not wish to force him. This must however dawn on him very gradually or chaos might easily result.[20]

Accordingly, in the next few years the Resident in Buea ordered the various DOs in no uncertain terms that they had to deliver their contingent of labourers by whatever form of pressure they saw fit. The DOs were apparently appalled. Especially the reactions of George Podevin, the DO in Bamenda (that is, in the famous 'Grassfields' with which so many colonials fell in love) are of interest in the context of this chapter, since this is also the area from where a big part of the labour force for the plantations was to come.[21] Apparently Podevin was so shocked by the orders to use, if necessary, force to make labour available, that he even dared to ask the Resident to send him the full text of Lugard's comments, not only the excerpt, '... as it is somewhat difficult to understand his Honour's observations without these references.' But the Resident refused this, using strong language to exhort this DO to finally take the recruiting of labour in his district seriously: 'If you still persist in this passive resistance, it may be found necessary to remove you from Bamenda.'[22] Apparently, even to the British, the desire to maintain the impressive plantation complex had priority over the official preference for the 'peasant option' – that is, cultivation for the market by independent peasants (by British officials at the time labelled as 'the Gold Coast option.'[23]

However, from 1920 on, the DOs in their annual reports triumphantly announced that labour was coming forth now 'voluntarily' and that the controversial

20 BNA, Qd(a), Lugard, 11 October 1917.

21 This Podevin must have been a charismatic figure. He is described as one of the first victims of the Cameroonian version of Masaitis (many British civil servants in Cameroon were as fascinated by these Grassfields, as their colleagues in East Africa were by the Masai). Podevin would even die in his beloved Bamenda.

22 BNA, Qd(a), 1916, letters by DO Bamenda (Podevin) to Resident in Buea (Young), 22 August 1917; and Resident Buea to DO Bamenda, 22 September 1917; Qe, 1917,2, letter by Resident in Buea to DO Bamenda, 1 November 1917. Podevin was not alone in his resistance against the new policy. In his 1918 annual report Rutherford, then DO in Victoria, still sharply protested against the imposition of forced recruitment (BNA, Cf 1918, 31 December 1918).

23 Cf. Clarence-Smith 1993 and Philips 1989 on British problems with the 'peasant option.' The Southwest Cameroon example suggests that if there seemed to be a more profitable alternative even people like Lugard or Hugh Clifford, his successor in Nigeria (both quoted by Philips as great defenders of the peasant option) did not hesitate to go against the peasant option. Cf. also Fred Cooper's critique (1981: 31 and 59 n.36) of Wallerstein for suggesting, in line with his world systems theory approach, that to the colonial state in Africa, the peasant option was 'the path of least resistance.'

German recruiting methods no longer had to be followed. Did this mean that Lugard's prediction had been right and that, indeed, coercion had been necessary only for a short intermezzo in order to make labour come forth 'voluntarily'? It seems that more hidden forms of force did play a crucial role in this surprisingly rapid solution to the labour problem by the British. Already by 1920, the British system of Indirect Rule had been installed, also in the populous Grassfields (the present-day Northwest Province). In their new role, the 'customary chiefs' were made to mediate in the recruitment of labour, sending their contingents of 'voluntary' labourers down to the coast. As Konings shows in his thorough studies of the evolution of the labour force on the plantations since the 1920s (1993, 1998, 2003, 2008), its composition was highly complex. At least initially there was also an important influx of labourers from the French part of Cameroon, who were fleeing the draconic *travaux forcés* imposed by the French. But in retrospect it would be especially the pressures by 'customary chiefs' in the Northwest to making labour come 'voluntarily' available that would have a great impact on subsequent developments in the Anglophone region. As said, this solution of mobilizing labourers through reinforcing the chiefs involved precisely the groups that are now at the heart of the autochthony issue in the Southwest: the Grassfielders, who are resented as 'came-no goes' in the local Pidgin.

After Lugard's forceful intervention to save the big plantations on Mount Cameroun's slopes – even if this meant recruiting labourers by force – the principle of Indirect Rule became sacrosanct for several decades. Subsequent generations of D.O.s remained obsessed with finding the 'true local authorities' in order to build their administration on them. In their application, Indirect Rule became a celebration of the local – a passionate search for the pure local form. Yet, as Lord Lugard must have clearly foreseen, in practice Indirect Rule was not only about localism and the fixing of people under the authority of their chief. On the contrary, the redoubtable power of the Grassfields chiefs, further fortified by colonial rule, played a pivotal role in making their young men migrate to the economic centres of the colony near the coast. Clearly the colonial paradox, noted before, is even present inside the model of Indirect Rule, which may appear as a celebration and affirmation of the local, yet in practice could imply mobilizing migrants, if need be by force.

'No taxation without representation' – early democratization under British rule

As Carola Lentz (2003 and 2006) signals for Ghana, the present-day conflicts over local belonging in a context of democratisation had clear precedents towards the end of the colonial period, especially with the gradual introduction of electoral procedures. In the Southwest this started relatively early, precisely because the British became increasingly uneasy over the balance between immigrants and natives in this particular area.

Indirect Rule had a particularly tortuous history here, since the 'traditional' pedigree of the chiefs among the Bakweri and other local groups was far from clear. For instance, the chieftaincy of Buea – to a certain degree seen as the Paramount of the Bakweri – was fiercely contested, right from the start of Indirect Rule in the region (see Geschiere 1993). But up to the 1930s the British stuck to the principle of ruling through 'hereditary chiefs' whoever they were supposed to be. In the wake of the Igbo 'Women's War' in Eastern Nigeria (1929) and the subsequent replacement of warrant chiefs by councils in areas where the traditional pedigree of local chiefs seemed to be weak, things rapidly changed in the Southwest as well. Successive D.O.s tried to outdo each other in tracing the true authority structure within the local communities, which led to a dazzling proliferation of village heads, local councils, and so on (see Geschiere 1989). However, this search for a more fine-tuned grid doing justice to the 'real' authority structures at the local level, automatically raised the thorny question of how immigrants, ever more present in the region, had to be represented in this multiplication of heads, sub-heads and councils. Striking are the inconsistencies that marked British policies on this issue, which became increasingly vital. In 1927, the Assistant DO in Buea proposed, for instance, to appoint a representative of the Hausa community in the town as a member of the Buea Native Court. Apparently, the chiefs and other court members – of course all Bakweri – agreed without any protest. But the Buea Resident, clearly a purist of Indirect Rule, had his doubts: was it possible to have a 'stranger' sit on a Native Court?[24] In the 1930's things changed. The British more and more came to realize that many 'strangers' intended to stay in the area; indeed, immigrant workers increasingly created their own farms there after the expiration of their labour contracts on the plantation (or also in combination with these contracts – see Konings 1993). In their search for a fair representative structure – Local Government rather than Indirect Rule (see Nicolson 1969) – the

[24] BNA Te (1963)1, letter by ADO Buea, 14-2-1927; and answer by Acting Resident Buea, 1-4-1927.

DOs increasingly emphasized the slogan 'no taxation without representation' as the very principle of British policy.

The Bakweri notables on their part seem to have foreseen quite rapidly that the diluting of the Indirect Rule idea and the undermining of the chiefly positions which the British had so strongly supported during the 1920s would have threatening implications. Already in 1942 a group of 34 Bakweri 'notables' protested angrily in the name of 'native custom' against the changes in Indirect Rule:

> The Bakweri ... had heads from time immemorial. The Government would appear to reduce us into a republic to admit the false history that our ancestors had no head.... We are sinking into a lethargy if this continues...[25]

Thus the British were confronted with their own constructions: not only that of a hereditary structure of chiefs within a group that seems to have been mostly ruled by some sort of 'big men' (Geschiere 1993), but also the lingering stereotype of a threatening indolence that would beset the Bakweri group. However, further reforms imposed by the British from the 1940s reflected their firm intention that one way or another the presence of so many immigrants in the area had to be addressed. These immigrants paid their taxes – in fact an increasing part of the total sum for the area; so, in the British view, they should be represented on way or another.

How threatening all this was to the Bakweri leaders is clear from the minutes of a 1944 meeting of the 'Bakweri Clan Council' in Buea. The DO opened the meeting by sternly admonishing the council to make at last a definitive decision on the reform of the 'Native Administration.' The councillors were clearly impressed by this opening shot and approved all his proposals without any discussion – until the issue of the 'strangers' representation' was raised. Then, a true firework of protest exploded. One after another, the councillors passionately argued why 'strangers' could never sit on any council of the Bakweri Native Administration:

> In our tradition, a stranger cannot become a chief – how can we call a stranger *sango boa* (litt.: "father of the village")? – We very much oppose it.

However, the DO stood firm:

> Here you are, the Bakweri Native Administration receiving approximately L 1500 a year in tax money of which the strangers in your midst pay almost exactly half. You benefit by their money and you decide how their money shall be used. This is absolutely contradic-

[25] BNA SAg (1934/38), petition of Bakweri Court members, 28-1-1941.

tory to the things we British believe in, and it is against the very things for which we are now fighting a war.

In spite of this passionate speech, the meeting broke up in complete chaos:

Whereupon all shout: "We will not admit strangers".[26]

The minutes of a Bakweri Clan Council Meeting later in the year quoted even stronger language:

The council without hesitation unanimously said that their answer [to the DO's proposal to have "strangers" in the council] is "no." They said that they had given reasons for their "no" in their previous meetings which they are not prepared to repeat, but if the Government wants to admit strangers in their Native Administration, that will be against their wish and that if the Government takes such steps, they will surrender all the Native Councils and Courts to strangers.[27]

The same question was to come up time and again during the last decade before Independence. The stubborn resistance of the Bakweri councils against any representation of strangers made the British push all the harder for open elections. However, still in 1957, the DO in Victoria proposed a highly complicated procedure for the elections for the Victoria Divisional Council in order to assure that at most 20 to 25 % of the elected representatives could be strangers.[28]

In subsequent years, however, party politics took over, leading to a deep split among the Bakweri notables themselves. With the institution of political parties, younger Bakweri took over, notably dr. Emmanuel Endeley who, for various reasons, fostered a deep grudge against his uncle, the proud 'Paramount' of the Bakweri, Mbele Endeley III. When a rival party emerged to Emmanuel Endeley's CPNC, chief Endeley even joined this new party (the KNDP) – which was all the more remarkable since this new party was led by John Foncha and other political leaders from the Northwest. Thus the segmentary structure of Bakweri politics – the constant rifts between their political leaders and their great problems in main-

26 BNA, Ag/15a, Minutes of the Bakweri Clan Council Meeting, 15-3-1944. Of interest is that this absolute refusal of having strangers represented in Native Administration was at the time quite new. In 1927, for instance, the Assistant DO proposed to appoint a representative of the Hausa community in Buea as a member of the Buea Native Court. The District Head (already Chief Mbele Endeley III) and the other Court Members agreed, apparently without any protest. However, then, the Resident (the ADO's superior), clearly a purist of Indirect Rule, blocked this innovation: 'How can we appoint a stranger on a Native Court?' (National Archives Buea, Te1, letter by ADO Buea, 14-2-1927 and answer by Acting Resident Buea, 1-4-1927).

27 BNA,Ag/15a, minutes of the Bakweri Clan Council Meeting, 21-11-1944.

28 Ja/e (1953)1, letter from DO Victoria, 18-2-1957.

taining a united front – further facilitated the imposition of a 'one man, one vote' procedure in the last years before Independence.

Epilogue

The preceding may have indicated that it is important to relate all the emotions and stereotyping of the present-day confrontations between 'autochthons' and 'strangers' in Southwest Cameroon to history and political economy. Indeed, this is why Piet Konings' studies are so valuable for understanding the upsurge of identity politics in this area. As said, autochthony always sits uneasily with history (see Geschiere 2009). It evokes history, but in the form of 'memory,' reducing it to a simple scheme of first- and late-comers.[29] Already the brief sketch above may have shown that the history of the Southwest is much richer and more variegated. The present-day opposition to the Grassfielders, as the autochthonous 'others,' is certainly not an historical inevitability. It is the outcome of specific historical turns and decisions, notably in the colonial history of the area. Even up to more recent times, alternative trajectories were present. For instance, the vital plebiscite of 1961, in which the area voted to join former French Cameroun rather than stay with Nigeria, was mainly determined by local resentment of Nigerians, notably Igbo immigrants from neighbouring East Nigeria. Several leading politicians among the Bakweri – notably Dr. Emmanuel Endeley – defended, at least for some time, the Nigerian option as the better one. In those days, the Igbo were 'the Other' to the locals, and hence the latter voted for the Cameroon option defended by Foncha and other Grassfields leaders. Even today, the realities of everyday life – the resentment of the *gendarmes* who always speak French (even if they come from the South- or the Northwest) – oppose people rather to the Francophones as their Other. Indeed, Konings and Nyamnjoh (2003) are right to emphasize that in many respects – in domains that are very important for people, like the school systems or the running of the administration – there is a common Anglophone identity opposed to the threat of Francophone domination. Clearly, some insight into the rapid switches from one 'Other' to the next one, depending on the changing politico-economic context is crucial since it may help to relativize the naturalizing self-evidence claimed by the advocates of autochthony – in Cameroon as elsewhere in our globalizing world.

[29] See Nora 1989 on the contrast between 'memory' and 'history'; and for an elaboration of this contrast with reference to autochthony in general and to Cameroon and the Netherlands in particular, Geschiere 2009, especially chapters 1 and 5.

References

Ardener, Edwin, 1962. *Divorce and Fertility – An African Study*. Oxford: Oxford University Press.

Arnaut, Karel, 2004. *Performing Displacements and Rephrasing Attachments: Ethnographic Explorations of Space, Mobility in Art, Ritual, Media and Politics*. Ph.D. thesis, Ghent University.

Arrighi, Giovanni, 1973, International corporations, labor aristocrats and economic development in Tropical Africa. In: G. Arrighi & J.S. Saul, eds, *Essays on the Political Economy of Africa*. New York: Monthly Review Press, pp. 105-151.

Bayart, Jean-François, Béatrice Hibou & Stephen Ellis, 1997. *The Criminalization of the State in Africa*. Oxford: James Currey.

Clarence-Smith, Gervase, 1993. Plantation versus smallholder production of cocoa: the legacy of the German period in Cameroon. In: P. Geschiere & P. Konings, eds, *Itinéraries d'Accumulation au Cameroun*. Paris: Karthala, pp. 187-217.

Cohen, William B., 1971. *Rulers of Empire: the French Colonial Service in Africa*. Stanford: Hoover Institution Press.

Cooper, Frederick, 1981. Africa and the world economy. *African Studies Review* 24 (2-3): 1-87.

Courade, Georges, 1982. Marginalité volontaire ou impose? Le cas des Bakweri (Kpe) du mont Cameroun. *Cahiers ORSTOM, Sciences Humaines* 19(3): 357-89.

Delafosse, Maurice, 1972 (1912). *Haut-Sénégal-Niger*. Paris: Maisonneuve.

Geertz, Clifford, 2000. *Available Light, Anthropological Reflections on Philosophical Topics*. Princeton: Princeton University Press.

Geschiere, Peter, 1989. 'Neo-traditional chiefs and the imposition of bureaucratic control – invention of tradition under French and British rule in Cameroon.' Paper for the Conference on relationships between State and Society in Africa and Eastern Europe. Bellagio, Como, Febr. 1990.

——. 1993. Chiefs and colonial rule in Cameroon: inventing chieftaincy, French and British style. *Africa* 63(2): 151-176.

——. 2004. 'Von Gravenreuth and Buea as a site of history – early colonial violence on Mount Cameroon.' Unpublisher Paper.

——. 2009. *The Perils of Belonging – Autochthony, Citizenship and Exclusion in Africa and Europe*. Chicago: University of Chicago Press.

Geschiere, Peter & Francis Nyamnjoh, 2000. Capitalism and autochthony: the seesaw of mobility and belonging. *Public Culture* 12(2): 423-453 (special issue on *Millennial Capitalism and the Culture of Neoliberalism*, ed. by Jean and John Comaroff).

Gruénais, Marc E., 1985. Du bon usage de l'autochtonie. *Cahiers ORSTOM – Série sciences humaines* 21(1): 19-24.

Izard, Michel, 1985. *Gens du Pouvoir, Gens de la Terre – Les Institutions Politiques de l'Ancien Royaume du Yatenga (Bassin de la Volta blanche)*. Cambridge: Cambridge University Press.

Konings, Piet, 1993. *Labour Resistance in Cameroon: Managerial Strategies and Labour Resistance in the Agro-Industrial Plantations of the Cameroon Development Corporation*. London – Portsmouth, N.H.: James Currey – Heinemann.

——, 1998. *Unilever Estates in Crisis and the Power of Organizations in Cameroon*. Hamburg: Lit Verlag.

——, 2003. Organised labour and neo-liberal economic and political reforms in West and Central Africa. *Journal of Contemporary African Studies* 21(3): 447-471.

——, 2008. Privatisation and labour militancy: the case of Cameroon's tea estates. *Journal of Contemporary African Studies* 26(1): 51-70.

Konings, Piet & Francis Nyamnjoh, 2003. *Negotiating an Anglophone Identity – A Study of the Politics of Recognition and Representation in Cameroon*. Leiden: Brill.

Lentz, Carola, 2003. 'Premiers arrivés' et 'nouveaux venus'- Discours sur l'autochtonie dans la savane ouest-africaine. In: R. Kuba, C. Lentz & C.N. Somda, eds, *Histoire du Peuplement et Relations Interethniques au Burkina Faso*. New York: Greenwood Press, pp. 113-134.

——. 2006. *Ethnicity and the Making of History in Northern Ghana*. Edinburgh: Edinburgh University Press for I.A.I.

Li, Tania Murray, 2000. Articulating indigenous identity in Indonesia: resource politics and the tribal slot. *Comparative Studies in Society and History* 42: 149-79.

Lombard, Jacques, 1967. *Autorités Traditionnelles et Pouvoirs Européens en Afrique Noire: le Déclin d'une Aristocratie sous le Régime Colonial*. Paris: Colin.

Loraux, Nicole, 1996. *Né de la Terre – Mythe et Politique à Athènes*. Paris: Le Seuil.

Luning, Sabine, 1997. *Het Binnenhalen van de Oogst – Ritueel en Samenleving in Maane, Burkina Faso*. Leiden: University of Leiden, Ph.D. thesis.

Malkki, Liisa H., 1995. *Purity and Exile – Violence, Memory and National Cosmology among Hutu Refugees in Tanzania.* Chicago: University of Chicago Press.

Mandeng, Patrice, 1973. *Auswirkungen der deutschen Kolonialherrschaft in Kamerun.* Hamburg: H. Buske Verlag.

Nicolson, I.F., 1969. *The Administration of Nigeria, 1900-60 – Men, Methods and Myths.* Oxford: Clarendon Press.

Nora, Pierre, 1989. Between memory and history: 'les lieux de mémoire'. *Representations* 26: 7-24.

Nyamnjoh, Francis, 1999. Cameroon, a country united by ethnic ambition and difference. *African Affairs* 98(390): 101-118.

Nyamnjoh, Francis & Michael Rowlands, 1998. Elite associations and the politics of belonging in Cameroon. *Africa* 68(3): 320-337.

Philips, Anne, 1989. *The Enigma of Colonialism: British Policy in West Africa.* London: James Currey.

Roitman, Janet, 2005. *Fiscal Disobedience: An Anthropology of Economic Regulation in Central Africa*, Princeton: Princeton University Press.

Rudin, Harry R., 1938. *Germans in the Cameroons 1884-1914.* New Haven: Yale University Press.

Rüger, Adolf, 1960. Die Entstehung und Lage der Arbeiterklasse under dem deutschen Kolonialregime in Kamerun 1895-1905. In: H. Stoecker, ed., *Kamerun under deutscher Kolonialherrschaft* I. Berlin: Deutscher Verlag der Wissenschaften, pp. 149-242.

Socpa, Antoine, 2003. *Démocratisation et Autochtonie au Cameroun – Variations Régionales Divergentes.* Münster: Lit Verlag.

Suret-Canale, Jean, 1964. *Afrique Noire Occidentale et Centrale II: L'Ère Coloniale 1900-1945.* Paris: Éditions Sociales.

Triaud, Jean Louis, 1998. "Haut-Sénégal-Niger", un modèle positiviste? De la coutume à l'histoire: Maurice Delafosse et l'invention de l'histoire africaine. In: J.-L. Amselle & E. Sibeud, eds, *Maurice Delafosse – Entre Orientalisme et Ethnographie: Itinéraire d'un Africaniste (1870-1926)*, pp. 210-33, Paris: Maisonneuve.

Waterman, Peter, 1978. Consciousness, organisation and action among Lagos portworkers. *Review of African Political Economy* 13: 47-62.

Wirz, Albert, 1972. *Vom Sklavenhandel zum kolonialen Handel: Wirtschaftsräume und Wirtschaftsformen in Kamerun vor 1914.* Zurich: Atlantis.

Zahan, Dominique, 1961. Pour une histoire des Mossi du Yatenga. *L'Homme* 1(2): 5-22.

Ganyu in Malawi: Transformation of Local Labour Relations under Famine and HIV/AIDS duress*

Deborah Fahy Bryceson

Ganyu labour, a longstanding form of ad hoc casualized rural labour, has come to the fore in recent years as the major coping mechanism for the rural poor to combat food insecurity in Malawi. This chapter explores ganyu in light of long-term trends in Malawi's local rural economies and the shocks of famine and the HIV/AIDS pandemic experienced at the outset of the 21st century. It is argued that ganyu, evolved from balanced to negative reciprocity over the past hundred years. During Malawi's 2001-02 famine, with many rural families adversely affected either directly or indirectly by HIV/AIDS morbidity and mortality, ganyu labour increasingly altered in character in terms of: growing inequalities of rural asset holdings, labour exchange negotiated under extreme duress, growing labour negotiations between members of the famine-affected rural areas with non-kin from outside of the local community, a diminishing ethical foundation to labour contractual terms and, in the case of women, sometimes the necessity of morally degrading sexual compromise for the sake of securing vital food supplies or cash.

Introduction

Livelihood studies have dominated the study of African rural economies for the last decade. However, as 'snapshots' of a given period of time they tend to pose as many questions as they answer. With their emphasis on workers' agency directed at coping in the here and now, the why and how of prevailing working conditions are circumvented. Diachronic studies of labour relations in Africa are an

* Parts of this paper derive from a longer study entitled: '*Ganyu* Casual Labour, Famine and HIV/AIDS in Rural Malawi: Causality and Casualty', *Journal of Modern African Studies* 44(2), 2006, 173-202.

invaluable resource to piecing together how it has all come to pass. Piet Konings has made a major contribution to the study of West African rural labour relations (1993, 1996, 1998, 2003). In particular, he has provided careful documentation of the changing contours of the labour force in a Cameroonian plantation owned by a multinational corporation. The declining bargaining position of the workers vis-à-vis management and their increasingly casualized and devalued remuneration under economic liberalization are counter to the higher living standards that national independence promised.

This chapter similarly adopts a long-time perspective to explore the changing nature of *ganyu* casual labour in Malawi. Unlike the plantation labourers Konings analysed, *ganyu* labourers are not employed by foreign investors. *Ganyu* is a local labour form whose origin can be traced back over a century, evolving largely outside of the sphere of commercial labour sale. It is best viewed as part and parcel of the local peasant moral economy.

Peasant moral economies are deeply embedded in a collective survival ethic in which rights of subsistence and norms of reciprocity are axiomatic (Scott 1976). The survival ethic of a peasantry evolves in response to locality-specific climatic and demographic fluctuations as well as internal and external economic, political and cultural processes over time. Europe's peasant populations dwindled over the last three hundred years in the face of industrialization and urbanization (Laslett 1965). Presently, global market forces are having an erosive impact on peasantries in Asia, Latin America and Africa. Thus, the world has witnessed the collapse of many peasantries' moral economies, sometimes simply through dissipation brought on by the opportunity for alternative modes of livelihood and generational rejection of time-honoured mores. In other cases, material deprivation and human suffering, often through worsening labour conditions, have been integral to the disintegration of the peasant moral economy.

Relying on historical literature and field evidence from a CARE International study[1] conducted between December 2003 and May 2004, I trace how *ganyu* em-

[1] The study took place in three off-road villages in Lilongwe rural district, Central Region. Data collection encompassed focus group discussions, key informant interviews, in-depth interviews with AIDS widows, orphans and foster carers, as well as a household survey of 141 randomly sampled households. I am grateful to CARE International, the Regional Network on HIV/AIDS, Rural Livelihoods and Food Security (RENEWAL) and IFPRI, who sponsored the study upon which this paper is based. Special thanks go to John Kadzandira of the University of Malawi, Michael Drinkwater, Jodie Fonseca, Nick Osborne and the CARE Malawi staff for their guidance and active involvement throughout the study. In addition John McCracken, Bridget O'Laughlin, Sarah Levy, Robin Palmer, Pauline Peters, Deborah Potts and Jan Kees van Donge offered advice on references, comments and criticisms while this paper was being writ-

ployers are increasingly challenging basic principles of both generalized and balanced reciprocity with deleterious effects on economic welfare and health. The first section of this chapter provides historical background on Malawian rural economies focussing on *ganyu* labour, a widespread labour form in Malawian history persisting to the present, followed by a consideration of agrarian policies during the colonial, Banda and post-Banda periods. Thereafter the expanding AIDS epidemic and household responses to the 2001-02 famine are discussed before returning to the analysis of *ganyu* labour and its transformation in the face of famine and HIV/AIDS.

Ganyu labour: origins and ethics

Malawi, formerly Nyasaland, attracted waves of in-migration over the centuries (Phiri 1976). The first Bantu-speaking 'Maravi' people migrated into the area more than two thousand years ago. The Chewa people, the country's largest ethnic group, are descendants from this migration. They are identified as part of a broad band of matrilineal Central Bantu speakers. However, Malawi has been subject to considerable ethnic mixing. The 19th century was a period of great upheaval, with Yao slave and ivory traders as well as the Ngoni entering the highlands of the Southern region. Slave trading severely disrupted the local agrarian economies during the 19th century. Early European explorers recorded heavily fortified settlements on hilltops (Phiri 1976, Mandala 1990).

Taking advantage of local chiefs' rivalries and general insecurity, European planters secured large tracts of land during the 1890s and used a variety of insidious tactics to gain access to labour for their plantation enterprises, with reverberations for tribute and reciprocal exchange labour traditions. Alongside lineage and tribal loyalties, *contractual* labour relations, known as *thangata*, became a prominent feature of Malawi during the British colonial period.

Much of the land debate in Malawi during the early 20th century revolved around Europeans' unsanctioned demand for *thangata* labour, i.e. forced labour. The Nyasaland colonial government did not officially sanction forced labour, but colonial district administrators turned a blind eye to it, relying on European planters to facilitate African tax collection through *thangata* labour service (White 1987). In this way, over the years *thangata* became entrenched. By the 1940s and 1950s rural population densities had mounted. European estate owners saw the responsibilities of providing family residence and work to increasing numbers as

ten, although I take full responsibility for the analytical interpretation of the historical record and survey data presented in this article.

more onerous than beneficial to their interests. *Thangata* labour gradually ebbed away but its exploitative practices continued to be vividly remembered by African farmers and politicians as they fought for independence from colonial rule.

Ganyu labour arose in the same historical context as *thangata,* but it denoted a distinctly different form of labour relations. The term has a Mozambican inflection related to the influx of African producers from Portuguese East Africa, the Anguru, who migrated to Nyasaland during the early decades of British colonialism. White (1987) used the word *ganyao,* Portuguese for 'bonus', to refer to the additional exchange that took place between the Anguru, as immigrants to Nyasaland and the local Yao chiefs. The Yao chiefs, eager to recruit labour for bush clearance, rewarded the Anguru's labour with food. At the outset, given the inter-tribal nature of exchange, it is likely that reciprocity was already veering towards a structurally balanced rather than more generalized form of open-ended exchange (Sahlins 1974). The Yao, who were in a superior position vis-à-vis land access and hence food production, could entice Anguru to work for them. Paradoxically, 'balanced reciprocity' may rest on imbalance in terms of asset holdings, whereas 'generalized reciprocity' is reflective of a more communally based society where people share relatively equal access to natural resources. Operating under more egalitarian circumstances, generalized exchange labour provides a means for gaining a critical mass of labourers temporally for specific tasks that the labour recruiter needs at that time.

O'Laughlin (2002) makes a connection between *ganyu* and *ganho-ganho*, the contemporary term for casual wage-workers labouring on a piecework or target basis across the border in Mozambique. She observes that the similarity between the two words and their identical meaning is reflective of the porous borders between Mozambique and Malawi throughout the colonial and post-colonial periods. The meaning of *ganyao*, *ganho-ganho* and *ganyu,* all variations on the Portuguese word for bonus, gain or profit, was markedly distinct from *thangata.* Far from any notion of forced labour, *ganyu* referred to mutually beneficial exchange of labour for cash or in-kind food payments between rural households.

During the first half of the 20th century, *ganyu* served different utilities. In densely populated rural areas, members of households lacking sufficient land with excess labour could resolve their land/labour imbalance by hiring *ganyu* labour. Labour-short households of any wealth standing, and notably those with absent male migrants, could gain access to additional labour seasonally. But generally, *ganyu* was associated with people from poorer households seeking goods or cash from better-off households through the sale of their labour (Vaughan 1987).

Various authors (Mandala 1990, Davison 1995, Englund 1996) note that work parties and other reciprocal forms of labour, not common during the colonial period, dwindled further during the decades following independence. In this way, relations of general reciprocity common amongst subsistence producers, as described by Sahlins (1974) and Sugimura (2004), were being replaced by morally constructed 'balanced reciprocity', alongside growing differential asset endowments between households. *Ganyu* became the main form of inter-household labour exchange between peasant households, continually adapting to changing economic actors and agendas. In some instances it did occur amongst equals seeking to alleviate temporary household labour shortages, but increasingly it was vested with the moral content of patron-client relations whereby patrons were obliged to award access to money or food to clients facing a deficit of either of these. Englund (1966) argues that the *ganyu* employers were optimising economic agents but their labour hiring was viewed by local people, notably those being hired, as altruistic in nature given the material imbalances between contractor and contracted labourers:

> *Ganyu* recruiters are self-interested actors whose concern is to protect, and possibly increase, personal wealth. Yet wealth (*chuma*) can only appear through mobilising others for, for example, *ganyu* labour. Wealth which is individual, mobilising no one but the self-interested actor him- or herself, constitutes its proprietor as the inversion of moral being, a witch... .Moral personhood, among 'rich' and 'poor' villagers alike, is predicated on the decomposition of constitutive relationships by performing deeds for others... (Englund 1996: 19).

Negotiating around differences of economic need and wealth demanded acute sensitivity. An embarrassment of riches was mirrored by an embarrassment of poverty. Whiteside (2000) observes how the social stigma of hunger, necessitating a transfer of food or cash between relatives or neighbours, was disguised as incidental labour exchange through *ganyu*. *Ganyu* was both an economic practicality and a cultural façade in which lineage relations were perpetuated yet kept in check. In a sense, *ganyu* was a means of socially saving face for both parties to the exchange.

Malawian women in matrilineal communities individualized their property and work effort to minimize the possibility of extended lineage claims which would necessitate sharing labour or property or having to pool labour and be held to account by lineage ties (Davison 1995). They preferred to engage in *ganyu* where payment was established at the outset without a deferred obligation to reciprocate. This eased the weight of moral responsibility illustrated by a Chichewa proverb translated 'to give is to place', meaning any favour will be placed in the recipient's memory and eventually the favour must be reciprocated (Englund 1996:7). The Malawian peasantry's historical familiarity with wage labour relations could have facilitated women's eagerness to keep lineage reciprocal obligations one or two degrees removed, providing an alternative model of exchange relative to traditional general reciprocal exchange. Furthermore, it had played a major part in increasing women's workload, creating the conditions in which deferred labour obligations would become more onerous with the threat of social shame in the event that they could not be repaid.

Economic needs, material practicality and social sentiments of the negotiating agents moulded *ganyu* contracts. Preference for open-ended negotiation seeking balanced reciprocity for that moment in time prevailed. In so doing, villagers did not have to confront the contradiction between the ideal of tribal egalitarianism and lineage responsibility and the reality of local wealth imbalances.

Change in local rural economies during the 20th century

Malawi's rural areas congealed around the tension between land and labour. The large tracts of land that had been awarded to European settlers for plantation production and the growth of rural populations translated into greater pressure on land resources entrusted to tribal authorities under colonial policies of indirect rule.

At the beginning of the 20th century, the colonial state had sanctioned male out-migration to the mineral-rich countries surrounding Nyasaland in addition to encouraging European plantations. In the regional colonial economy, Malawi functioned as an outpost of the Southern African regional economy and a source of cheap labour for European settler and mining enterprises. The Rhodesian Native Labour Bureau began recruiting in Nyasaland in 1903. While large segments of the male population migrated away from their families on a circular basis, their wives were remained in rural areas engaged in subsistence farming.

Economic dualism of rural labour reserves

Male labour migration generated a rigid gender division of labour and dual character to the household labour effort. Women laboured to produce basic subsistence food needs in households with shrinking land assets, while their men worked on plantations or mines inside or outside Malawi. Within the village community, wives and traditional leaders faced labour shortages caused by the absence of male labour. Households short of labour, with cash remittances of male migrants or other household wealth on hand, could hire *ganyu* labourers to make up their labour shortfall.

Women faced the structural challenge of inducing their cash-earning husbands to send remittances and to physically return home, a concern particularly in matrilineal areas where husbands had no land inheritance rights and marital instability was high (Reniers 2003). Men's return migration was also of concern to employers and Native Authority chiefs and headmen. The power of the latter was based on the size of their population and its tax base. With men's outward migration, it was imperative that women were obliged to stay behind in the village with various moral sanctions against female mobility. The centrality of tribal identity, custom and obligation were continually stressed by male elders and colonial officers. But there was a more pleasurable side to the migrant's sense of belonging and desire to return home – the conviviality of village life and the comforts of home.

The local rural economies that men returned to afforded few cash cropping or other productive opportunities. After independence, village cash cropping became more commonplace, particularly that of tobacco production in Central Province. However, in government policy, plantation agriculture continued to be prioritized over smallholder production (Kydd and Christiansen 1982, Peters 2006). In 1975, the crash of a plane with migrants destined for South Africa caused President Banda to call a temporary halt to Malawian men's international migration. Banda had become concerned with the restricted wage labour supplies to Malawi's large-scale tea and tobacco plantations. By the early 1990s, the flow of export labour had virtually stopped; its demise hastened by the unravelling of the apartheid economy and its final dismantling by the Mandela government (Chirwa 1998). Meanwhile, Malawi's plantation wage labour opportunities were shrinking in the face of declining world agricultural commodity prices. As the migrant labour system collapsed, cash circulation in the Malawian countryside contracted.

Banda had actively discouraged urbanization and left governance of the countryside firmly in the hands of local tribal leaders answerable to the country's ubiquitous single political party, the Malawi Congress Party, and ultimately to himself. Rural infrastructural investment in roads, schools and health facilities had been minimal. Literacy rates and health indicators were exceptionally low by African standards.

Putting peasants first but far too late under economic liberalization of the 1990s

Towards the end of Banda's long presidency, as Malawi's export labour economy disintegrated and massive rural poverty loomed ahead, a government programme supporting peasant smallholders' production of burley tobacco and agricultural credit became a focus. The country was already well-known for its good-quality tobacco exports produced primarily on plantations but the measures to encourage peasant commodity production could not make up for the regime's preceding neglect. Banda relinquished power in 1994 and the Muluzi government that followed gained western donor backing to develop the country's smallholder peasant sector.

However, smallholder development goals were ambiguously positioned between the international financial institution's desire to alleviate poverty, on the one hand, and exhortations for peasant producers to conform to the competitive demands of the world market (Bryceson 2000, 2002a and b). Under the sway of structural adjustment and economic liberalization policies, it became glaringly apparent that Malawi's rural service and productive infrastructure were severely under-resourced. ADMARC, the national crop-buying parastatal, was downsized at the insistence of the World Bank. This move undermined cotton and tobacco producers' main market outlet and source of supply for improved inputs and the position of poor peasants as net food purchasers needing access to ADMARC's low, stable consumer prices (Mvula *et al.* 2003: 20).

During the 1990s, Malawi was one of Africa's poorest countries, sharing this label with a number of war-torn or extremely badly governed countries. The Muluzi government directed its efforts towards food security and poverty alleviation, along lines championed by Western donors' stated goals, by introducing a flint hybrid maize package for peasant farmers. Counterpoised to this, under pressure from the World Bank, the government gradually removed the fertilizer subsidy (Edriss *et al.* 2004).[2] Our 2003 CARE village focus group discussions revealed that 10 years after the government's removal of the subsidy, peasant farmers were still resentful, seeing this move as a government betrayal of their efforts to increase yields.[3]

---

2 Between 1991 and 2002 the price of fertilizer rose from MK 45.50 to MK 1650.50 per 50 kg bag: an increase by a factor of 36, giving Malawi one of the highest price ratios of nitrogen to maize in the world (Edriss *et al.* 2004).

3 Subsequently, in 2005, the newly elected Bingu Wa Mutharika, acting on rural pressure, introduced a universal fertilizer subsidy which has facilitated a bumper harvest in 2007 (Dugger

Government investment was also insufficiently directed at the rural poor. The prosperity of an upper stratum of burley tobacco producers did not percolate down to the majority of peasant farmers (Peters 1996, Tellegen 1997, Shah *et al.* 2002, Takane 2005). Malawi's smallholder agricultural sector stood out in the region as extremely low-yielding and limited by heavy mono-cropping of maize as a food crop and tobacco as a export crop (Ellis 2003). Government policies, giving priority to poverty alleviation, offered too little too late to peasant farmers.

Rural non-farm activity was severely constrained by the lack of local purchasing power. Tellegen's (1997) survey of income diversification in Central Province revealed that the production of alcoholic drinks was the most ubiquitous rural enterprise. Dominated by women producers, a third of all entrepreneurs in Tellegen's study were involved in brewing. The vast majority of female entrepreneurs were engaged in the production and sale of the local brew *masese* or distilled *kachasu.* In the early 1990s, a bag of maize sold to ADMARC earned 25 kwachas as opposed to quadrupled earnings that could be obtained when maize was used for beer brewing (Englund 1996, Tellegen 1997). Even higher profits were to be had from distilling *kachasu.* The inputs and skills were readily available and initial capital outlays were small because sophisticated equipment was unnecessary.

Men, and increasingly women, used alcohol to relax, have a good time and escape from the realities of their unpromising agricultural existence as well as serving as an important point of contact for soliciting *ganyu* contracts.[4] It is in this context of sinking rural economic prospects that the risk of famine emerged as a major threat to peasant welfare as outlined in the next section.

The bottom line: famine's impoverishing effects

Over the last half of the 20th century, Malawi experienced fluctuating grain harvests and food insecurity influenced by adverse climatic conditions, low-yielding female subsistence farming, and growing over-concentration on a single staple food, maize. The poor harvest of 2001-02, which triggered the most recent famine, had been preceded by a bumper harvest. De Waal and Whiteside (2003) argue that household famine vulnerability increased with the rising prevalence of HIV/AIDS, to produce a 'new variant famine' phenomenon. Certainly the 2001-02 famine was considered to be out of proportion to the level of the harvest shortfall. Rural food insecurity persisted during 2003.

2007).

4 In the poverty monitoring programme of the 2000s, alcohol abuse was cited as an attribute of the poor (Malawi, NEC 2002a, p. 15)

Rural households had relied heavily on remittances of male migrants working in distant places during earlier famines. Vaughan (1987) documents how male migrant labourers' earnings represented a vital support during the severe famine of 1949 as rural households experienced a narrowing range of local options for meeting their food needs. The government prohibited alcohol production to conserve cereal stocks. Beer brewing and petty trading were the first activities to cease during this famine, along with most *ganyu* labour. This placed women in a situation of unprecedented dependence on men. Those whose husbands were in wage employment stood a far better chance of gaining access to food than did those married to unwaged men (Vaughan 1987).

By contrast, during the 2001-02 famine the cushioning effect of migrant labourers' remittances was largely absent. Those who had offspring in urban areas had some recourse to funds/resources, but most rural households had to fend for themselves. *Ganyu* labour was the main sustainable way of obtaining food when people's household supplies ran out. Citing data from the nation-wide Targeted Input Programme (TIP), Table 1 shows rural households' changing portfolio of food sources during the course of the famine and its immediate aftermath (Nyirongo *et al.*, 2003 a and b'). In the 2001-02 agricultural season and also in the period after the 2002 maize harvest, *ganyu* food payments were the main means of obtaining food excluding consideration of own production and market purchase of food. In 2002-03, when donors had taken the famine situation seriously and made their major food relief effort, households' participation in *ganyu* to obtain food remained high at 46 per cent, topped by food aid at 56 per cent. In all three periods, the incidence of *ganyu* food payments superceded reliance on help from relations and external aid interventions. It should be noted that the incidence of *ganyu* paid in food may have been understated in this survey, because it is considered shameful to have to resort to it for provisioning household food needs. Roughly 98 per cent of households in 2001-02 resorted to maize purchase, compared to 75 per cent in 2002-03 when availability of food aid improved (Nyirongo *et al.* 2003b). *Ganyu* labour was most dominant in the Central Region where the CARE survey took place (see Table 1).

Table 1: Malawian rural households' non-market sources of food during the famine and its aftermath, 2001-03*

Source of food	% of households accessing source: 2001-02 Main season	2002 Post-harvest period	2002-03 Main season	Pre-harvest 2003 by Region: South	Central	North
Obtaining food through *ganyu*	53%	29%	46%	44%	61%	31%
Food aid	8%	10%	56%	54%	59%	53%
Food from friends/relatives	30%	17%	31%	23%	36%	39%
Food-for-work programmes	8%	3%	5%	1%	1%	17%
Under-5 programme	1%	4%	4%	3%	3%	9%
Other	2%	3%	9%	10%	10%	4%
No. of respondents	1411	1407	2750	1227	905	618

(Source: Nyirongo *et al.* 2003a, 43 & 2003b, 90-1 and personal communication with S. Levy, July 2005).

* It should be noted that this was a detailed study to determine the impact of targeted inputs (TIP) on rural households. The household figures are those shown for the non-TIP recipient households (2001-02 main season and 2002 post-harvest period) and all households (2002-03 main season). Generally there was very little difference between recipient and non-recipient households. Recipient households resorting to *ganyu* constituted 50 percent in the 2001-02 main season and 25 per-

cent in the 2002 post-harvest period, only 3 and 4 percent less than non-recipient households in each year respectively.

Ganyu labour's changing economic and moral content

From being an institutionalized form of *ad hoc* labour dating back to the 19th century, *ganyu* labour became a form of negative reciprocity (Sahlins 1974). During the 1990s *ganyu* contracts based on relations of reciprocity or patron-client ties dwindled, with a declining number of *ganyu* employers according preferential hiring or better remuneration to relatives or neighbours as a means of maintaining a local safety net (Whiteside 2000). Older women, however, were sometimes employed as *ganyu* labour 'out of kindness'. Englund (1996) argues that the reciprocity of *ganyu* contracts disintegrates the more distant the relational ties between labour contractor and labourer. In his Dedza district case study, when contractors hired Mozambican rather than local labour, wages and working conditions deteriorated. However, orphan focus group discussion participants in our 2003-04 CARE study mentioned a reversal of this practice:

> We prefer working for strangers rather than relatives because they offer lower wages as well as make upsetting remarks concerning the death of our parents. A stranger can offer twice as much money as a relative for washing clothes. (Orphan girls, FGD, matrilineal village 30 km from Lilongwe, 12 March 2004).

Several factors may account for *ganyu*'s *ad hoc* labour relations becoming more skewed to the economic interests of employers during the 1990s. Labour supply was outstripping demand, reducing the bargaining position of labourers with respect to wage levels and the nature of work tasks demanded. The removal of the fertilizer subsidy caused farmers to drastically reduce their improved input usage causing maize productivity to decline and shifting the allocation of rural labour from one's own family farm to other larger farms producing at scale or to non-agricultural activities. Suboptimal labour inputs depressed productivity further on peasant smallholdings (Edriss *et al.* 2004). Meanwhile the growing prevalence of HIV/AIDS compounded by the 2001-02 famine reinforced this tendency by limiting the number of people who were able to employ *ganyu* labour, on the one hand, at the same time as more and more rural dwellers, particularly women and youth, sought employment as *ganyu* casual labourers. The following sub-sections consider *ganyu* labour's changing characteristics in more detail.

Influence of food insecurity on ganyu labour

With the removal of producer subsidies over the preceding decade, commercial maize production ceased to be remunerative for farmers other than those producing on a large-scale with adequate capital to buy fertilizers (Levy *et al.* 2004). Farming households failed to achieve their households' basic food security from their small plots. Per capita maize production was on average: 49 kg for the ultra-poor, 63 kg for the poor and 116 kg for the non-poor, all falling short of the average 155 kg minimum staple food requirement, leaving even the non-poor in a deficit position (Malawi, NSO 2002 and FAO/WFP 2002).

Increasing resort to *ganyu* labour in the preceding decade had been intimately related to the worsening of both chronic and acute food insecurity. Mvula *et al.* (2003: 21) identified three main rural strata on the basis of their level of food insecurity: the 'well-to-do' who had food stocks that on average last eight to nine months of the year, the 'a bit well-to-do' who had food sufficient to cover four to six months and finally the 'have-nots' who usually had less than one hectare of land and harvest only one to two months of their household's food supply needs. While everyone's food security had deteriorated the latter group experienced a precipitous slide downwards:

> . . . a decade ago, the 'have-nots'/poor households used to have maize for 6-8 months, they had more livestock which have been sold off to cushion the effects of hunger and they had more *ganyu* opportunities compared to the current situation where the demand has highly superseded its supply. (Mvula *et al.* 2003: 26).

When a household has to contend with a near continuous state of food uncertainty, their livelihood strategies revolve around the imperative of obtaining food on a day-by-day basis. Under these circumstances, *ganyu* labour can become a way of life, but one that was likely to exacerbate rather than solve the household's food production constraints. Opportunities for *ganyu* employment increased during the peak agricultural seasons posing an allocative dilemma for *ganyu* labourers. Trying to satisfy their immediate need for food, they were forced by circumstances to do *ganyu* labour at the critical time when they should have been preparing, planting and weeding their own fields. In doing so, they were likely to exacerbate their future food insecurity.

Poor households were likely to be planting late because they first had to do *ganyu* to earn enough to buy seeds. Some employers allowed their labourers to work on their own fields in a timely fashion, but Whiteside (2000: 5) saw the benefits of this benevolence being counteracted by an entrenched and rising section of the population becoming dependent on *ganyu* for an increasing proportion of their livelihood in some districts. During the 1990s, the extent of *ganyu* in a particular area was seen as a sensitive poverty measure (Whiteside 2000: 3-6).

Acute food insecurity in the form of famine had a profound impact on the nature and extent of *ganyu*. Generally during a famine the incidence of *ganyu* labour rose, far exceeding demand as many smallholders previously able to hire *ganyu* labour could no longer do so, as observed by Peters (1996) during the 1992/93 famine. When food supplies improved due to famine relief, increased market supply, or the following year's harvest, the supply of *ganyu* labour usually contracted (Table 1).

During 2001-02 *ganyu* food payments superceded food aid as a source of food (Nyirongo *et al.* 2003b). In early 2003, the World Food Programme and other donors delivered their major famine relief effort, household reliance on *ganyu* food payments displayed an interesting pattern. The very poor and poor continued to depend heavily on *ganyu* food payments on a par with food aid, whereas the ultra poor and the two most well-off income categories, the moderate and least poor groups, had stronger leanings to food aid. The ultra-poor were considered to have far more households who lacked adult labour or were incapacitated by age or disease, especially AIDS, which would have hindered their participation in *ganyu* labour. The more well-off groups, on the other hand, could choose to avoid doing *ganyu* once their hunger was alleviated by food aid. In general, and with the exception of the ultra-poor, food from relations and *ganyu* food payments tended to vary inversely with a household's poverty status.

Ganyu labour and rural economic differentiation

There was a widening gulf between the shrinking number in rural Malawi who could afford to hire *ganyu* labour and the expanding number who had to seek *ganyu* labour during the eight-year inter-famine period between 1993 and 2001. *Ganyu* was an integral part of deepening rural impoverishment. Leach's (1995) study of 420 smallholders found the majority of *ganyu* labour was being performed by smallholders for other smallholders. Pearce *et al.* (1996) reckoned that three-quarters of villages in Salima District had at least one better-off farmer who hired *ganyu* in 1994/95, hiring between two to twenty labourers often for two to three times a week for several months (cited in Whiteside 2000). The terms of *ganyu* contracts were worsening. Edriss *et al.* (2004) estimates that real wages declined from a 1985-94 average of 13.8 Kwacha per person day to an average of 4.8 Kwacha over 1995-2000, with *ganyu* accounting for 67 per cent of rural households' total income in 2000 (Malawi, NEC 2002b).

The famine accentuated existing tendencies towards mass impoverishment and recourse to *ganyu* labour. Figure 1 shows household income sources by poverty group in 2002-03.* *Ganyu* labour was the predominant income source for all rural strata except the least poor, who reported a higher incidence of crop sales and the very poor who relied roughly equally on the two sources.

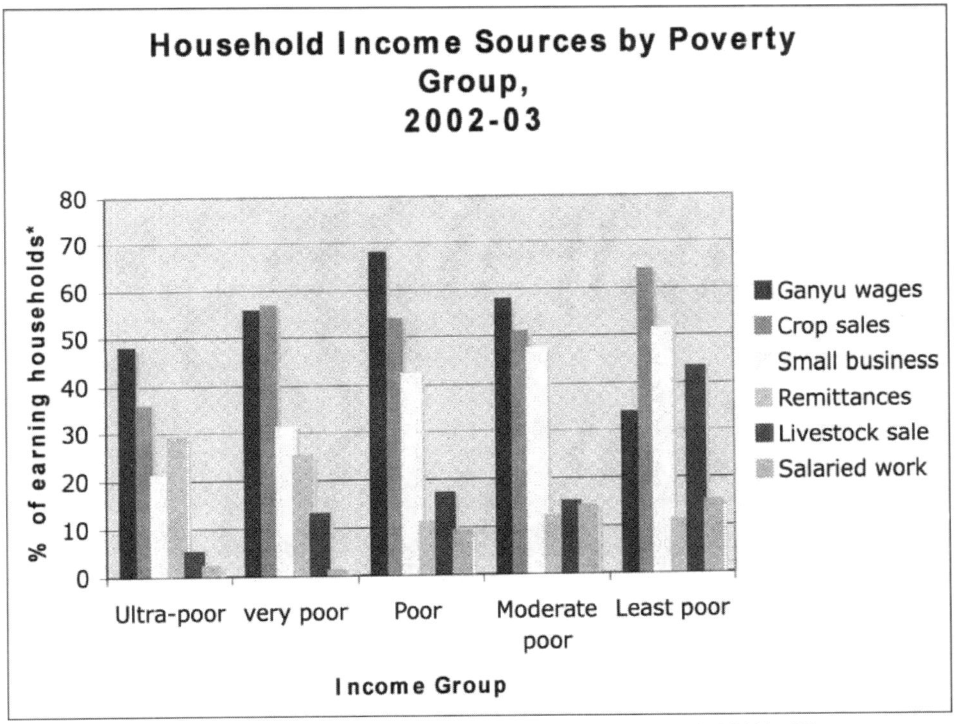

Figure 1. Household income sources, 2002-2003 (Source: Nyirongo et al. 2003b, 82).

* Survey of 859 households who did not receive TIP inputs in 2002-2003.

The famine's 'winners' and 'losers' coalesced in the interplay of land, labour and capital allocation. Widespread famine distress and destitution were inevitable given the protracted nature of villagers' food insecurity and the fact that it was compounded by the prevalence of HIV/AIDS. Chirwa (2004), on the basis of a comparison of rural household panel data in 1998 and 2002, provides insights into the welfare dynamics of the famine. In 1998, 80 per cent of all households in the sample were considered impoverished. Four years later during the famine the figure was 91 percent. In 1998, 36 percent of household heads were reported to be ill. In 2002 the likelihood of these households moving into more serious poverty was 16 percent higher than average.

Ganyu employers have to have surplus food or cash, both of which become relatively scarce in rural households during a famine. In Peters' (1996) rural case study, the least poor 10 to 20 per cent of rural households were employers of *ganyu* labour during the 1990s. Within the rural areas, there was a cadre of civil servants, teachers, and health workers who received salaried income, which in the above Figure ranges from 1 and 2 per cent for the ultra and very poor to 14 and 15 per cent for the moderate and least poor respectively. The fortunes of the rural households who had salaried incomes during the famine were distinct. In Chirwa's (2004) study, they constituted 11 per cent of all households in 1998 and were 13 per cent more likely during the famine four years later to have economically advanced given their reliable earnings compared with households based on agricultural commodity and labour sales. Many straddled agricultural, trading and community organizational activities in their villages (van Donge 2004).

The 'winners' with cash for food and labour were also in a strategic position for asset purchase. Mvula *et al.* (2003: 19) observed households in Lipiri and Mikundi leasing productive pieces of their land. Leasing can signal distress on the part of households who have insufficient labour or capital to work the land, or alternatively face a food security crisis necessitating their access to food or cash to buy food immediately. Complicated interlocking contracts involving land and labour markets emerged. Land leasing and sharecropping arrangements often signalled polarization between those forced by declining economic circumstances to rent or sell their land as opposed to those of growing affluence, either salaried rural dwellers and entrepreneurs or urban-based patrons, who took advantage of the opportunity to expand their rural assets. In our 2003-04 CARE study villages, households experiencing impoverishment had increasingly been resorting to a range of asset-depleting measures like mortgaging their crops and selling household or agricultural assets.

Leasing land in these circumstances means foregoing subsistence production and cashcrop earnings from cultivation. When this divestment tendency persists, broad swathes of rural households relinquish the agrarian assets that enable them to secure their basic needs independently of casual wage labour. Renting their land further undermines their already low bargaining position pushing them more deeply into a future of casual *ganyu* labour.

Ganyu labour and transactional sex

Women have been involved in *ganyu* for probably as long as men but there are large gender differentials in *ganyu* remuneration. Whiteside (1998) reported piecework daily rates of 20 Kwacha for men, 5-10 Kwacha for women and 2-3 Kwacha for children. These differentials were locally justified by the view that men were putting in a full day's work whereas women were distracted by domestic duties. Besides attitudinal difference regarding the value of female labour, there were the very real issues of need for cash. During the 1990s, female heads of households became especially identified with *ganyu*. Their lack of other income sources lowered the opportunity costs of their labour. Furthermore, it was noted that women were restricted to *ganyu* work close to their homes, influenced by notions of social propriety as well as childcare responsibilities, whereas men ventured further distances and across the border into Mozambique where they could find higher wage levels.

The 2001-02 famine catalyzed changes in female *ganyu* labour patterns. First, women increasingly left the confines of the village to seek labour opportunities in more distant markets. Second, in the face of fierce competition for work they were increasingly conceding to additional 'tasks', notably the provision of sexual services. These tendencies were strongly associated with and rationalized in terms of women's perception of themselves as food provisioners under the duress of famine. The household welfare crisis was dramatized by women's term for their *ganyu* labour search; '*kusokolo*' literally translated 'looking for food'.

The incorporation of women's transactional sex into *ganyu* contracts on a widening scale surfaced in response to deepening household impoverishment (Shah 2002, Shah *et al.* 2002). The lack of local purchasing power prompted women to travel to trading centres, Lilongwe and other nearby places to earn cash or food. En-route or at their destinations, they encountered economic propositions that sexually compromised them. For example, in our study village closest to Lilongwe, the women had been going to the grain mill in Area 25 desperate to collect the maize bran that was left after the milling process. This often involved staying overnight on site to get access to this resource. Men working at the mill took advantage of this and offered the women *ganyu* contracts. The Village Action Committee in our study area described the phenomena as follows:

> We think mostly people are getting infected with HIV/AIDS because of poverty. What usually happens at the household level is that the woman is affected seriously because of her deep concern for her children. She starts looking for *ganyu* opportunities that are not easy to find in the village so she goes to Area 25 where there are different types of *ganyu*

like cultivating in people's gardens, doing household chores. Some decide just to go to the mill to look for maize bran that they can use for food at home... When our women go to Area 25 they meet men who are ready to release quick money if they sleep with our women which in most cases they do comply because of the magnitude of their food supply problems and its impact on their families and the suffering of the children. This situation is rampant in months like January when the hunger is at its peak. (VAC FGD, patrilineal village 30 km from Lilongwe, 4 December, 2003)

Village men in the FGD explained the situation as follows:

The men offer them the *ganyu* but also entice them to sleep with them. Since the women are bringing food [maize bran], we cannot object [as husbands]. (Men's FGD, patrilineal village 30 km from Lilongwe, 4 December, 2003)

Transactional sex in rural Malawi must be distinguished from prostitution. Prostitution refers to people soliciting sex as an occupation and frequently entails women moving away from their home areas to seek their livelihood as a prostitute in a town or trading settlement. They have a vested professional interest in adopting safe sex practices and can impose safe sex as a contractual condition of their service to their clients (Campbell 2003, van den Borne 2005). Rural peasant women who happen to enter into sexual encounters are ill-prepared to bargain the terms of such a happenstance sexual liaison. To feed their families, they risk exposure to HIV/AIDS. The diffuse, haphazard nature of transactional sex in Malawi's rural areas makes safe sex practices far more difficult to promote.

The widely reported cases of women and girls exchanging sex for basic foodstuffs have taken place in the context of having nothing else to offer in exchange. Rural peasant women are reduced to transacting an 'essential exchange' in all respects: sex for basic food needs.

Conclusion

Ganyu, as a traditional labour exchange arrangement originally embedded in affective ties, has historically encapsulated aspects of subsistence labour, local moral economies and collective responses to community-experienced threat. This chapter has probed the contradictory nature of *ganyu* tracing it from its origins as the *ad hoc* exchange of casual labour for food or cash in a pioneer land clearance setting to its current form, a means of surviving deepening rural duress in a peasantry wracked by insufficient land, rising economic differentiation, HIV/AIDS and famine. Rural land-labour ratios have experienced a complete inversion. Land abundance and labour scarcity have evolved towards land scarcity and labour gluts.

Malawian smallholder farmers are at a crossroads both economically and politically. Throughout the 20th century, famines imposed sporadic hunger and economic distress, but village life proceeded on the basis of a *dual system* of female subsistence production and male remittances that converged with the regularized return of male migrants to their home villages. After being articulated to Southern Africa's wage labour economy for almost a century, rural men have now faced redundancy of their export wage labour and international donors' expectation that they become *in situ* peasant commodity producers.

Now growing landlessness and rural distress are taking the form of classic patterns of agrarian dispossession and proletarianization akin to the historical experience of Europe and Asia. Increasing peasant economic differentiation during the 1990s followed by the 2001-02 famine greatly enhanced the bargaining position of rural elites and other external agents pursuing economic accumulation, social aggrandizement and pleasure-seeking through *ganyu* contractual relations at the expense of desperate, food-seeking peasants. Weighed down by the growing prevalence of HIV/AIDS, local village economies contended with famine in the absence of reliable income flows from labour remittances, cashcropping or female brewing. In this context, *ganyu* labour became crucial to the welfare of Malawi's peasant farming households. Tragically at the same time as *ganyu* became so critical to rural welfare, its norms of reciprocation and welfare orientation were undermined. The historical tension between the moral empathy embedded in *ganyu* and its role in optimizing rural factor exchange tipped in favour of the latter.

Having previously argued the economically and socially responsive nature of *ganyu* and its changing etymology, it is useful to consider what *ganyu* has become with its growing ubiquity. *Ganyu* offers extremely low pay and demeaning work conditions – a quick fix for hunger rather than a long-term earning or accumulation strategy. As soon as hunger or the emergency is over, people are eager to forsake *ganyu* activities if they can. Remuneration levels during and in the aftermath of the famine were barely enough for one's day's food needs.

Defining 'proletarianization' as a process in which growing numbers are divorced from their land and other means of independent livelihood and become dependent on wage labour for daily subsistence, the evidence presented here suggests that Malawian peasant households' dwindling land assets, increasing food insecurity and growing reliance on *ganyu* casual wage labour was a classic example of a proletarianization trajectory. In the aftermath of famine in 2003 and 2004, *ganyu* labour represented a vortex of impoverishment, intensifying the unequal exchange between haves and have-nots in Malawi's local rural economies.

References

Bryceson, D.F., 2000. African peasants' centrality and marginality: rural labour transformations, in Bryceson, D.F., C. Kay & J. Mooij, eds, *Disappearing Peasantries: Rural Labour in Africa, Asia and Latin America*. London: Intermediate Technology Publications, pp. 37-63.

Bryceson, D.F., 2002a. The scramble in Africa: reorienting rural livelihoods. *World Development* 30(5): 725-39.

Bryceson, D.F., 2002b. Multiplex livelihoods in rural Africa: recasting the terms and conditions of gainful employment. *Journal of Modern African Studies* 40(1): 1-28.

Campbell, C., 2003. *'Letting Them Die': Why HIV/AIDS Prevention Programmes Fail*. Oxford: James Currey.

Chirwa, W.C., 1998. Aliens and AIDS in Southern Africa: the Malawi-South African debate. *African Affairs* 97: 53-79.

Chirwa, W.C., 2004. 'Access to land, growth and poverty reduction in Malawi', Paper prepared for the research project Macroeconomic Policy Choices for Growth and Poverty Reduction funded by the North-South Institute, Canada, www.sarpn.org.za/documents/doo/007/index.php.

Davison, J., 1995. Must women work together? Development agency assumptions versus changing relations of production in Southern Malawi households, in: Bryceson, D.F., ed., *Women Wielding the Hoe*. Oxford: Berg Publishers, pp. 181-99.

De Waal, A. & A. Whiteside, 2003. "New variant famine": AIDS and food crisis in Southern Africa. *The Lancet* 362: 1234-37.

Dugger, C.W., 2007. Ending famine, simply by ignoring the experts. *New York Times*, 2 December 2007.

Edriss, A., H. Tchale & P. Wobst, 2004. 'The Impact of Labour Market Liberalization on Maize Productivity and Rural Poverty in Malawi', Robert Bosch Foundation under Policy Analysis for Sustainable Agricultural Development (PASAD) Project at the University of Bonn, Germany (http://www.pasad.uni-bonn.de/pasadJournalpaper.pdf).

Ellis, F., 2003. 'Human Vulnerability and Food Insecurity: Policy Implications', Forum for Food Security in Southern Africa, Overseas Development Group, University of East Anglia, July 2003.

Englund, H., 1996. 'The Self in Self-Interest: Change and Agricultural Labour in Malawi', Paper presented at the Workshop 'The Dynamics of Local Economy in Africa', 19-20 May, 1996, Institute of Development Studies, University of Helsinki.

FAO/WFP 2002, FAO/WFP Crop and Food Supply Assessment Mission to Malawi, 29 May 2002 (http://documents.wfp.org/stellent/groups/public/documents/ena/wfp036450.htm)

Konings, P., 2008. Privatisation and labour militancy: the case of Cameroon's tea estates. *Journal of Contemporary African Studies* 26(1): 51-70.

Konings, P., 1998. *Unilever Estates in Crisis and the Power of Organizations in Cameroon.* Hamburg: Lit Verlag – Leiden: African Studies Centre.

Konings, P., 1996. Chieftaincy, labour control and capitalist development in Cameroon. *Journal of Legal Pluralism and Unofficial Law* 37/38: 329-346.

Konings, P., 1993. *Labour Resistance in Cameroon: Managerial Strategies & Labour Resistance in the Agro-Industrial Plantations of the Cameroon Development Corporation.* Portsmouth, N.H.: Heinemann.

Kydd, J. & R. Christiansen, 1982. Structural change in Malawi since independence: consequences of a development strategy based on large-scale agriculture. *World Development* 10(5): 355-75.

Laslett, P., 1965. *The World We Have Lost*. London: Methuen and Co. Ltd.

Leach, M., 1995. '*Ganyu* Labour: The Implications of Off-Farm Labour for Alley Cropping in Malawi', Addfood Project (mimeo), cited in Whiteside 2000.

Levy, S. with C. Barahona & B. Chinsinga, 2004. 'Food Security, Social Protection, Growth and Poverty Reduction Synergies: The Starter Pack Programme in Malawi' 95, September 2004.

Malawi, National Economic Council (NEC), 2002a. *Qualitative Impact Monitoring (QIM) of the Poverty Alleviation Policies and Programmes in Malawi, Volume 1: Survey Findings*. Lilongwe.

Malawi, NEC, 2002b. *Economic Report 2001*, Government Publications, Zomba.

Malawi, National Statistical Office (NSO), 2002. *Statistical Yearbook 2002*. Government Publications, Zomba.

Mandala, E.C. 1990. *Work and Control in a Peasant Economy: A History of the Lower Tchiri Valley in Malawi, 1859-1960*. Madison: University of Wisconsin Press.

Mvula, P.M., E.W. Chirwa & J. Kadzandira, 2003. Poverty and Social Impact Assessment in Malawi: Closure of ADMARC Markets, Zomba, Wadonda Consult and World Bank, Social Development Department, April 2003.

Nyirongo, C.C., H.C.Y. Gondwe, F., F.B.M. Msiska, H.A.J. Mdyetseni, F.M.C.E.

Kamanga, with S. Levy 2003a, '2001-02 Targeted Inputs Programme (TIP) 'Evaluation Module 1 – Food Production and Security in Rural Malawi: Main Season Post-Harvest Survey', Malawi, Ministry of Agriculture and UK, Department for International Development, March 2003.

Nyirongo, C.C., F.B.M. Msiska, H.A.J. Mdyetseni, F.M.C.E. Kamanga, with S. Levy, 2003b, '2002-03 Extended Targeted Inputs Programme (ETIP) 'Evaluation Module 1 – Food Production and Security in Rural Malawi: Pre-Harvest Survey', Malawi, Ministry of Agriculture and UK, Department for International Development, August 2003.

O'Laughlin, B., 2002. Proletarianisation, agency and changing rural livelihoods: forced labour and resistance in colonial Mozambique. *Journal of Southern African Studies* 28(3): 511-30.

Peters, P., 1996. Failed Magic or Social Context? Market Liberalization and the Rural Poor in Malawi, Cambridge, Mass.: Harvard Institute for International Development (http://www.hiid.harvard.edu/pub/pdfs/S62.pdf).

Peters, P., 2006. Rural income and poverty in a time of radical change in Malawi. *Journal of Development Studies* 42(2): 322-345.

Phiri, K.M., 1977. Cultural and political change in the pre-colonial history of Malawi. *The Society of Malawi Journal* 30(2): 6-10.

Phiri, K.M., 1984. Production and exchange in pre-colonial Malawi, in *Malawi: an Alternative Pattern of Development*. Edinburgh: University of Edinburgh, African Studies Centre.

Reniers, G., 2003. Divorce and remarriage in rural Malawi. *Demographic Research* 6: 175-205 (www.demographic-research.org).

Sahlins, M., 1974. *Stone Age Economics*. London: Tavistock Publications.

Scott, J.C., 1976. *The Moral Economy of the Peasant*. New Haven: Yale University Press.

Shah, M.K., N. Osbourne, T. Mbilizi & G. Vilili 2002. 'Impact of HIV/AIDS on Agricultural Productivity and Rural Livelihoods in the Central Region of Malawi', CARE International Consultancy Report, January 2002.

Shah, M.K., 2002. 'Buying Sex for Three Sweet Potatoes: Participatory Assessment of Adolescent Sexual and Reproductive Health in Makala Village, Lilongwe', CARE International Consultancy Report, August 2002.

Sugimura, K., 2004. African forms of moral economy in rural communities: comparative perspectives. *Tanzanian Journal of Population Studies and Development* 11(2): 21-37.

Takane, T., 2005. Tobacco and smallholders in Malawi: village case studies in the

Mchinji and Mangochi districts, *African Research Series* (Institute of Developing Economies, Chiba, Japan) 11: 93-119.

Tellegen, N., 1997. *Rural Enterprises in Malawi: Necessity or Opportunity?* Aldershot: Ashgate (African Studies Centre Research Series 12).

Van Donge, J.K., 2004. 'Exploring the "real" maize market in Malawi', Paper presented at the African Studies Association of the UK Biennial Conference, Goldsmith's College, University of London, 13-15 September 2004.

Van den Borne, F., 2005. *Trying to Survive in Times of Poverty and AIDS: Women and Multiple Partner Sex in Malawi.* Amsterdam: University of Amsterdam (PhD thesis).

Vaughan, M., 1987. *The Story of an African Famine: Gender and Famine in 20th Century Malawi.* Cambridge: Cambridge University Press.

White, L., 1987. *Magomero: Portrait of an African Village*, Cambridge: Cambridge University Press.

Whiteside, M., 1998. 'When the whole is more than the sum of the parts: the effect of cross-border interactions on livelihood security in Southern Malawi and Northern Mozambique', Report for Oxfam GB (www.ids.ac.uk/eldis/malmoz.htm).

Whiteside, M., 2000. '*Ganyu* Labour in Malawi and Its Implications for Livelihood Security Interventions – An Analysis of Recent Literature and Implications for Poverty Alleviation'. London, Overseas Development Institute, Agricultural Research & Extension Network Paper no. 99 (http://www.odi.org.uk/agren/papers/agrenpaper_99.pdf).

Labour migration from the Gold Coast to the Dutch East Indies: Recruting African troops for the Dutch colonial army in the age of indentured labour

Ineke van Kessel

Labour migration – both forced and voluntary – has been a defining feature of Ghana's history over many centuries. In popular memory and in the academic literature, the Atlantic slave trade is the most prominent example of labour migrations from West Africa. In recent decades, large numbers of Ghanaian migrants have fanned out to Europe, the United States and the Middle East. Less known is an episode in between the age of the slave trade and the contemporary period of voluntary migration. After the abolition of the slave trade, indentured labour became the preferred method of meeting global labour demands. The terminology of indentured labour is usually associated with Asia and the Americas, but certain recruiting practices used in 19th century West Africa fall into the same category. One example is the recruitment of West African soldiers for the Dutch colonial army in the Netherlands East Indies.

The story of the African troops in the Dutch East Indies Army is the subject of my book Zwarte Hollanders *(Black Dutchmen), published in 2005. While the book focuses on the history of these 3,080 West African men and their Indo-African descendants, in this contribution I interrogate my research material from a fresh perspective. Inspired by the work of my long-time colleague Piet Konings, I analyse the recruitment of African troops for the Dutch colonial army from the vantage point of labour studies. Ever since his dissertation on the trade union movement in Ghana (Konings 1977), labour movements, labour militancy, labour conditions and workers' consciousness have been a prominent theme in Konings' prolific research. While most of Piet Konings' work concentrates on post-independence West Africa, this chapter will explore labour practices in the 19th century, with a focus on indentured labour.*

Widely practiced in the transitional decades between slavery and free labour, indentured labour is a form of contract labour. A worker under the indentured labour system agreed to work for another person for a given period of time (usually between 3 and 7 years) in exchange for payment of passage, accommodation and food, and sometimes a modest wage. After expiry of the contract, the indentured worker was free to establish him or herself in the new land, and was sometimes entitled to a bonus in the form of money or land. Indentured servitude was instrumental in the European colonisation of the Americas and was again widely used in the 19th century when Asian workers were recruited for employment elsewhere in European colonial empires. Apart from South Africa, indentured labour did not become common practice in Africa, but this chapter will argue that certain recruitment schemes in West Africa can best be understood in the context of indentured labour.

Introduction

Labour shortages were endemic in colonial societies. Plantation labour and mining were notoriously unattractive, but the army posed problems of its own. In their search to satisfy the voracious appetite for labour in commercial empires and colonial societies, rulers developed racial and ethnic stereotypes as to which 'race' was most suitable to perform certain jobs. Africans were deemed most suitable for hard physical labour in tropical climates. They were also portrayed as 'martial races', fit to fill the manpower needs of both Islamic and European armies (Killingray 2000; Segal 2001). This article will first give a brief overview of the indentured labour system, followed by some remarks on the recruiting practices of colonial armies. Next, I discuss in more detail one peculiar aspect of inter-colonial labour migration in the Dutch colonial empire: the recruitment of West African soldiers for the Dutch East Indies army in the 19th century. In the concluding section, I situate their experience within the context of the indentured labour system.

Indentured labour

As David Northrup (1995) has pointed out, indentured labour was not a 19th century innovation: indenture had a long history in British colonies of the Americas. More than half of all European migrants to the British colonies in the 17th and 18th century are estimated to have been indentured. A trickle continued to arrive in the first quarter of the 19th century, until the new, largely Asian, indentured migrants began to arrive in the 1830s (Northrup 1995: 4):

> These new indentured migrants differed from their European predecessors in more ways than their origins. Indentured Asians, Africans, and Pacific Islanders of the nineteenth century went to a wider variety of destinations in the Americas, as well as to islands in the Indian and Pacific Oceans, to Australia, and to parts of East and Southern Africa, making theirs more global than the European migrations across the Atlantic. Unlike the earlier European indentured servants who generally received only their maintenance, the indentured labourers of the nineteenth century received wages along with free housing and medical care, along with clothing and full rations in many cases.

The earlier indentured migrants had largely been displaced by slaves. Now the new indentured migrants were recruited initially as successors to the slaves freed in the British colonies in the 1830s. When the French, Dutch and Spanish colonies ended slavery, they too turned to indentured labour, as would the owners of plantations and mines in areas that had never had slavery.

Some commentators have portrayed indentured labour as little else than a disguised continuation of slavery. In the case of African indentured labour, Monica Schuler has argued that, "in practice... African indentured labour recruitment cannot be distinguished from either the 'legal' or the 'illegal' slave trade." (Schuler 1986: 125-127). Northrup admits that there are certain similarities, such as harsh treatment and tough working conditions, but believes the differences to be more striking. Contract labour was a voluntary bondage of limited duration. After expiry of the contract, workers had the option to return to their country of origin, in most cases with free passage and often with substantial savings (Northrup 1995: 7).

In terms of supply and demand, or the factors of 'push' and 'pull', the migrations of free and bonded migrants followed largely similar patterns. Both 'free' Europeans and indentured non-Europeans were pushed to leave their home and friends by economic misery, discrimination, and famine at home and pulled to new locations overseas by hopes of better conditions and opportunities. Both resulted in permanent settlement as well as cyclical migration. After the abolition of slavery, many planters' first preference was for European labourers, whose work habits they believed superior. But in spite of massive out-migration from Europe in this century, most preferred temperate climates and avoided plantation labour. Several British colonies attempted to meet their labour needs by recruiting Africans freed from slave ships. British naval patrols policed the West African coast to search ships suspected of illegal slave trading. As it was not feasible for liberated Africans to return to their home countries, most of them were brought to Sierra Leone. Between 1841 and 1850, the British West Indian colonies imported some 13,500 liberated Africans from Sierra Leone plus an equal number from other liberation depots. But these numbers fell as the naval patrols proved successful in ending the slave trade. However, much larger numbers of indentured workers were obtained from India, initially for Mauritius and later for British Guyana and the West Indies (Northrup 1995: 22-23).

The French experimented with the 'rachat', the repurchase of slaves in Senegal to secure labour for public works, on 14-year contracts. From 1854, repurchased Africans began to be transported to the French Caribbean colonies on six-year contracts. During the eight years of its operation some 18,400 African contract workers went to French Guyana, Martinique and Guadeloupe on conditions that differed little from slavery. As abolitionist lobbies sounded the alarm and scandal mounted, the British agreed to give the French access to the better regulated Indian labour market on condition that labour imports from Africa were terminated (*ibid.*: 27-28).

Planters in Surinam preferred Chinese workers, who were seen as the most industrious and dependable. However, after China in 1873 banned further indentured labour migration, Dutch planters turned to India. The treaty with Britain to allow the Dutch access to the recruitment of labour from India coincided with the cession of Elmina to the British in 1872. As the transfer of its last foothold on the Gold Coast to Britain was linked to two other treaties with London, the deal enabled the Dutch government to persuade parliament that at least the Netherlands was receiving some compensation for the loss of Elmina. Some 34,500 Indians were introduced over the next 44 years with the right of a free return passage after a five-year contract. Between 1853 and 1920 Surinam planters also imported 19,000 indentured labourers from Java. After China lifted its ban on labour recruitment in 1893, the country became an important source of manpower for the Dutch plantations on Sumatra. At the beginning of the 20th century, some 100.0000 'Coolies' worked on Sumatra's East Coast (Breman 1989: 2).

In Africa, recruitment of indentured labour was closely linked to the ending of the long-standing slave trade. African slaves had constituted the bulk of the intercontinental slave trade, but the portion of Africans in the new indentured labour migrations was modest. Asians dominate the global picture of the indentured labour force, with a limited number of Africans for the period up to 1870. Recruitment on a voluntary basis was not successful, because the 'push factor' was lacking: Africans saw no compelling reasons to venture overseas for long periods of hard physical labour. Unlike Asia, land was abundant in most parts of Africa, and long distance travel within the continent was expensive and cumbersome. Europeans were only in control of scattered coastal settlements.

Indentured labour from Africa had its origins in the British suppression of the Atlantic slave trade. From 1808, when the Abolition of the Slave Trade Act (adopted on 25 March 1807) took effect, able-bodied young men were inducted into the West India Regiments or into the Royal Africa Corps of the British navy, on the basis of lifetime service. Except for these military recruits Britain resisted shipping liberated persons out of Sierra Leone for several decades, as trans-Atlantic migrations were reminiscent of the slave trade. The end of slavery in the British West Indies and Guyana made the problem of labour shortages more acute. Restrictions for recruiting liberated Africans in Sierra Leone for overseas employment were lifted in 1840. Faced with a lack of volunteers, recruiters began exploring the potential of neighbouring populations. Along the Liberian coast, Europeans had a longstanding practice of hiring local men, known as Kru, as hands on European vessels trading along the West African coast. They were highly regarded and praised for their 'hard work, loyalty and thrift' (Northrup 1995: 45-46). However, they proved unwilling to sign up for the Caribbean colonies, as they preferred short term contracts and disliked plantation work. Between 1841 and 1857, the British and later the French succeeded in recruiting only some 2,400 Kru for the Caribbean colonies. The Dutch contemplated recruiting Kru labourers for Surinam, but never got around to doing so. Later in the 19th century they did turn to Liberia to recruit soldiers for the East Indies army, an ill-fated venture that will be described later in this chapter.

Having abolished the slave trade, the British were determined that other European countries should follow suit in order to prevent unfair competition. The Dutch, by now a small nation, had no option but to heed British warnings, but the French, Spanish and Portuguese proved less receptive. Meanwhile, the slave trade continued from West Africa to Brazil and Cuba on a much larger scale than the transports of indentured Africans to the Caribbean. Northrup estimates that less than 10 percent of over 60,000 overseas indentured workers from Africa were completely voluntary: the Kru and a number of liberated Africans from Sierra Leone. He ranks the slaves redeemed by the French and the Dutch for an overseas destination in the category of forced labour (Northrup 1995: 51). This is a conclusion that I will contest, as far as the Dutch military recruitment on the Gold Coast is concerned. The later Dutch effort in Liberia can indeed be categorized as forced migration.

Africa was not only a source of labour, but also became a destination for indentured labour from Asia. Best known is the story of indentured Indians who built the East African railways and worked in the sugar plantations of Natal. They left a lasting Indian presence in East and Southern Africa, unlike the 60,000 Chinese miners who were recruited on three-year contracts for the goldmines of the Transvaal. This experiment was terminated because of opposition by white workers. A Dutch governor in Elmina, C. Nagtglas, at one point contemplated the importation of Chinese workers for plantation labour, because local Africans were not willing to work on plantations.[1] Nothing came of it, but the British did later experiment with bringing Chinese mineworkers to the Gold Coast. In discussing the 'Native labour question', British colonial officials expressed a firm belief in the superiority of Chinese over African labour. The Chinese were depicted as hardworking, disciplined and productive, while Africans were seen as racially inferior: unskilled, indolent and unproductive (Akurang-Parry 2001: 372).

In discussing the differences between slave labour and indentured labour, Northrup compares the mortality on board ship and for the duration of the contract. Unlike slaves, indentured workers received a wage. One other important distinction is of course the option to return home after expiry of the contract. In nearly all cases, a majority of ex-indentured workers opted to settle in their new environment. In terms of strategies of protest and resistance, both slaves and indentured workers could resort to suicide, desertion, absenteeism, strikes and open rebellion. In most cases, these protests were aimed at securing proper treatment and not at contesting the status of bonded labourers. Direct confrontations however were rare: most indentured migrants accommodated to the new life and made the best of it. We will return to these issues when discussing the experiences of African soldiers in the Dutch colonial army as compared with the general patterns of indentured labour.

African soldiers in colonial armies

Enlisting Africans in colonial armies was common practice during the 19th and 20th centuries. Like the Africans in the Dutch East Indies army, the famous Tirailleurs Sénégalais, established in 1857, were also largely of servile descent (Echenberg 1986). African soldiers were not only instrumental in wars of conquest and in the consolidation of empire in Africa but were also used for military expeditions overseas. In 1827 the French sent 200 Wolof soldiers to Madagascar, followed in 1831 by the dispatching of 220 troops to Guyana. As we have already seen, the British recruited among freed slaves in Sierra Leone to swell the ranks of the British West India regiments. In the 20th century, the King's African Ri-

[1] Nationaal Archief, The Hague (hereafter NA), Verslag wegens de overdragt aan Engeland van de Nederlandsche Bezittingen ter Kuste van Guinea. Kamerstukken zitting 1873-1874.

fles played a vital role in the consolidation of British rule in East Africa (Parsons 1999).

The rationale for African recruitment was remarkably similar in all cases: a shortage of European recruits and high mortality rates among European soldiers who, voluntarily or involuntarily, were dispatched to the tropics. The lower cost of local personnel could also have been a compelling argument, although there were obvious limitations to cost cutting. The loyalty of African troops was generally ensured by granting them special benefits and privileges. Thus, even when they were of servile origins, African soldiers used their newly acquired corporate identity as military men to enhance their status *vis-à-vis* civilian society. It fitted the purposes of colonial rulers to instill their African soldiers with a sense of superiority over their civilian colonial subjects. In his history of the King's African Rifles, Parsons pointed out that African servicemen both consciously and unconsciously exploited the contradictions of the colonial state to seek greater rights and status. He aptly quotes Ann Laura Stoler and Frederick Cooper who remind us that: "One of the most basic forms of colonial control (...) depended on soldiers who were simultaneously coerced and coercing, who enforced the will of the elite yet made demands themselves" (Parsons 1999: 6).

Certainly in the phase of conquest and early consolidation, imperial rulers generally deemed it advisable to use foreign-born Africans rather than locals. But even foreign-born African soldiers were not always reliable tools of imperial expansion. It is noteworthy that, in the phase of conquest, the British preferred to strengthen their colonial forces in East Africa with Indian troops. As the Inspector-General of the King's African Rifles put it bluntly in 1912: "The Indian contingents were introduced in order that we might have a body of troops with no religious or local sympathies, and therefore no incentive for throwing in their lot with the native inhabitants" (Parsons 1999: 6). The same rationale underpinned the Dutch decision to recruit African soldiers for the East Indies rather than expand local recruitment in the Indies.

Conquest, control and coercion

The West African men who served in the Dutch East Indies army were not the first Africans to arrive in the Indonesian archipelago. During the 17th century, the Dutch East India Company (Verenigde Oostindische Compagnie – VOC) brought large numbers of Malagasy slaves to Sumatra to work in the gold mines at Sillida (Barendse 2002; Ranjeva-Rabetafika, Baesjou & Everts 2000).

The most intriguing occupation mentioned for 18th century African slaves is the duty of assistants to the bailiff. As we have seen, in every colonial empire the jobs of conquest, control and coercion posed particular problems. These duties were often performed by outsiders, men who would not be tempted to make common cause with the colonial subjects and who inspired fear into the local population. Thus the VOC employed visible foreigners to apprehend fugitives and administer physical punishments. Both at the Cape and in the East Indies, these servants of justice were called Kaffirs. At the Cape, they were eastern slaves or convicts who functioned as auxiliary police to apprehend escaped slaves and to act as disciplinarians. Punishments, whether judicial or not, were usually administered to slaves and sometimes to Europeans by these 'servants of justice'. On this account the Kaffirs were hated and feared by the slaves, and indeed by some whites. It is noteworthy that at the Cape this function was performed by Asians; at Batavia the Kaffirs or *dieffleyders* ('thief-catchers') were African slaves, most likely from Mozambique (Armstrong and Worden 1998: 128; De Haan 1922, vol. I: 292). To some extent, it was this experience with the Kaffirs that inspired the experiment with recruiting African soldiers for the Dutch East Indies Army after 1830.

Responding to a proposal from The Hague to recruit Africans, the commander in chief of the Dutch East Indies army reacted favourably. Major General De Stuers had had personal experience with African policemen, slaves from Mozambique or Angola who had long been used as police auxiliaries.[2] He was convinced that Africans would be able to withstand the climate and the strenuous army campaigns and that they would serve loyally, provided that they were well treated and that proper discipline was maintained:

> It is beyond doubt that the Negro instills great fear in the natives, and that he is unlikely to fraternize with the natives. As an example, the undersigned can state that he personally experienced during his stay as military commander and civil administrator on Sumatra's West Coast how the Africans among the police auxiliaries caused great alarm. Therefore Africans were favoured for policing duties.[3]

The paradox of military labour under colonial conditions was obvious to contemporaries. Indigenous soldiers were trained to fight, provided with arms but low in status and subservient to foreign occupying forces: how to secure their loyalty? In opting for the experiment with African soldiers, the Dutch government was mainly

[2] NA, Algemene Staatssecretarie en Kabinet des Konings 1813-1814, inv. no. 5743, Nota van De Stuers, exh. 1 Juni 1831, no. 75.

[3] Source: see previous footnote.

inspired by the example of the British West India regiments. Between 1808 and 1833 the British colonial army enlisted about 3,147 liberated slaves. They received the same uniforms and the same pay as white soldiers in these regiments, but while whites served a seven-year contract, for black soldiers the army was a lifetime occupation. As part of their training, it was impressed on the African soldiers that as servants of the British king their status was way above the slave population (Buckley 1979). Dutch officials based in Surinam and in the Dutch West Indies had had the opportunity to see the West India Regiments in action. They reported most favourably about the professional performance of these soldiers and their loyalty to the regiment. These regiments were not only employed in the Western hemisphere. In 1823, the West India regiments were used in the British war against Ashanti, and again in later expeditions against the Ashanti kingdom. The locally recruited Gold Coast corps proved useful for policing duties, but useless in a war against a powerful opponent. After the Indian Mutiny, major A.B. Ellis, who had served with the West India regiments, proposed their deployment in India. "For service in India, Negroes seem the very thing; they are sure not to fraternise with the natives. By and by, unless we first lose our Colonial Empire, we shall practically recognise the wisdom of the Romans, who garrisoned each province with troops from a distance" (Ellis 1885: 2).

This particular advice remained unheeded, but it is illustrative of the dilemmas posed by colonial armies. Much the same logic inspired recruitment policies for the Dutch East Indies army. After the first phase of colonial conquest, it was feasible to recruit local troops for army and policing duties, but every colonial ruler harboured doubts about the loyalty of indigenous troops. It was imperative to prevent fraternisation with the locals and instead to promote identification with the army. Particularly for men far away from home, the army became a substitute family.

The Dutch East Indies Army

In the 19th century, the East Indies were the only profitable part of the Dutch overseas empire. At the beginning of this century, Dutch rule was limited to Java, some coastal regions of southern Sumatra, the Moluccan islands and some footholds on the other islands. By 1900 colonial rule had been consolidated throughout the vast Indonesian archipelago. African soldiers played a part in this process of imperial expansion. African companies fought in Dutch army campaigns in southwest Sumatra, Borneo (Kalimantan), Celebes (Sulawesi), Bali, Timor and, not least, the protracted Atjeh (Aceh) war.

Throughout the 19th century the Dutch East Indies army or KNIL (Koninklijk Nederlands-Indisch Leger) operated on the principle that roughly one half of the troops ought to consist of Europeans. However, the numbers of volunteers in the Netherlands always fell short of the manpower needs. Mortality in the tropics was high and the status of colonial soldiers was low. Conscription had been introduced for the national army, but enlistment for the colonial army was on a voluntary basis. As more and more European countries introduced conscription, it became more difficult to hire mercenary soldiers. After the secession of Belgium – an important source of manpower– in 1831, most mercenary soldiers came from Switzerland and Germany. The Java War (1825-1830) highlighted the dilemmas of the colonial army: the loyalty of local troops could not be taken for granted and the losses among the European troops were quite dramatic.

It was during this period that various alternative recruitment strategies were explored. Quite influential were the recommendations made by major Charles Hamilton Smith, who had served twelve years with the British West India regiments. Hamilton Smith (born as Karel de Smet, near Antwerp) was a personal acquaintance of the Dutch royal family. He was held in high esteem because of his services to the Dutch army in the 1815 army campaign against Napoleon. Hamilton Smith praised the strength, discipline, courage and endurance of African troops and emphasized the crucial importance of equal treatment of black and white troops. Provided that they were treated properly and humanely, African troops would serve loyally. Hamilton Smith saw no danger whatsoever of fraternisation between Africans and Asians, as he believed that Asians regarded Africans as cannibals. It was therefore advisable to send also a number of black women in order to establish small African communities around Batavia, which would also serve to reproduce new manpower for the army. He also volunteered some practical details, notably that half rations of rum would be sufficient but that it was absolutely vital to allow them to dance at night, "because all of Africa dances at night".[4]

Hamilton Smith believed that volunteers could be found among free blacks and slaves in Surinam and the Dutch West Indies, but these colonies suffered already an acute shortage of manpower due to the abolition of the slave trade. After some further explorations, the Dutch government turned to its almost forgotten

4 NA, Ministerie van Koloniën (Department of Colonies, hereafter MK) MK I, verbaal 558, Hamilton Smith to the Minister of Colonies, exh. 30 mei 1827 no. 79; verbaal 615, Hamilton Smith to Min. of Colonies, exh. 7 mei 1828 no. 78; verbaal 615, Prins Frederik to Min. of Colonies, exh. 7 mei 1828, no. 78.

Possessions on the Coast of Guinea, where commercial activity had all but halted since the abolition of the slave trade.

The beginnings of African recruitment

Recruitment in St. George d'Elmina began in 1831. Governor F. Last received orders from The Hague to assemble a detachment of 150 'Negro soldiers' for Java. If the experiment proved successful, African recruitment would be expanded to some 2.000 men. Last was under strict instructions to enlist volunteers only, without resorting to coercion. In the East Indies, the African soldiers would be paid and treated on an equal basis with the European troops. After the expiry of their six-year contract, they had a choice between re-enlistment, repatriation to Elmina or settling on Java. In 1831 and 1832, three ships were sent from the Netherlands to Elmina to transport the 150 African troops to Batavia. But in spite of sustained efforts, Last managed to recruit only 44 men. The prevailing impression in The Netherlands was that Africans would be eager to escape from poverty and misery, but Last reported to The Hague that the experiment was totally alien to local custom. According to his report, emigration, even of a temporary nature, was an unknown phenomenon on the Gold Coast: nobody here even contemplates leaving the land and place of his birth, because their main concern is to look after the graves of their ancestors, while the women work on the land.[5]

Some of the 44 recruits had previously served with the Dutch in the small Elmina garrison, but most were debtors or pawns in debt arrangements. They used their army pay to pay off debts. Some were slaves, who transferred part of their army pay to their masters in Elmina or other coastal towns. Some were free men who had been attracted by the possibility to delegate part of their army pay to their parents or other relatives. Because of these small numbers of men, the costs of this experiment proved excessive. However, reports about their military qualities were quite favourable.

In 1836, major general Jan Verveer embarked on a mission as envoy of the Dutch King Willem I to the court of Ashanti. Recruitment along the Coast had yielded only a trickle of volunteers. For lack of volunteers, the new Governor Lans had resorted to the practice of buying slaves and enlisting them for long periods of service of up to 20 years. Since these slaves had not been manumitted, this type of recruitment amounted to a violation of the international treaties banning the slave trade. After his arrival in Elmina, Verveer immediately ended this practice

5 NA, MK I, Ingekomen stukken van de Kust van Guinea 4001, Last to Min. of Col., 7 dec. 1831.

and Lans, now living in retirement in the Netherlands, was severely censored. His recruits were retroactively manumitted. The British, who policed the ban on the transatlantic slave trade, had strongly objected to Lans' recruitment methods, but initially they raised no objections against Verveer's scheme, after he had ensured that only free men or manumitted slaves would be enrolled.[6]

In the new, expanded recruitment scheme the focus was on the Kingdom of Ashanti, an old ally of Elmina and the Dutch. In the past, Ashanti had been a major supplier of slaves. The Dutch believed that Ashanti still commanded a surplus of manpower, some of which surely could be made available to the Dutch colonial army. After long delays and the exchange of lavish gifts, the contract between King Willem I of the Netherlands and Kwaku Dua I of Ashanti was duly signed in the Ashanti capital Kumasi on 18 March 1837. The contract stipulated that the Ashanti king would deliver 1000 able-bodied men within a year, in exchange for 6000 guns with powder. In addition, Verveer obtained permission to open a recruitment bureau in Kumasi, where individuals could enlist. The African soldiers would be entitled to equal pay and equal treatment, in every respect, with the European troops.[7]

One exception to this rule however was their term of service. While Europeans generally enlisted for six years, the Africans who entered Dutch army service after 1837 were contracted for a period of 15 years or an indeterminate period. The latter applied to slaves from the distant lands beyond Ashanti: the Dutch undertook to provide free passage home for retired soldiers to Elmina, but it was inconceivable that the home-bound trip would extend into the area of present-day Burkina Faso or Northern Nigeria. Although this was never clearly spelt out, these men were considered lifetime soldiers. However, in 1844 the indeterminate period of service was converted to 15 years.

After expiry of their contracts, the soldiers could opt for re-enlistment, repatriation to Elmina or permanent residence on Java. In the first phase of African recruitment, most chose to return to their native lands. Men from the coastal areas mostly returned to their former place of residence, while those from northern re-

6 NA, Ministerie van Koloniën voor 1850 (Department of Colonies before 1850, hereafter MK I), Geheime Verbalen, inv. no. 4243, exh. 6 Dec. 1836 no. 292, correspondence by the British envoy in The Hague, Disbrowe, to the Netherlands Department of Foreign Affairs; MK I, Openbare Verbalen, inv. no. 1076, exh. 11 Feb. 1837 no 24, ibid.; MK I, Geheime Verbalen, inv. no. 4257, no. 410, 28 Dec. 1839, Department of Colonies to the Governor-General of the Dutch East Indies.

7 NA, MK I, Openbare Verbalen, inv. no 1223, exh. 16 April 1839 no. 20, report by Verveer to the Dept. of Colonies; MK I, Geheime Verbalen, inv. no 4246, Treaty between Jan Verveer on behalf of the Dutch King and Kwaku Dua, 18 March 1837.

gions generally opted to settle in Elmina. Veterans were allocated plots of land on a hill just behind the Castle of St. George. From the 1840s, the hill became known as Java Hill. Although the name is still in use today, very few present-day inhabitants are familiar with the historical background of Java Hill. With two exceptions, I have not been able to locate descendants of returned KNIL veterans.[8]

As the numbers of Africans in the East Indies increased, veterans increasingly decided to settle with their Indo-African families in one of the garrison towns on Java, often maintaining close contact with fellow Africans. Particularly for ex-slaves, settlement on Java could be the more attractive option. On the Gold Coast, they would be regarded as former slaves, while on Java they were entitled to European status. Soldiers had a lowly position in colonial society, but, on the other hand, Europeans were considered superior to the native population. Most African soldiers however were never faced with this choice: they died during their long periods of army service. Few actually died on the battlefield. As with the Europeans, most Africans succumbed to diseases.

On the invitation of King Willem I, the Ashanti king entrusted his young son and his nephew to Verveer, to be taken to the Netherlands for a European education. The nephew, Kwamena Poku, later returned to Elmina as an army corporal. His intention had been to return to Kumasi, but he had become alienated from the land of his birth. No longer able to speak his native Twi, he wasted away in Elmina and ultimately committed suicide on 22 February 1850. The son, Kwasi Boakye, studied in Delft to become a mining engineer and eventually died of old age on Java.[9]

Verveer initially had hoped to enlist Ashanti men for the Dutch army. The Ashanti had a great reputation as a warrior nation, but it rapidly transpired that enlisting Ashanti men in foreign armies was out of the question. In practice, the troops recruited in Kumasi were the slaves of the Ashanti, captured in war, rendered as tribute or bought at slave markets such as Salaga. Their regions of origin were north of Ashanti, perhaps even as far as the bend of the Niger River. They

8 Contact was established with the Witts family and the Ulzen family. The Witts family are descendants of soldier Jan Wit, who returned to Elmina in 1880 after 12 years of army service. He left his son Melchior behind on Java. Jan Wit began a new family life in Elmina, while young Melchior joined the Dutch army. The descendants of Melchior Wit now live in the Netherlands. The Ulzen family was no longer living in Elmina, although they maintained strong bonds with their place of origin. Their forefather is corporal Manus Ulzen, who was among the first volunteers to enlist in 1832.

9 For the story of the two Ashanti princes, see Yarak 1987. The story has acquired international fame after the publication of a historical novel by Dutch author Arthur Japin, that has also been published in English translation.

were generically known as Donkos. Enlisting free Africans as volunteers proved a pipe dream. In order to reconcile the recruitment effort with the obligations of the treaties banning the slave trade, the recruits were issued with an Act of Manumission. They purchased their freedom with an advance on their army pay of about 100 guilders, to be repaid over the years by deducting 8.5 cents a day from their pay. Verveer reckoned that the soldiers would be able to pay off their debts in two years, after which they would enjoy equal status in every respect with the European soldiers.[10]

The Asantehene Kwaku Dua proved negligent in fulfilling the obligations in the treaty. When recruitment ended in 1842, he had delivered only 235 men.[11] Numerous recruits sent by the King were returned to Kumasi because they were too young, too old or not in good health. Instead, most African recruits were obtained from the recruitment agency in Kumasi, which was staffed by a Eurafrican official in Dutch service, Jacob Huydecooper.

Meanwhile, recruitment also continued along the Coast. By 1842, some 2,200 men had been sent from Elmina to Batavia. The procedure prescribed by Verveer required that all recruits ought to be asked explicitly and individually whether they voluntarily accepted to enlist. In quite a few cases, the Dutch governor concluded that the men had been brought against their own will. They were sent away or returned to their owner.[12] As long as the proper procedures were adhered to, the recruits did have a certain choice in the matter. Some governors undoubtedly were more lax than others, but judging from the Elmina journals after 1837, it was fairly routine procedure to inquire whether the recruits consented, although this probably could not have applied to the recruits sent from Kumasi. The price for their freedom had already been paid to the owners in Kumasi. The recruitment system had no provisions to recuperate these sums, or to book these amounts as losses.

Military merits

Initial army reports on the performance of the Africans were largely favourable, in spite of the numerous communication problems that made their training both

[10] NA, MK I, Openbare Verbalen, inv. no. 1223, exh. 16 April 1839 no 20, report by Verveer to the Dept. of Colonies.

[11] NA, MK I, Ingekomen stukken van de Kust van Guinea inv. no. 4012, Governor Van der Eb to Dept. of Colonies, 31 Oct. 1842.

[12] These cases are mentioned in the journals kept by the Governor in Elmina: NA, MK I, Journalen van de Kust van Guinea, inv. no 3964-3975. For the places of origins of the men recruited in Kumasi, see LaTorre 1976: 31-42.

difficult and time-consuming. The Africans spoke a variety of African languages which often were not mutually intelligible. They understood neither Dutch nor Malay, the languages of instruction in the army. A few Eurafricans and Africans could act as interpreters between Dutch and Fanti or Twi (the languages spoken on the Gold Coast and in Ashanti), but there were never sufficient interpreters to serve in all the African companies. Because of the language problem, the Africans were not yet fully subjected to the army's code of discipline. Army command had issued instructions for lenient treatment, and therefore their misdemeanors were rarely punished.

According to their commanding officers, the main vice of the Africans was laziness, resulting in uncleanliness. They took better care of their weapons than of their uniforms. The Africans kept their distance from both Europeans and native Indonesians. It was emphasized that they looked down on the native population. The officers remarked that they were very distrustful, always worrying about being cheated. The character of the Africans was described as "hot-tempered, irascible and often very insolent". Another officer remarked that they were "of a rough nature, jealous, distrustful and greedy". On the other hand, they were honest men. No instances of thievery had been reported. The Africans were strong, muscled, indefatigable and very well adapted to the tropical climate. In battle, they demonstrated bravery and fearlessness, even more so than the Europeans. In combat, their ardour needed to tempered, otherwise they ignored the orders of their officers. Some reports complain about substantial drinking, but alcoholic excesses were less serious than among the European soldiers.[13] On balance, the judgment was largely positive, certainly in comparison to the bitter complaints that were regularly voiced about drunken, lazy and undisciplined European troops.

Some reports indicate that some of the Africans suffered from homesickness or had otherwise problems to adapt to their new lives. A number of those cases were repatriated to Elmina, considered unsuitable for army service.

Mutinies[14]

By and large however, the Africans seem to have adjusted well to their new role, jealously guarding their status as European soldiers. Most causes of discontent were related to infringements on the promise of equal treatment. Nothing would

[13] NA, Ministerie van Koloniën na 1850 (hereafter MK II), Generaal Overzigt van hetgeen betrekking heeft tot de werving van Afrikanen en van de verkregen resultaten, inv. no 49, exh. 4 Nov. 1850, no. 24, Verslag over bij het leger dienende Afrikanen, 3 Sept. 1838 no. 3 geheim.

[14] For a more detailed account of the mutinies, see Van Kessel 2003.

cause more resentment than the belief that they were being treated as natives, not as Europeans.

Widespread discontent began erupting from 1838, when the Africans were ordered to exchange their (European) straw mattresses for (native) sleeping mats.[15] Coming on top of accumulating grievances about unequal treatment, the issue of the mattresses became the final straw. Other grievances were related to their longer term of service and lower pay, as a result of the deduction of 8.5 cents to repay the costs of manumission. These deductions had become a permanent feature, continuing long after the due amount of about 100 guilders had been repaid. This meant that the Africans were no longer paying off a debt, but that they received a structurally lower pay than the Europeans.

In mid-1838, a mutiny erupted among the Africans of the 1st infantry battalion on Sumatra. Brought before a military tribunal on Sumatra, the case remained inconclusive because of language problems. The spirit of rebellion became more widespread in 1840 and 1841. Several instances of armed revolt were reported from Sumatra and central Java.[16] For the first time, the Africans were court-martialed. The sentences passed by the Supreme Military Tribunal in Semarang on 18 December 1840 were remarkably lenient. The five ringleaders in the Kedong Kebo mutiny were sentenced to two years in prison and 25 strokes, with lighter sentences for the remaining mutineers.[17]

Army command expected that the court martial would set an example. Rebellious behaviour would no longer be tolerated. It is not certain whether the news of the court martial spread around to garrisons on other islands. If it did, it did not deter other discontented Africans from staging armed protests. After another mutiny on Sumatra's West Coast, army command concluded that the experiment with African recruitment had miscarried. Experience proved that the 'Negro race' was not as suitable for the military as had initially been thought.

When African recruitment was abandoned in December 1841, the army

---

[15] NA, MK II, Generaal Overzigt, Missive van den kommandant van het observatiekorps dd. 6 Feb. 1838 no. 186.

[16] NA, MK II, Generaal Overzigt, Missive van den militairen kommandant te Kedong Kebo, 17 April 1840.

[17] NA, MK II, Generaal Overzigt, Missive van den kommandant van het leger dd. 21 april 1840, no. 12 spoed;

Generaal Overzigt, Missive van den Advocaat Fiscaal voor de Land- en Zeemagt dd. 22 April 1840, no. 171, spoed. Data on the sentences are taken from the individual army records: Stamboeken onderofficieren en minderen van het Nederlandsch Oostindisch Leger. The records are incomplete, and therefore this account of the sentences might be incomplete as well. The corporal punishment consisted of "*klingslagen*", strokes with a sword blade.

counted 1318 Africans. After the initial panic had calmed down, the KNIL command believed that the problem of the 'haughty' Africans would solve itself, as they would gradually be phased out from the army.[18] Throughout the 19th century, the position of the Africans remained ambiguous. In most respects, they were indeed treated as Europeans. But in other respects, regarding terms of service, reenlistment premiums, pensions, and – perhaps most importantly – the continuing deductions which no longer could be justified as restitution of the manumission payment, the KNIL treated the African soldiers as a special category. Full equal treatment was only achieved by the second generation, the Indo-African sons who were born free in the East Indies. Growing up in army barracks, most sons followed their fathers' footsteps in becoming professional soldiers.

Army opinion about the qualities of the African soldiers saw another unexpected twist after the Third Expedition to Bali in 1849. The African troops earned the admiration of several military observers, including the newly arrived Commander-in-chief of the KNIL, Duke Bernhard van Saxen-Weimar Eisenach, a German aristocrat who had made his career in the Dutch army. He reported to The Hague that the Africans compared favourably with the European part of the army.[19]

The new Commander-in-chief, supported by the new governor in Batavia, urged a resumption of African recruitment. The Dutch government initially declined, but in 1855 recruitment in Elmina was reopened, although on a much more modest scale than before. The new effort had a very slow start. The first detachment left Elmina only in 1860. Recruitment ended with the transfer of the Dutch possessions on the Guinea Coast to Britain in 1872. When the ship Robertus Hendrikus left Elmina on 12 April 1872 with the last batch of 78 soldiers, a little over 800 African recruits had sailed to the East Indies in this second phase of African recruitment. The total number of soldiers from the Coast of Guinea in the KNIL adds up to about 3080. Most of these 800 new troops served in the Aceh war, the longest and deadliest war in Dutch colonial history.

By 1915, there were no more African soldiers serving in the Dutch East Indies army (*Encyclopaedie* 1917-1921 vol. I: 13-14). Army periodicals reflected on the African troops with considerable nostalgia. Surely, they were impetuous when not treated properly, but who would hold that against them? The Africans were generally praised for their courage, loyalty and stamina (*Indische Gids* 1886: 611-617).

---

[18] NA, MK I, Geheime Verbalen, inv. no. 4294, Cochius to Governor-General 11 Nov. 1842.

[19] NA, MK II, Generaal Overzigt, Missive van Zijne Hoogheid den kommandant van het leger dd 21 August 1849 no. 4, zeer geheim.

The Indo-African offspring of the African soldiers remained a permanent feature of the KNIL, until the end of colonial rule in 1949. The veterans settled in garrison towns on Java – notably Batavia, Semarang, Purworejo, Salatiga, Solo – where their pensions were paid out. Known in Malay as *Belanda Hitam* (Black Dutchmen), they largely assimilated with the Indo-European population. After Indonesian independence, most Indo-Africans opted for 'repatriation' to the Netherlands, as they considered themselves 'born Dutch'.

Unwitting Liberians

The saga of a failed recruitment experiment in Liberia had no happy ending. After the transfer of Elmina to the British, the Dutch maintained a consulate in Elmina to deal with longstanding obligations such as the payment of pensions to army veterans and others who had worked in Dutch service, but also as a lookout for new opportunities to recruit for Surinam or the East Indies. Various options in the Congo, Dahomey, Grand Bassam and even Ethiopia and Zanzibar were explored without any success. Liberia however seemed more promising. The Kru had a good reputation. After several failed ventures, at long last a German steamer was chartered to take about one hundred Liberians to Java. However, as soon as the distant destination and the nature of job were explained, almost all the men ran away. They were willing to engage in short terms contracts for the coffee and cocoa plantations in West Africa, but not in army service in some unknown part of the world. After this botched attempt, the recruitment agents decided to keep the destination secret. At long last, 188 Liberians were taken on board ship but when they disembarked in Semarang on 13 January 1891, they were still ignorant about their assigned job. Only when they were handed military uniforms and formed into two army companies did they realize that they were meant to serve as soldiers. They refused to sign their contracts for a 3 year period of service. During the first months of their military training, they repeatedly went on strike, refusing to carry out orders. Finally admitting that these men were recruited under false pretences, the army command decided to repatriate the unwilling soldiers to Liberia. Only four Liberians stayed behind, volunteering for a 6 year contract (Kalff 1928).[20]

---

[20] NA, MK II, verbaal 1099, exh. 14 sept. 1861; verbaal 6204, 26 nov. 1890 D17 no 746; verbaal 6203, 13 juni 1891; verbaal 6209, 19 april 1892 R5 geheim no 238; verbaal 6207, 20 feb. 1892 P2; 'Het Afrikaansch Recruten Korps', 1892, pp. 2-13.

Conclusions: African soldiers as indentured labourers

How does the experience of the African recruits for the Dutch East Indies army compare with the experiences of indentured workers in the same age? In some respects their fate seems worse, but in terms of their position in the social and racial hierarchy of the Dutch East Indies they were much better off than workers on plantations.

In terms of mortality on board ship, an important criterion for Northrup in distinguishing the transport of indentured workers from the transatlantic slave trade, the African soldiers compare very favourably. Losses on ships with British migrants for New York were around 1% for the period 1836–1853. Mortality among Indian migrants to the West Indies between 1851 and 1870 was 6.5% and among indentured Africans to the West Indies 3.5%. Mortality in the 19th century Atlantic slave trade averaged 7%. (Northrup 1995: 89).

In comparison, the mortality on the Dutch troop ships destined for the East Indies was very low: 0.28% for the period 1826-1894 (Bossenbroek 1992: 90). This voyage took on average 100-120 days, much longer than the trip London-New York, or Sierra Leone-Guyana. The Dutch government chartered private ships for the troop transports and issued strict regulations for sleeping quarters, food, water and physical exercise en route. Mortality among African recruits during the voyage from Elmina to Batavia was 0.84%.[21]

How voluntary was African recruitment? With few exceptions, the African recruits had been slaves. This condition no doubt limited the exercise of free choice, more so in the case of men brought from Ashanti than along the coast. The rules introduced by Verveer were designed to make sure that every individual consented. Every man was to be asked individually, in the absence of his owner, whether he voluntarily agreed to enlist in the Dutch army. This procedure was to be repeated before boarding ship. It cannot be ascertained that this practice was adhered to throughout the period of recruitment, but dozens of men did make clear that they did not wish to become soldiers, and they were indeed turned away. In the case of recruits from Ashanti, it is unlikely that this procedure applied, as there was no way of recouping the money that had been paid for them in Kumasi.

Did the recruits understand what they were consenting to? There is reason to believe that overall this was indeed the case. Recruits were trained and housed along with the small Elmina garrison, and thus had a foretaste of military life in

[21] The records are not complete. I have made my calculations on the basis of 2,336 records out of a total number of 3,080 soldiers over the period 1831-1872. These records relate to 28 ship transports.

Dutch service. The military escorts sent from Elmina to Kumasi to accompany new recruits to the coast often included men who had also been recruited for the East Indies: they were in position to explain the arrangement to the newcomers. On the other hand, it is likely that the recruits had no notion of the distance of their destination: a voyage of three months over the oceans. But here are similarities with the Asian indentured workers who also had no understanding of the geographical location of Guyana or Trinidad. However, the West African recruits clearly understood that they would be serving under the same conditions as European troops: infringements on their status as 'European' were immediately noticed and resented.

In the case of the Liberians, they certainly were neither aware of their destination nor of their military destiny. However, the Liberians cannot be categorized as slave labour, because the Dutch agreed to bring them back home when they refused service, in spite of all the means of coercion at the disposal of a colonial army.

Wages for an African soldier in the 1830s averaged around fl. 122 p.a. plus free clothing, food and lodgings. Average annual earnings for Indian indentured workers in British Guyana was 54 $ per year.[22] However, soldiers who served at least 20 years were entitled to a pension, a rare privilege for 19th century workers. Veterans who did not qualify for a pension but who were physically or mentally disabled, could be granted a pension if this condition was due to army service, and a half pension if their disabilities were deemed to have other causes.

In terms of the duration of their contract, the African soldiers were worse off than most indentured workers. The contract period for indentured labour could vary from one to ten years, but a five-year contract was fairly typical. This was the norm for Indian workers in British Guyana and in Surinam. Only the first batch of African recruits, with contracts for a six-year term, would fit in this category. By far the largest number of African recruits enlisted for a period of 15 years. Soldiers serving in the second period of African recruitment, after 1855, all served on a 12-year contract.

Mortality among the African soldiers throughout the duration of their contracts was much higher than among indentured workers, but not much different from the losses among their European fellow soldiers. Northrup gives the following statistics for indentured immigrants – largely plantation labour – for British Guyana in 1853. Mortality was highest among the Chinese, with 11.3%, followed

[22] This means that cash income was roughly comparable. Using the IISH List of Datafiles of Historical Prices and Wages, 122 guilders in 1830 would amount to $ 1.430 in terms of 2007 wages and prices, while $ 54 amounts to about $1.252. www.iisg.nl.

by Portuguese with 7.9%. Losses among Indians were much less, with 3.6%. Africans – both newcomers and local Creoles – figured at the bottom end of this scale, with a mortality of only 1.4%. Turning to the Dutch colony Surinam, the calculations (for a later period) are less favourable. For the decade 1871-1880, mortality among adult indentured workers was 5.36%. However, by 1890-1900, this figure had declined to 1.68% (Northrup 1995: 122).

For the Dutch East Indies, the statistics show substantial variations over time. It might be assumed that soldiers run higher risks than plantation workers, but deaths in battle were very few. Not more than 1.7% of the African dead were casualties on the battlefield. The vast majority of African troops succumbed to diseases, just like the indentured workers in the western hemisphere. Epidemics – dysentery, cholera – were the main killers. Living conditions for the indentured workers were of course more stable than the circumstances of soldiers who had to endure primitive living conditions during army campaigns. The first year after arrival was the most critical, accounting for about one fifth of the total number of African deaths. Those who survived the first year in their new environment stood a good chance.

The bulk of the African recruits (2283 men) arrived between 1832 and 1844. Over this period, mortality among the Africans was calculated at 8.16%, lower than the 9.24% figure for European troops. Mortality among Africans reached a peak in 1836 with 15%, possibly reflecting the poor health condition of the slave-soldiers recruited by Governor Lans. However, in 1841 the Africans compared very favourably with European troops, with an 8% loss compared to 17% among the Europeans. From 1841, a clear improvement is visible, with African mortality falling to 5.2 and 5.3%. However, the declining trend does not continue in the next decade. For the period 1850-1869, the army calculated African mortality at 8.75% while losses among European troops averaged 5.89%. Looking at these figures in more detail, an interesting pattern emerges: Africans were apparently at the highest risk in the coastal garrisons of Java, with mortality figures exceeding 20%, while European deaths were limited to 7.81%. The reverse situation prevailed in the interior, where African deaths were considerably less than European deaths. Apparently the Africans could adjust better to the primitive conditions prevailing at remote outposts.

While working conditions may have been more trying for the African soldiers than for the indentured workers, they were better off in terms of their status in colonial society. In the army, the Africans enjoyed almost equal status with European troops, while veterans retiring from army service easily found employment with the police or prison service and other public service sectors, or as overseer on plantations. Lastly, an important indicator for satisfaction is the choice made at the end of the contract: re-enlisting, settlement on Java or repatriation to Elmina. Re-enlisting was common practice. The Dutch honoured their undertaking to provide free passage home for retired soldiers, even after the cession of Elmina to the British in 1872. As is the case with indentured labour in Surinam, the percentage of settlers is higher than the percentage of returnees. Roughly two-thirds of the indentured Indian workers in Surinam opted to stay after expiry of their contract. Comparing the figures here becomes difficult, as we are comparing choices made after a 5-year period and after a 15-year (or much longer) period of army service. The majority of the African soldiers (some 60%) died during their long period of army service, a figure that indeed looks bleak in comparison to the statistics for indentured workers. Of the 3,080 African recruits for the KNIL, roughly 15% percent returned to Elmina, while a little over 20% opted for settlement in one of the garrison towns on Java.

A comparison of living conditions in terms of family life is inevitably speculative. The proportion of women among the indentured workers was small, at best around one third of the labour force. Competition for women was a cause of much violence on the plantations. No women ever accompanied the Africans recruits to Java. Paradoxically, this may have made life easier. The African soldiers followed the practice established among European troops: they lived with their indigenous wife and children in army barracks. Thus competition for women may have been less acute, while living with indigenous women facilitated their contacts with Indonesian society. Most Africans of the first generation were more fluent in Malay than in Dutch.

In an article that focuses only on the terms of recruitment, not on actual conditions of service in the East Indies, Larry Yarak concludes that the episode of African recruitment for the Dutch East Indies army fits in with the general pattern of indentured labour, not with previous patterns of the slave trade. On the basis of an overview of the entire spectrum of experience of the African recruits for Java, I come to the same conclusion.

Like indentured labour, African soldiers did not come cheap. Only when the Africans served the full term of 15 years were they cheaper than European troops. Recruitment costs for a European soldier in 1837 were calculated at 430 guilders, while the costs of an African recruit rose to 535 guilder, due to a higher enlistment bonus and a longer period of waiting for the opportunity to board ship. Costs of manumission are not considered in this calculation, as the army would recoup that amount by deducting 8.5 cents from his daily wage. Costs of repatriation were 282 guilder per person for the voyage Batavia-Netherlands, but African veterans caused additional costs because they had to be accommodated in the Netherlands while waiting for a ship to Elmina, for which another 92 guilder per person had to be paid.

In any case, African soldiers were far more expensive than Javanese soldiers. Costs for an African were calculated at 205 guilder per year for wages, food, clothing and equipment, while only 116 guilder p.a. was spent on a Javanese soldier.[23] The Belanda Hitam were not soldiers on the cheap.

References

Encyclopaedie van Nederlandsch Indië. 1917. Part I. 's Gravenhage: Nijhoff, pp. 13-14.

Het Afrikaansch Recruten Korps, *Indisch Militair Tijdschrift* 23 (1892): 17-28.

Het behoud van het Afrikaansche element bij het Indische leger. *Indisch Militair Tijdschrift* 12 (1-6), (1881), pp. 372-386.

Iets over de militaire politiek in Indië. *Indische Gids* 1 (1886): 611-617.

Gedenkschrift Koninklijk Nederlandsch Indisch Leger 1830-1950. Dordrecht, 1990.

Akurang-Parry, K., 2001. We cast about for a remedy: the opposition of the Gold Coast press to the Chinese mine labour experiment in the Gold Coast, ca. 1874-1914. *International Journal of African Historical Studies* 34(2): 365-384.

Armstrong, J.C. & N.A. Worden, 1988. The slaves, 1652-1834, in: R. Elphick & H. Giliomee, eds., *The Shaping of South African Society 1652-1840*. Middletown, Conn.: Wesleyan University Press & Cape Town: Maskew Miller Longman.

Barendse, R., 2002. *The Arabian Seas: the Indian Ocean World of the Seventeenth Century*. Armouk, N.Y.: Sharpe.

Blussé, L., 1997. *Bitters Bruid: een Koloniaal Huwelijksdrama in de Gouden Eeuw*. Amsterdam: Maarten Muntenga & Uitgeverij Balans.

[23] NA, Generaal Overzigt II, bijlage La C Vergelijkende nota tot effenstelling der Engagementskosten van den Afrikaanschen recruut over deszelfs geheelen diensttijd in tegenstelling van den Europeaan. Bijlage L A, Vergelijkende nota van kosten voor een Infanterist der ondervolgende natien op Java, voor rond een jaars. NA MK I, verbaal 4294, legercommandant aan de Gouverneur-Generaal van Ned. Indië, 7 feb. 1843 exh. 20 nov. 1843 no 482; NA, MK I, verbaal 5820, Nota over de Negerwerving. "Het behoud van het Afrikaansche element bij het Indische leger", *Indisch Militair Tijdschrift*, 12^e jrg, no. 1-6, 1881, pp. 372-386.

Bossenbroek, M.P., 1986. *Van Holland naar Indië: het Transport van Koloniale Troepen voor het Oost-Indisch Leger 1815-1900*. Amsterdam: De Bataafsche Leeuw.

Breman, J., 1989. Taming the Coolie Beast: Plantation Society and the Colonial Order in Southeast Asia. Oxford: Oxford University Press.

Buckley, R.N. 1979, *Slaves in Red Coats: the British West India Regiments 1795-1815*. New Haven: Yale University Press.

Echenberg, M., 1986. Slaves into soldiers: social origins of the Tirailleurs Sénégalais, in: P. Lovejoy, ed., *Africans in Bondage: Studies in Slavery and the Slave Trade*. Madison: University of Wisconsin Press.

Echenberg, M., 1991. *Colonial Conscripts: The Tirailleurs Sénégalais in French West Africa, 1857-1960*. Portsmouth, N.H.: Heinemann.

Ellis, A.B., 1885. *History of the 1st West India Regiment*. London: Chapman and Hall.

De Haan, F., 1922-1923. *Oud-Batavia, Gedenkboek uitgegeven door het Bataviaasch Genootschap van Kunsten en Wetenschappen naar Aanleiding van het Driehonderdjarig Bestaan der Stad in 1919*, 3 volumes. Batavia: BGKW.

Kalff, S., 1929. Inlanders en Afrikanen in het O-I Leger. *Indisch Militair Tijdschrift* 51: 779-788.

Killingray, D., 2000. Imagined martial communities: recruiting for the military and police in colonial Ghana, 1860-1960, in C. Lentz & P. Nugent, eds., *Ethnicity in Ghana: the Limits of Invention*. Basingstoke: Macmillan.

Konings, P., 1977. *Vakbeweging en Ontwikkelingsstrategie van de Overheid in Ghana, 1874-1976*. Tilburg: Katholieke Hogeschool.

Northrup, D., 1995. *Indentured Labor in the Age of Imperialism, 1834-1922*. Cambridge: Cambridge University Press.

Parsons, T.H., 1999. *The African Rank and File: Social Implications of Colonial Military Service in the King's African Rifles, 1902-1964*. Portsmouth, NH: Heinemann.

Ranjeva-Rabetafika, Y., R. Baesjou & N. Everts, 2000. Of paper and men: a note on the archives of the VOC as a source for the history of Madagascar. *Itinerario* 24(1): 45-67.

Schuler, M., 1986. The recruitment of African indentured labourers for European colonies in the nineteenth century, in P. Emmer, ed., *Colonialism and Migration: Indentured Labour before and after Slavery*. Dordrecht: Nijhoff, pp. 125-161.

Segal, R., 2001. *Islam's Black Slaves: a History of Africa's Other Black Diaspora*. New York: Farrar, Strauss & Giroux.

Van Kessel, I., 2003. African mutinies in the Netherlands East Indies: a nineteenth century colonial paradox, in J. Abbink, M. de Bruijn & K. van Walraven, eds., *Rethinking Resistance: Revolt and Violence in African History*. Leiden – Boston: Brill, pp. 141-169.

Van Kessel, I., 2005. *Zwarte Hollanders: Afrikaanse Soldaten in Nederlands-Indië*. Amsterdam: KIT Publishers.

Yarak, L.W., 1996. New sources for the study of Akan slavery and slave trade: Dutch military recruitment in the Gold Coast and Asante 1831-72, in: R. Law, ed., *Source Material for Studying the Slave Trade and the African Diaspora: Papers from a conference of the Centre of Commonwealth Studies*. Stirling, UK: University of Stirling, pp. 35-60.

Economic crisis and imaginative response: the upsurge in traditional medical practices among youths in Cameroon

Robert Mbe Akoko

Within the last decades, Cameroon has been going through an economic crisis, which has resulted in much poverty among the ordinary population. Even though conditions seems particularly frustrating to the young generation, the paradox is that many of them are increasingly devising alternative strategies to survive, and succeed in earning a living and even to accumulate capital. Several authors have revealed some domains in which this has been occurring. With examples drawn from the city of Buea and its environs, this chapter examines one of these activities: the exercise of 'traditional medical practice', a domain which before the coming of the economic crisis was associated with elderly people and most often with skills acquired through inheritance, but that has recently been embraced by many young people. The study reveals that many youths have not only inventively embraced this activity, are making their own drugs from plants and barks of trees, but have also displayed with enough evidence that they accumulate lots of money through it.

Introduction

Within the last decade or so Cameroon, like most countries in Africa, has been grieved with a serious economic crisis[1] that has left few untouched and has retarded economic progress significantly. Although predictable and indeed foreseen, the crisis seems to have taken the government by surprise, since very little was done to avert or prepare for it. The crisis, coupled with the devaluation of the

1 GDP in late 1980s and early 1990s was estimated to be -8.6% but after the implementation of certain measures which included the devaluation of its currency, a structural adjustment program and the enhanced HIPC initiative between 1994 and 2006, the economy is said to have started stabilizing (see Fambon 2010).

CFA franc in 1994 by 50 percent and fixing its parity at 100 Franc CFA against the then French Franc and implementation of a Structural Adjustment programme imposed by the IMF in the 1990s has exacerbated poverty, misery, unemployment, fear, and uncertainty among Cameroonians. From the onset, the state was faced with difficulties in paying employees and had a hard time in honoring its other obligations. Public and private institutions laid-off personnel and continue to do so. This situation was worsened as the recruitment of new workers was drastically reduced. Salaries of workers were slashed several times and this inflicted and continues to do so, great hardships on them and their families, resulting in a sharp increase in social insecurity (cf. Jua 1991, Konings 1996, Takougang and Kriegar 1998). In addition, armed banditry is now commonplace, with bandits operating in broad daylight even in homes, markets, buses, financial institutions,[2] and often with impunity.

The government has all through been taking some measures to reverse the economic downturn. In addition to the devaluation of the CFA Franc and the implementation of the structural adjustment programs, it initiated in 2000, the implementation of a 3 year economic and financial program supported by the IMF in the context of a Poverty Reduction Growth Facility (PRGF) covering the period between October 2000 and September 2003. The finalization of the Program, in 2003 allowed the authorities to negotiate with the IMF, the enhanced Heavily Indebted Poor Countries (HIPC) initiative's completion point which was reached in April, 2006 (Fambon 2010). Since getting to this point, the government gives the impression that the economy has experienced overall macroeconomic stability. From about -8.6% GDP, they argue it has gone up to about 4% in 2011. While one may be tempted to believe that the economy has improved somehow beginning from 2006,[3] a vast majority of the population is living below the international

2 On September 28 2008, a group of heavily armed robbers with explosives, attacked Amity Bank Limbe in the early morning for more than 3 hours, destroyed the safe and took away about 250 million francs CFA. In the early morning of March 18 2011, another heavily armed gang of about 25, attacked ECOBANK Douala for more than four hours. Despite the intervention of security forces, they escaped through the sea after killing five people on the spot and injuring eight others and went away with huge sum of money. The government reportedly arrested some of the robbers in the ECOBANK case. In each of these cases, some passer-byes were killed. On June 5 2011, four armed robbers pretentiously boarded a night seventy-seater passenger bus as normal passengers, which left Yaounde for the West region town of Dschang and a few kilometers to the destination, they attacked the passengers, taking away valuables and monies but unfortunately for them the police were quickly informed and two of them arrested.

3 Some recruitment on a small scale is always done, salaries of state employees has not only been been paid regularly, there was even an increase of about 12% in 2008. Some infrastructural development is taking place all over the country, for instance, construction of highways and

poverty threshold of US$1.25 a day. Unemployment is still rife. From 2000 to 2009 the rate of unemployment has remained stable at 30% each year (See Index Mundi 2010 report on unemployment in Cameroon) and inflation rate too has been fluctuating through out. Index Mundi report of March 11 2010 reveals that in 2003, inflation rate was 4.5%, in 2004 it dropped to 2.3%, 2005 was 1%, 2006 was 2% 2007, 2.4%, 2008, 1.1%, 2009, 5.3% and 2010, 3%. The unemployment and inflation figures are indications that the living conditions of the population is still to be improved significantly.

To show the gravity of the unemployment situation in the country, in his address to the Cameroon youth on 11 February 2011 (Youth Day, celebrated as a public holiday) President Paul Biya announced the recruitment of 25,000 (a figure he believed was so much to please the youth) youth into the public service in 2011 but unfortunately when call for applications was made, more than 350.000 candidates applied within one month. This number is indicative of the high rate of unemployment in the country.

Even though the situation seem particularly frustrating to the young generation, the paradox is that many of them are increasingly devising alternative strategies to survive, earn a living and even to accumulate capital. In addition to the crisis, this has been enhanced by an ongoing political liberalization in the country. Liberalization, no doubt, has been expanding the private sector, and people continuously straddle the formal/informal divide (see Niger-Thomas 2000). In course of this, youths have shown a remarkable degree of creativity and imaginative innovation to improve their living conditions and developed various strategies to achieve this.

Several authors have pointed to this high degree of creativity and imaginative innovations among Cameroonian youths during this period of economic and political crises (see Malaquais 2001, 2002, Konings 2006, Ndjio 2006). In a book edited by Konings and Foeken of 2006, entitled *Crisis and Creativity: Exploring the Wealth of the African Neighborhood*, Konings and Ndjio have revealed certain activities in which Cameroonian youths have shown remarkable ingenuity in overcoming the effects economic crisis. In the volume, Konings has shown how the youths of New Bell (a neighbourhood in the city of Douala), taking advantage of the government liberalization of the transportation sector, invented a new activity, using motor-bikes as taxis. Commonly known as *bendskin*, this activity has not only secured them a livelihood in crisis conditions and structural economic problems but contributed to reducing the acute transportation problem

roads within towns, schools and hospitals.

that is typical of the town (Konings 2006). In addition, Konings revealed that this activity equally stimulated the growth of other local activities directly linked to this business. For instance, the importation and sale of bike parts and the new local repairers have become foci of brisk businesses. He shows how the 'bend-skin' drivers have tended to organize themselves in small groups based on ethnic and friendship bonds, with each group having its own parking space in a strategic position in the neighbourhood where passengers can easily reach them. Though in groups, they tend to demonstrate much solidarity both during working hours and in leisure time. Though in competition with each other, they appear nevertheless capable of overcoming group boundaries and they rally together in defense of common interests against 'outsiders', such as other road users and more particularly, government authorities and the police.

Basile Ndjio on his part has revealed another activity which shows creativity among the youths (see this volume, below). This is popularly known as *feymania*, a Pidgin English expression for 'swindling' (see also Malaquais 2001, 2002 and Konings 2006). Within the last decades of the economic crisis, Cameroonian youths have increasingly been involving themselves in illegal activities such as scamming[4] and counterfeiting of bank notes and fiscal stamps,[5] credit cards and passports and international trafficking of drugs and human parts.[6]

---

4 See for instance, APA-Douala of August 11, 2010, article entitled 'Worrying Rise in Cyber Criminality in Cameroon'. The paper reveals that the rise in this scourge has been spectacular over the years. It reveals that it takes the form of forgeries, frauds and swindling, hacking of electronic addresses, as well as the duplication of official websites via the internet. The post newspaper of May 10, 2011 reveals Cameroon is one of the countries that had been voted as the most unsafe in cyber world. Hacking, scams and other cyber crimes from the country have caused many countries including the United states and The United Kingdom to advise their citizens to beware of transacting with companies and businesses whose URLs trace down to countries like Nigeria and Cameroon

5 In February, 2011, the government announced the recruitment of 25,000 youth into the civil service and requested interested unemployed to compile documents and apply. Some of these document required fiscal stamps for certification. At the end of it the government realized that most of the fiscal stamps used were counterfeited stamps circulating all over and people buy without knowing that these are fake.

6 On November 10, 2008, a girl, Ngeyi Xaverie Marie, was gruesomely murdered in Yaounde by her boy friend. It was discovered that her body parts, like eyes and private parts had been removed and before it could be discovered and reported to the police, the man had escaped to Nigeria with the parts. It was known that he escaped to Nigeria because, the family of the girl reported that they received a call from the criminal using a Nigerian cell number telling them to go to his residence and collect the remains of their daughter. Also beginning from May 2011, there has been confirmed reported cases of beheading people and equally extracted other parts in Fako Division of the South West Region (see also www.thepostwebedition.com). The

Konings reveals that some of them can apparently count on the support of some leading figures in the Cameroonian regime and its security network. As a result of these activities, they have been able to amass fabulous wealth in a short period of time, and they are not ashamed to display their material success in the form of conspicuous consumption. With regard to the international dimension of *Feymanism*, Malaquais (2001) reveals how one of Cameroon's notorious gangsters, Donatien Koagne, popularly known as *Le King,* established close ties with some African leaders, which he exploited in order to ease the swindling of huge sums of money out of these people and others. For instance, he managed to create close ties in 1994 with members of the Mandela team in South Africa, so as to become a guest of honour at Mandela's presidential inauguration. One of the gangster's proudest possessions is a series of photographs of him posing side by side with some African leaders of the 1990s, for instance, Nelson Mandela, Mobutu Sese Seko and Denis Sassou Nguesso. There is no evidence that his relation with Mandela, whatever they were, became at any point unpleasant but with others he swindled huge sums of money from them. Malaquais reveals that he swindled fifteen million dollars from Marshal Mobutu and forty million dollars from Blaise Compaore of Burkina Faso. Sassou Nguesso, Etienne Eyadema of Togo, several high officials of Gabon, Tanzania and Kenya, a member of the Spanish government and an ex-operative of the Israeli Mossad were bamboozled as well. Koagne has been linked to a wide range of illicit practices – drug dealing, money laundering and trade in controlled substances (blood diamond, uranium), among others. Malaquais reveals that the means he used to defraud Mobutu and his colleagues, however, were something else altogether. The modus operandi was a fabulous con job, a sham money multiplication scheme involving a top-secret portion, allegedly concocted by the United States Department of Treasury for use in the manufacture of dollars bills. He concocted this scheme to give the impression to his potential victims that he had the ability to double any sum of money. He cheated many other people by collecting huge sums of money from them for this purpose, which they never got back.

In every big town in Cameroon, you find many of such young men *(feymen).* Many Cameroonians have fallen victim (and continue to do so) to these con men, and because of their connections to some high officials in the state security forces,

online paper reports that within three weeks, (between four people have been killed, their heads removed and female parts extracted. One of the suspected killers, caught with such parts, was arrested and handed to the military on June 3th, 2011 where he revealed that they had a mission to kill ten people, but had just killed four. The popular belief is that they have a ready market in neighboring Nigeria where the parts are used for rituals.

other state officials and they have the ability to bribe, so they are quickly released if detained. In this chapter, the legality or illegality, the deceit or extortion exhibited in this practice are not the central issues. What concerns me here is the knack or the tactics used by these youths to extract money from various people on an almost daily basis and the degree of success they attain in accumulating it in a country hard hit by economic crisis. Ndjio (2006) reveals that the popular perception of *feymen* is that these *nouveaux riches* are involved in 'occult-related' practices, and their success or failure rests not so much in their cunning and skill, but their talismans or 'magical powers'. For these people, as for many Cameroonians, one cannot operate successfully in *feymania*-related practices unless you are a 'sorcerer' or a member of a 'mystical society. It is difficult to subscribe to such an argument. More plausible is that these youths use their intellect and social skills to manipulate people in various ways. They use various methods of deceit to get people, and new methods are quickly adopted as people discover the old ones. Being able to manipulate people with great success is indicative of the high degree of ingenuity among these young men.

Some of these criminal activities existed before the economic crisis but the degree was not high and this probably accounts for why the state could not come out strongly with legislations against them. For instance, swindling, which most often took the form of sham money multiplication scheme, known popularly as 'money doubling', was done on a small scale without the use of modern communication systems such as the internet and cell phones and only practiced within the country. Hardly did you hear of someone scammed of millions of FCFA. Amounts were so small compared to the ongoing scamming of millions of FCFA not only from nationals but also from foreigners with the use of modern communication systems.

Just like the ordinary citizen, the Cameroon government is disturbed over this rise in crime wave and has been compelled to take some measures aimed at regulating them. For instance, relating to Cyber security and Cyber Criminality, Cameroon Law Number 2010/012 of 21 December 2010, was adopted by the Cameroon legislative body. This law governs the security framework of electronic communication networks and information systems, defines and punishes offences related to the use of information and communication technologies in Cameroon. The law which does not provide for suspended sentences for any offence provides sanctions of up to five years imprisonment and a fine of up to 100.000.000 FCFA.[7] In compliance to this law, many scammers have recently been arrested in many

7 One euro (in 2009) was about 655 FCFA.

parts of the countries and some of their names were published in newspapers and circulated on the internet as a deterrent. The state also recently created two special units to fight crime wave (One of the police core called the *Special Rapid Intervention Unit* created some four years ago and the other of the military called the *Battalion d'Intervention Rapide* (BIR) created some two years ago). These are specially trained and well equipped to fight criminality in the country. They are placed in major cities in the country and in some rural areas noted for high crime wave. Even though it can be argued that their activities have reduced crime wave wherever they are found, much still needs to be done. For instance, the state needs to recruit many more people into these units so that they can cover the entire country and also be made available in most neighborhoods of towns where they are located.

The aim here is to look at another activity which has had an upsurge among the youths within this period of the economic crisis: traditional medical practice. Before the coming of the economic crisis, 'tradi-medical' practice was associated with elderly people, and most often the skills were acquired through inheritance (see, for instance, Lantum 1985). However, many youths have now become strongly involved and inventive in this field, and like in *feymania* and *bendskin*, one can see them displaying a high degree of success in accumulation through it (see Ndjio, in this volume). These young men make their own drugs from plants and barks of trees and administer them to people. Unfortunately this is an activity which has not yet been regulated by the state. They could be seen all over advertising and selling their drugs unperturbed as there is yet no state regulation on the practice I focus here especially on practitioners in Buea municipality and begin with a presentation of the history of traditional medicine and a general picture of the practice in the country, followed by examining specific practitioners in Buea and then give some general impressions and responses of the ordinary people and clients on this practice. Buea is the regional capital of the South West region of Cameroon. The last sixteen years have witnessed an exponential growth of its population because of the creation of a state university in this town. The university has attracted students and business people from all over the country.

The history of traditional medicine and its general picture in Cameroon

Before the colonial era Western hospitals were nonexistent in Africa. However, traditional healers, nurses and midwives provided widely accessible and effective services to local populations. African traditional medicine was in its full bloom, as it was a 'people's culture' without alternative or competing medicinal systems.

Colonial rule, which was indeed a cultural invasion, brought along a new Western culture of diagnosis and medication of which allopathic or conventional medicine, developed on scientific basis, was an essential component. Its aim was to first of all protect and heal their citizens working in Africa before focusing on the Africans. As a policy in all colonies, the imported medicinal system was instituted as part and parcel of the government administration, to the exclusion of indigenous medicine. The latter was devalued with the arrival of Europeans and other foreigners on the continent. Thus, as traditional African medicine was negated in favour of their Western equivalents and conventional medical practices expanded, the traditional practices dwindled (cf. Lantum 2007, Toussaint, undated). Acknowledging this and in appreciation of African traditional medicine, Aujoulat (cited in Zingui 1976) lamented:

> A form of indigenous medicine existed in Black Africa before the coming of Europeans; today it carries on functioning but more or less in hiding — It is unfortunate that it has been reduced to the state of heretical medicine, pitilessly harassed for its errors or its accident, but hardly ever honoured for its victories. Thus finally collapse to nothing while its body of clinical knowledge and therapeutics should have profited universal medicine (p. 7).

This attempt at sweeping away traditional medical practices did not however work for obvious reasons. Lantum (2007) argues that it would have succeeded if the allopathic system was 100 percent efficient and efficacious, and could assure coverage for all the population sectors to palpably and satisfactorily reduce morbidity, mortality and prolong life. It is clear that conventional medical practices are not 100 percent efficient, their coverage low and they are not affordable to many people in the developing world.[8]

Realizing this loophole, international organizations, for instance, WHO and UNICEF, came in with a new conscience with regards to traditional medicines – the need to promote and sustain the practice. A combined WHO/UNICEF study commission came out with results in 1975 on the encouragement of traditional medicine, which were approved by the UNICEF Executive Board as UNICEF policy, and adopted by the World Health Assembly as Resolution WHO 22.88. The evidence content of this world policy is summarized in "Alternative approach to meeting basic health needs in developing countries" as follows:

> Despite great efforts by governments and international organizations, the basic health needs of vast numbers of world's people remain unsatisfied. In many countries, less than

[8] See, for instance, the WHO Media Centre Report, no. 134 of May 2003.

15 percent of the rural population and other underprivileged groups have access to health services. More serious still, these people are both partially exposed and particularly prone to disease. A hostile environment, poverty, ignorance of the causes of disease and of protective measures, lack of health services or inability to seek and use them-all may combine to produce this sorry situation"... The strategy adopted to meet the main health needs of the underprivileged by many developing countries has been modelled on that of the industrialized countries, but as a strategy, it has been a failure.

This was a radical departure from the repression of traditional medicine by the colonial administrations. Countries, especially in Africa, were encouraged to resurrect the practices and enact laws that could enhance its smooth functioning. The World Health Organization (WHO) Media Centre revealed in its May 2003 publication that the WHO launched its first comprehensive traditional medicine strategy in 2002. The strategy was designed to assist countries to:

- Develop national policies on the evaluation and regulation of traditional medicine (TM) and 'complementary' or 'alternative' medicine (CAM);[9]
- Create a stronger evidence base on the safety, efficacy and quality of the TM/CAM products and practices;
- Ensure availability and affordability of TM/CAM including essential herbal medicines;
- Promote therapeutically sound use of TM/CAM by providers and consumers;
- Document traditional medicine and remedies.

According to the publication, there is an increasing use and popularity of traditional medicines in the developing world and its use is rapidly spreading in industrialized countries. For instance, up to 80 percent of the population of Africa uses traditional medicine for primary health care and in Europe, North America and other industrialized regions, over 50 percent of the population have used complementary or alternative medicine at least once.

Considering the importance of this practice and in compliance with the WHO policy, Cameroon has made a lot of progress to encourage traditional medicine. It has enacted laws aimed at encouraging this sector. For instance, Law No. 81/12 of 27 November 1981, which approved the Fifth Five-Year Social, Economic Political Development Plan (1981-1986) provided measures to lay down a joint strategy and method to effectively integrate traditional medicine into the national health plan by implementing a program on traditional medicine in conjunction with some of the neighbouring countries. Under this plan, Cameroon created the Traditional Medicine Service within the Unit of Community Medicine in the Yaounde Central

[9] In industrialized countries, the equivalent of traditional medicine is 'complementary' or 'alternative' medicine, usually abbreviated 'CAM'.

Hospital. There have been other developments since then. For instance, a service for traditional medicine was created in the Ministry of Public Health in 1985; the Centre for the Study of Medicinal Plants set up within the Institute for Medical Research; the authorization of the formation of the tradi-practitioners' association in 1990 and the upgrading of the service of traditional medicine in the Ministry of Public Health to a Directorate in August 2002. This department already spear-headed the elaboration of a 'National Strategic Plan for Traditional Medicine' and initiated a preliminary draft of the law organizing the practice of traditional medicine in Cameroon. It equally included some traditional medicine practitioners in Cameroon's primary health care program. The encouragement of the traditional health practices has led to the opening of private traditional medicine hospitals in Buea and Melong. Furthermore, Cameroon has since 1980 authorized the setting up of three Chinese traditional medicine hospitals in Guider, Yaounde and Mbal-mayo. A special convention has been signed between the University of Yaounde 1 and China to promote the research valorization and development of traditional medicine. These various links with Chinese traditional medicine stimulated the widespread use of these medicines in the country. Also significant is the fact that the Ministry of Public Health in collaboration with the WHO took it a duty to organize the annual celebration of the 'African Day of Traditional Medicine'[10] all over the country every August 31 (Lantum 2007, WHO 2001).

Although the government encouraged traditional healing, before the economic crisis only a few people actually went into the practice on a full-time basis. The belief was that it was a practice reserved for old people because most of those involved in it were old people. Moreover, all traditional medical practices were still categorically condemned as 'witchcraft' and 'sorcery' by some religious groups (Lantum 1985). But within the last decades, there has been an upsurge in the number of traditional healers in Cameroon particularly among the youths. This has been enhanced by the increasing number of people that take recourse to their services. Their services are used by Cameroonians of all ranks and backgrounds, often simultaneously with conventional care. Some scholars have attributed the increase in their services to the economic crisis which Cameron has been facing in the last decades. Hillenbrand 2006 argues that they turn to traditional medicine

[10] In their meeting in Abuja in April 2001, African heads of states declared that research into traditional medicine be made a priority among members states. As a follow-up, in April 2003 in Tripoli, African Ministers of Health adopted a plan of action for the decade of African traditional medicine after their AU meeting. In July 2003, after another summit in Maputo, African heads of states endorsed the 'African Traditional Medicine Day', set on August 31, to be celebrated each year to create greater awareness of traditional medicine.

because they cannot afford pharmaceuticals or conventional medical care due to the economic crisis. A 2002 report from the Ministry of Public Health confirms that the economic crisis and the failure of the social security system have created an intensive return to traditional health services. The report reveals that today, 45 percent of the average household health budget goes to traditional medicines. Nearly twice as many people from poor households rely on traditional medicine, as do people from rich households (*Stratégie Sectorielle de Santé*, 2002: 32-39). It is understandable why the youths are so much involved in this activity. They are the most affected by the economic crisis. Many of them remain jobless, despite the academic certificates they may have. Employment in the civil service has been minimized and the country's taxation policy does not encourage entrepreneurship, making many youths to either look for greener pastures abroad or remain jobless in the country. Rather than continuously remaining without a source of income, they now take traditional healing as an activity they can lean on, because taxes cannot only be easily evaded but are minimal in the practice (Njimanted, 2006). Many youths have become strongly involved in it, and like in *feymanism* and *bendskin* one can see them displaying a high degree of success in the business. As evidence of ingenuity, they conceive and make the drugs themselves. Although the question of the safety of their drugs to human life is crucial, what struck me more during research was the ability of the youths to exploit the economic crisis to conceive and make something so crucial and delicate as people's health the issue of their business and making an economic success of it.

Tradi-practitioners are now found in every part of the country. My findings revealed that there are two types of traditional healers in Cameroon: herbalists and diviners. While the herbalist uses herbs and barks of trees to remedy illnesses and discomfort which are associated with natural causes, the diviner specializes in diagnosing and treating of illnesses which are associated with 'mystical causes', for instance, 'revenge of a neglected spirit', or of an 'ancestor unhappy with the violation of time-honored custom' or 'witchcraft' or 'sorcery'. Findings also revealed that some of them are both herbalists and diviners. This chapter, however, focuses on herbal traditional healers because the upsurge has been more in this direction. While some of them are part-time practitioners and could treat only a particular illness (for instance, typhoid) others are full-timers. Full-timers treat a variety of illnesses. For instance, Mami Kankang of Buea 'treats' up to 59 different types of illnesses. My findings revealed that one drug could be used in treating several illnesses: for instance, *Ginseng tea*, produced by Dr Mofor Pride[11]

[11] Though no formal academic qualifications to be called 'doctors', traditional healers in

of Buea, treats more than 32 illnesses. Another drug produced by Dr Mofor, *German Liniment,* is used to treat 21 illnesses. Although one drug could be meant to treat a variety of illnesses, the method of application varies with the illness. For instance, to use *German Liniment* to treat malaria, typhoid, yellow fever and jaundice, Dr Mofor recommends that the patient boils 6 packets of *Ginseng tea* in 6 litres of water, with 5 lemons added to it, for 30 minutes and drink a glass every morning and evening for 18 days and to use the same drug for the treatment of gastro-intestinal tract infections, stomach ulcer, constipation, intestinal fungi, amoebiasis, pile, stomach disorder, ported belly or reduction of excess fat, he recommends that 6 packets of *Ginseng tea* should be fermented in 6 litres of water, with 10 lime fruits added to it, for ten minutes and a glass should be taken every morning and evening for 21 days.[12]

Another issue typical of the healers is the *packaging* of their drugs and the inclusion of instructions on how to use them. Criticisms often labelled against traditional practitioners are the poor packaging of drugs and the dosage prescription (Lantum 1978, Hillenbrand 2007). The modern healers (the youths) try to overcome these problems by packaging their drugs in sealed papers and bottling those that are in liquid form, with instructions on how to use them either placed on them or written on a separate paper. Some of these healers not only limit their activities within the towns where they are located, but have pharmacies for their drugs in other towns where they also go from time to time to do consultations.

The upsurge has brought keen competition leading to a high rate of advertisement on traditional healing. This is done on radio, newspapers, in highway commercial buses, on streets in urban areas, motor parks and in vehicles equipped with a public address system for communication. Over local radio stations you find slots reserved for commercial announcements, most of which are centered on traditional healers, and in newspapers you find some of them occupying a whole page or half of it. Some of the tradi-practitioners, for instance, Dr Fru of Buea, Dr Ambeno Maurice of Tiko, Dr Dewah of Kumba, Dr Dan Baba of Buea and Dr Abiodum of Douala frequently make use of the radio and the newspapers. There is no doubt that they spend a lot of money on adverts. For instance, it cost 10.000 FCFA to read a commercial message two times on the radio and for a newspaper a full page cost 500.000 FCFA and 300.000 FCFA for half page and only for a single edition. One thing I tried to find out was whether the profession pays de-

Cameroon attribute themselves this title. They are called by this title by the population and I have maintained it all through the work.

12 The various illnesses and methods mentioned here were given to me from Dr Mofor himself. I have merely reproduced them as given to me.

spite the money spent on advertisement and in running pharmacies in hired houses in other towns. Some of them, for instance, Dr Fru of Buea, confirmed that they accumulate money through traditional healing. Dr Fru's flamboyant lifestyle, his many expensive brands of cars, well constructed clinic and the many facilities, including full-time workers of the clinic and the fact that he is full-time in the profession attest that he is actually accumulating through the practice.

The Buea experience

The town of Buea has witnessed a phenomenal increase in traditional healers within the past 10-15 years. There are more than forty professional traditional healers in the town. If we include the non-professionals[13] the number would definitely be above a hundred. A good number of them live around the university neighbourhood and some of them are university students. It is obvious that they target this area because of the increasing population and students get involved in traditional healing as a means of raising money to take care of themselves in Buea. Some of them have become famous through adverts on various radio stations, in motor parks and by the reputation of their performance. The Buea and FM Mount Cameroon radio stations, *The Post*, *The Humorist* and *Cameroon Express* newspapers are the media frequently used by these healers. The *Mile Seventeen* motor park which ferries people from Buea to other parts of the country is a popular location used by some of them to advertise and market their products. In order to understand the phenomenon and the performance of the new healers, I present some case studies below.

Case 1: Dr Fru Richard

Dr Fru Richard,[14] a lively and neat gentleman of about 34, was born in Mankon Bamenda of the Northwest region Cameroon. He did his primary education in Bamenda, where he started secondary education before completing it in the South West region. He obtained the General Certificate of Education (GCE) Advanced level in 1994 in Biology, Chemistry, Physics and Mathematics. When he was a child, he nursed the interest in becoming a medical doctor. This explains why he opted for the sciences in secondary school. Unable to gain admission to do medicine in a university after obtaining his GCE 'A' level, he switched to traditional healing in 1995. He began the practice in Kumba and later in 1996, moved

13 The non-professionals here are mostly those that do not rely solely on traditional healing for a living. They do purport to treat only one illness, for instance, typhoid, frontal headache, or infertility.

14 Dr Fru was interviewed in his office at his clinic in November 2007.

to Limbe. While in Limbe, he made trips to the creeks of Ndian Division of Cameroon for research on medicinal plants. Dr Fru told me that he made his first discovery in 1997, which to him was like a miracle. It was a drug he named *Secret solution* for treating a skin infection (locally called *come-no-go*) which was attacking many people and was resistant to modern drugs at the time. This drug was tested and found effective in the treatment of the infection by the regional delegation of public health in Buea. He was invited to the delegation and congratulated. This drug, which could allegedly treat the patient in less than three days, became widely used and it was being recommended to patients by conventional health practitioners.

After this discovery, Dr Fru decided to move to Buea where he started to operate an institute called *Garden of Eden: Institute of Natural Medicine Cameroon (GAEINAMED-CAM)*. He told me that he strongly believes in the healing power of *canda stick* and that *canda stick is a miracle for all health hazards. (Canda stick* is a pidgin word meaning 'bark of a tree'). Most of Dr Fru's drugs are made from barks of trees. His institute, which has been running for about 15 years, has a training school for traditional medicine and a clinic where he does consultations and treats his patients.[15] The idea of attaching a training school to the institute came later. The well-constructed institute has facilities like lecture and conference halls, a canteen, a modern laboratory, a research and production department, a school van and a garden for medicinal plants.

Admission to his three-year training programme is open to people of all academic levels. A student who successfully goes through the programme is awarded a diploma in traditional medicine. Since its inception and approval by the state in 2003, it has trained more than 100 youths. Some of the graduates have established their own clinics while others make drugs and sell through hawking. The programme recruits staff on part-time basis.

The clinic on some days gives consults up to 70 patients. For now, it provides only out-patients services but Dr Fru made arrangement for hospitalization some years ago. He told to me that the clinic used to employ more than 50 full-time workers but after some restructuring, he brought down the number to 42, supported by part-timers. Some of his workers, particularly those working in the laboratory, are graduates from the Faculty of Health Sciences of the University of Buea. On recruitment, they undergo another brief training in the institute on the traditional concepts of illness, healing and medicinal plants.

Dr Fru also revealed that at his *Garden of Eden Institute* he produces 180

[15] The website of his institute is www.candastick.org.

multi-purpose drugs, produced from over 500 medicinal plants. The drugs have various names, some of them very interesting: for instance, *Dosolin CPX, Candastick 2000A, Try me, Fru-vax, Fru-marcs, Good day and good night, Secret solution, C-none, Prosta O, Prosta E, Happinone-C, Spring wash.* He alleged that his drugs treat several illnesses, including affliction from 'witchcraft' and 'evil forces', HIV/AIDS, cancer, all venereal diseases, diabetes, impotence, epilepsy and all skin infections. Each drug is used to treat several illnesses. For instance, he told me that *Try-me,* in particular, is a "supernatural and holistic healing panacea for all illnesses you could imagine on earth". In his clinic, consultation is free but patients pay for the laboratory tests and drugs. At the time I was conducting this research, Dr Fru was carrying out an operation to treat people suffering from diabetes free of charge, although this only applied to the first 100 patients. This was repeatedly announced over the radio. He revealed to me that it was going to cost him millions of francs to go through the exercise but he did not mind it because he wanted to help people.

On where he gets the raw material (plants and barks of trees) for his drugs, he revealed that they come from all over Africa and even parts of Asia. In Africa, he mentioned specifically Cameroon, Nigeria, Ghana and the Central African Republic. Dr Fru either goes to these places to look for the plants himself, or his foreign suppliers send them to him. He equally revealed that some of the plants are cultivated in his *Garden of Eden* campus, but he still relies heavily on foreign supply because those in the garden are limited. Dr Fru has branches of his clinic in some major cities (Kumba, Bamenda, Yaounde, Douala, Dschang and Limbe) in the country where he occasionally goes to consult his patients.

Dr Fru maintains a good working relationship with some conventional healers and he told me that he sometimes refers cases he cannot treat to them and they too refer cases they cannot handle to him. On his relationship with other traditional healers, he expressed disgust at elderly healers who still do not believe in young traditional healers. As he puts it: "Most of them are less informed and are only contented with what they know, with no zeal to learn from especially younger people: there is this superiority complex." This confirmed to me that there is no good relationship between the old generation of traditional healers and the young. The young ones are coming up in their numbers and they seem to be exploiting the weaknesses of the elderly ones to make themselves popular, which of course does not please the elderly healers.

Dr Fru no doubt is popular, not only in Cameroon but also abroad. For instance, apart from attending many international conferences on traditional medicine, the University of Guinea-Conakry once invited him to give lectures on traditional medicine. He received a press award of excellence as the number one and most reliable traditional medical practitioner in Cameroon for the year 2007. His garden is like a touristic site in Buea, visited by many foreigners (at the time I interviewed him, they were some five visitors from Holland). There are indications that he accumulates substantial funds through traditional healing. The wonderfully constructed *Garden of Eden Institute* and its facilities, the number of workers he employs, his cars, residence, etc. are all indicative of his success. I realized that he spent a lot of money too to make himself popular. He used many radio stations and newspapers to make his adverts quite frequently.[16]

Case 2: Dr Obale Aku

Dr Obale,[17] a Rastafarian of North West region origin, was born in 1979 in Bolifamba, Buea, where his parents are based. He did his primary education in his native village, Ngwo, in the North West region. After completing this he went and did his secondary education in Calabar, Nigeria. On completing it he developed an interest in medicinal plants in Calabar. While there, he was able to discover the medicinal value of many plants, which he used in treating people. After working in Nigeria, he returned to Cameroon to do healing in Bolifamba, Buea. He told me he was inspired to do traditional healing by his parents, who are also traditional healers. His father, mother, younger sister and brother are traditional healers in Bolifamba. His mother is secretary of the association of traditional healers of the South West region. Dr Obale has been in practice for more than 18 years.

Dr Obale does not do divination. He uses herbs and barks of trees to heal his patients. He revealed to me that, though he does not do divination, if a diviner confirms that someone is suffering from a 'witchcraft'-related illness, he would heal the person. When I asked him how this is possible, he said that there are herbs which he uses in driving away a witchcraft attack. He treats more than 40 illnesses, among which are malaria, typhoid fever, stroke, chronic sexually transmitted infections including HIV/AIDS, and cases of infertility and impotence.

Unlike Dr Fru he gets his medicinal plants from within Cameroon, especially in Mamfe area, which he told me has big forests that are rich in medicinal plants. Also unlike Dr Fru, who never wanted to reveal the transformation process of his raw material, Dr Obale revealed to me that on bringing home his plants or barks of trees, he dries them every day for about a week under a very low temperature

[16] See, for instance, *Cameroon Express* no. 027 of Tuesday 29 January 2008 and no. 028 of Thursday 6 March 2008 and *The Humorist* no. 44 of 15 February 2008.

[17] Mr Obale was interviewed on 25 November 2007 in his residence at Bolifamba Buea

before grinding them to the required level. He argued that a plant or bark of a tree loses its medicinal value if dried under very high temperature.

Dr Obale does not have pharmacies for his drugs but he has agents in various towns that sell them at an agreed commission. In addition, he has employed eight workers who move round selling the drugs for him. He equally advertises and sells them on streets corners. A greater quantity of it is stocked in his house for sale or administered to patients. He does not charge for consultation but patients have to pay for their drugs. He revealed that in some cases, for instance a stroke, he tells his patients to bring certain things which he uses in preparing his treatment. In other cases he treats the patients free of charge though expecting him to reciprocate. He reveals that this method sometimes pays. As supporting evidence, he said that he treated the wife of a customs official in Douala of a pregnancy problem and the man dashed him a car, which he uses now. The customs official has continuously been helping him.

Dr Obale does consultations in his house in Bolifamba, and he contends he gives consultation to up to 45 people on some days. Cases he cannot treat are sent to other healers who are specialist. For instance, he revealed that cases of epilepsy are referred to another young healer, Dr Besong of Bolifamba, who is a specialist on epilepsy. More serious 'witchcraft' cases are referred to his younger brother (Gilbert). Gilbert is a diviner who knows little on herbal treatment. With regard to his relationship with conventional medical practices, he claimed that some hospitals have been inviting him to treat difficult cases, for instance stroke, which they cannot treat effectively.

Although based in Bolifamba, Dr Obale travels to many parts of the South region of Cameroon to treat people. He told me that when he goes to a place for the first time for healing, he goes straight to the chief's palace to introduce himself to the chief, who then introduces him to his subjects. The first twenty persons are usually treated for free after which the rest pay for their drugs. This free treatment is usually meant to let them assess his capability. More difficult cases or those that need to take long to treat are brought to his home in Bolifamba.[18]

Dr Obale admitted to me that he accumulates money through this practice. As evidence, he pointed to his two cars, a nice house and another one under construction, and his sponsoring his two kids in an expensive primary school in Buea.

18 While interviewing him in his home on 2 December 2007, I saw three young girls he brought from Ebolowa to be treated for pregnancy problems.

When compared to other young men in Buea, he dresses expensively and uses the most recent and expensive watches and cell phones.

Case 3: Dr Mofor Pride
Dr Mofor,[19] a calm and soft spoken young man, was born in 1980 in Santa, North West region of Cameroon. He graduated from the department of Political Science, University of Buea in 2008 with a B.Sc. in political Science. Before he enrolled in the university, he had started practicing traditional healing. He has been in the practice for over 11 years, and Mofor said that he got his inspiration for traditional healing from his parents and other traditional doctors in the town of Santa.

He deals only with medicinal plants. Most of the plants he uses come from the North West region. In Santa, he has a herbarium of some of the plants, which is visited by many people for research.

Dr Mofor has produced seven drugs, which are *Ginseng tea, German liniment, Africansa, family cure, quina cure, period cure* and *Indian remedy* which he told me is made from the mustard seed. He revealed to me that although his drugs are few, each of them is 'holistic'. By 'holistic' he means using one drug to treat several illnesses, but with different modes of application. For instance, *Ginseng tea,* he told me, restores strength, reduces impotence, stress, extends life, and revitalizes the cardiovascular system. Although he said he could not diagnose witchcraft cases, he uses medicinal plants to handle such problems after diagnoses confirmed by an expert. Dr Mofor revealed that his breakthrough has been the healing of heart diseases, which modern hospitals have failed to do. Another interesting thing he revealed to me was that many patients, particularly university students, come to him for gynaecological complications and venereal diseases, and he had been solving their problems. However, I could not confirm this from any one he treated and he too did not reveal any person he treated to me. He has no laboratory to diagnose certain illnesses but worked closely with some private laboratories. However, he revealed that he would soon set up his own laboratory. Dr Mofor does not charge money for consultations, but the patients pay for their drugs.

Unlike Dr Fru, who sells his drugs in pharmacies, Dr Mofor's drugs are marketed either in his home where he gives consultations or in highway commercial transportation buses. He has employed over 30 young men to advertise and sell the drugs in buses. He negotiates with the bus service the amount to be paid to them for using their buses. He recruits his workers and trains them in the various

---

[19] Dr Mofor was interviewed in my office in the University in November 2007 at a time he was still a student in the University of Buea.

strategies to be used in persuading travellers to buy the drugs. Each worker is paid depending on his output. He revealed that the least amount each of them can make in a month is 35.000 FCFA.

Dr Mofor claimed to be very unhappy with the field of traditional healing in Cameroon. He frowned at the proliferation of traditional healers in Cameroon. He believed that most of them are charlatans and he attributed this to effects of the economic crisis. He argued that with the crisis, many young Cameroonians are venturing into it; they spend much on advert claiming they could treat all diseases, thereby putting the lives of Cameroonians at risk. He was particularly worried about charlatanism in this domain, because it also affects him. He expressed worry that the proliferation of fake traditional healers and their drugs in Cameroon has made many Cameroonians to lose faith in traditional healing. He revealed that he was writing a book on economic crisis and traditional healing in Cameroon.[20] He equally frowns at traditional healers who try to make traditional healing mystical. As he puts it: "Secrecy is the worst problem." He believes that this attitude makes Cameroonians to be sceptical of traditional healing: "Many people think there are a lot of mystic and secrets in it because an African medicine man hardly shows you what he does; he prepares and puts in a container dries it and put in a paper before selling."

Other issues which Dr Mofor frowned at are the unhygienic conditions[21] under which some of the drugs are made and the inability of some healers to identify the right plants. He revealed that once a couple died in Bamenda because a traditional healer gave them a drug made from a plant which he mistook for another.

Dr Mofor also told to me that he accumulates money through healing. He cited examples to show his success, for instance the sponsoring of himself and a girl in the University, enough money to buy his car and set up a laboratory. It is evident that he accumulates if one were to consider the number of people that buy his drugs. During three trips which I made from Buea to Yaounde in buses in which some of his drugs (*Ginseng tea*, *German Liniment,* and *Africa panasia*) were sold, I observed that many people buy them. Of over 30 passengers in the bus during the first trip, 16 bought one, two or three of the drugs that were sold by his agent. On the second trip, 14 persons bought, and in the third 21 did. In each case, a few people who did not buy expressed the desire to do so, but said they did not have the money. From my observations, some people buy them for the first time for

20 Dr Mofor has written a few books on medicine, among which is *Feminine Hygiene: Problems and Solutions of the Female Anatomy and Physiology.*

21 He cited dirty water, hands, homes and non-packaging, which expose the drugs to flies, dust, etc.

two reasons: first, the persuasive manner in which the agents advertise them, and second, some passengers who had used them testify to their efficacy. As further evidence of high demand, within one hour that I was interviewing him in my office for this work, he had two different calls[22] from people he did not know requesting him *Ginseng tea* because the stock with his agents was finished.

Four issues can be observed from these three traditional healers: The first is that they are relatively young men. The second is that each of them started traditional practicing, as an occupation, within the period of the economic crisis. The third is that, none of them actually went through any formal training or claimed to have inherited the practice from an ancestor but made it through their own inventiveness. Although Mofor and Obale said they were inspired by other traditional healers, they all believe that they have perfected and modernized traditional healing practice, and fourth, they are able to produce new 'drugs' from medicinal plants that sell and have contributed to achieve economic success during a difficult time.

Reactions of people

In order to know the reactions of ordinary Cameroonians and clients to traditional healing at this time that the ordinary Cameroonian is yet to benefit from the positive economic growth which the government is claiming, I interviewed over 40 people, selected from among modern health personnel, students, farmers, civil servants, and business people in Buea. An examination of the answers revealed that some people 'believe' in traditional healing (make use of it along with the conventional services) particularly during this period of the economic crisis, while others are completely against it.

Of these two groups, those who believe in them often stated that the healers are rendering 'a wonderful service to Cameroonians'. The general impression of members of this group is that traditional healing is as good or as bad as conventional healing. They make use of the two services but argue that one must be selective when it comes to choosing *which* traditional healer or conventional service to make use of. They argue that selection is important because there are good and bad or fake traditional healers as well as good and bad or fake conventional medical practitioners.

On the first issue, Sakwe, a teacher,[23] believed that a good traditional or conventional healer is not money-minded when it comes to healing people. He is

[22] Labels of his drugs usually carry his contact number.

[23] Mr. Sakwe was interviewed on 8 December 2007 in his Buea residence.

efficient and charges very little money for his services. Sakwe admits making use of the two services in his health-related behavior. On the second issue, the problem is how to discern who is a charlatan or a credible healer. Dr Njei, a private medical doctor[24] who interestingly falls in this first group, argued that there has been an invasion of the medical field (both conventional and traditional) by self-proclaimed doctors during this period of the economic crisis in Cameroon. He explained that for the tradi-practitioner, it is easy to differentiate between the two. Being a cultural heritage from the ancestors, a tradi-practitioner does not need advertisements or formal training. According to him, a charlatan is a self-proclaimed traditional doctor. They can be recognized by the fact that they are involved in a lot of commercial activities but a tradi-practitioner needs no publicity. For the conventional practitioner, Dr Njei explains that he should be well trained, efficient, recognized by the National Union of Cameroon Medical Doctors, abides by the norms of the profession and does not exploit patients. As a medical doctor, he reveals that he himself works closely with some traditional healers. He refers patients suffering from certain illnesses to them and they too send patients to him. According to Dr Njei, the economic crisis is at the root of the upsurge in charlatanism in traditional healing because young men, despite the dangers to human life, venture into it in a bid to make money to overcome the crisis.

Most members of the first group admit having been cured or know of a relative cured through traditional healing after failures in conventional health centres. Common illnesses they mentioned that were cured by traditional healers after they had tried conventional medical services with no success were: epilepsy, typhoid fever, frontal headache, reproductive problems (low sperm count, infertility, impotence, etc.) and skin infections. Marie, a graduate of the University of Buea,[25] revealed to me that typhoid fever had been her greatest problem during her first two years in Buea. Unable to get a cure from various conventional healers, she was referred by a student to Pa Tantoh, of Buea, who treated her traditionally. She told me that for about three years, she has not had any traces of the illness again. On his part Mr Sube, a carpenter,[26] revealed to me that his second son was epileptic up to the age of nine but was eventually treated by Dr Besong of Bolifamba, after several failed attempts in various hospitals. For more than ten years (the son is about nineteen years now) the child has not been attacked again. Niba, a student, revealed that he suffered from a fungus infection between his laps for long. After several attempts at healing failed, he was prescribed Dr Mofor's *Ger-*

24 Mr. Njei was interviewed on 10 December 2007 in his private clinic.

25 Marie was interviewed on 10 December 2007 in Molyko, Buea.

26 Mr. Sube was interviewed on 14 December 2007 in Bomaka, Buea.

man liniment, which he used for a few weeks and the fungus was cleared. The treatment convinced him that traditional healing could be efficient.

Some members of this group also revealed that they prefer traditional healing because it is cheaper. For instance, Marie had spent more than 130.000 FCFA within this period in various hospitals with no success, but with only 1000 FCFA Pa Tantoh performed the magic with only five litres of a mixture of herbs, which she took for one week. Mr Sube on his part revealed that he spent close to 30.000 FCFA to treat his son with Dr Besong, an amount he believes is small compared to what he had spent in various conventional hospitals. Because of costs and the treatment of certain illnesses which conventional practitioners had failed to handle, Marie and Sube, just like others in this category, believe a lot on traditional healing. Each of them castigated conventional practitioners, accusing them of money mindedness despite their inability to treat certain illnesses.

The second category believes that traditional healers are not doing any good to Cameroonians. They argue that they are a health hazard to Cameroonians. Based on comparisons with conventional services, some of them argue that traditional healing is not based on any scientific premise, full of secrecy, unhygienic, poor prescription and preservation, etc. In addition, some of them accused tradi-practitioners of contributing in the spread of HIV/AIDS through their activities, for instance, the use of a single blade in extracting blood from many patients. In addition, they castigate some of them for either denying the existence of this pandemic or claiming they could cure it. Mr Mokube, senior health officer[27] in one of the government health establishments in Buea, even argued for legislation banning the activities of traditional healers. He said that he would never advise any person to go for traditional healing, nor refer a patient to any of them. Based on past experience some of them have decided to avoid traditional healing at all cost. Mrs Ayuk, a business woman,[28] revealed that what caused her to hate traditional healing was the death of her brother seven years ago. Her brother was ill of HIV/AIDS and instead of taking his anti-retroviral drugs, a traditional healer deceived her that he could treat the brother. But when he was taken to him, he made things worse and her brother ended up dying. On his part, Mr. Ngwa, a teacher,[29] revealed that he nearly died because of fake drugs produced by a traditional healer purported to be for cleansing the human system. His wife had bought for him during a trip from Bamenda to Buea. He said if he had not been not quickly rescued

27 Mr Mokube was interviewed on 14 December 2007 in Bomaka, Buea.

28 Mrs Ayuk was interviewed on 13 December 2007 in Muea, Buea.

29 Mr Ngwa was interviewed in Bolifamba, Buea, on 15 December 2007 in a bus I boarded with him to Bamenda in which traditional drugs were being sold.

in the Divine Providence Clinic, he would have died. He told me that after this horrible incident he developed a deep scorn for traditional healing, particularly fearing the fake drugs sold by them in buses or cars. Miss Njamnsi, a laboratory technician,[30] said that her problem with the drugs marketed by these healers was the method of preservation. As she puts it,

> Drugs, particularly those in liquid form, get bad if not preserved under a certain temperature but the so called drugs produced by these people are carried about under hot sun, in parks, streets etc and sold to ignorant people. How can I, a person of the medical field, take them serious?

Conclusion

In this paper, I have shown that there has been an enormous upsurge in traditional healing, especially among youths in Cameroon. This, as argued above, can be attributed to conditions of durable economic crisis, which instilled a spirit of creativity among the youths to develop new survival and income strategies. They make their own drugs and sell. The demand for their services or drugs is on the rise, because when compared to conventional health services they are cheaper and many people increasingly believe in their efficacy. Moreover, the crisis has rendered Cameroonians poorer, to the extent that they tend to go to where it is cheap for their health problems. The case studies in Buea testified to the high demand for their services: none of them receives less than 35 patients a day. When this number is compared to what is received by conventional private practitioners in Buea, it is very high. I visited some of the private conventional clinics in Buea to make a comparison and the numbers were indicative: for instance, the Solidarity Clinic receives on average 18 clients daily, the Good Shepherd Clinic 14, the Divine Providence 12 and the Joan of Arc 15. The ingenuity of this new young generation of traditional healers has enabled some of the youths to get involved in such practice that allow them to make a fortune.

One issue that can be underscored in observing this development is that it has not only provided self-employment to the healers but contributed in the employment of other youths. For instance, Dr Fru revealed that he has up to 36 full-time workers in his Garden of Eden Clinic and also that since the inception and approval of his training school he has trained more than 70 youths. Some of the graduates have established their own clinics, while others make drugs and sell

[30] Miss Njamnsi was interviewed on 15 December 2007 in a bus to Bamenda I boarded with her and in which traditional drugs were being sold.

them through hawking. Dr Mofor, on his part, has 21 employees, with a minimum of 35.000 FCFA made by each of them daily. This amount is not small and allows them to meet much of their basic needs at this time of the crisis.

A final issue to be pointed out is the need for the state to put more sanity in the profession in order to discern who is a charlatan or a *bona fide* tradi-practitioner. Though everything is done to encourage the sector, Cameroon has no legal framework that regulates the activities of traditional practitioners. So long as this is not done, charlatans will continue to increase in number, thereby exposing the lives of Cameroonians to unhealthy practices and making casualties.

References

Ajoulat, L.P., 1969. *Health and Development in Africa.* Paris: Armand Colin.

Cameroon, Law no. 81/12 of 27 November 1981 approving the fifth five year Social, Economic and Political Development plan (1981-1986). (Section 16-1 on the integration by its Ministry of Public Health of traditional medicine into the country's Health Care Delivery System).

Cameroon Law no. 2010 of 21 December 2010, relating to Cybersecurity and Cybercriminality, deliberated and adopted by the National Assembly and enacted into law by President Paul Biya.

Hillenbrand, E., 2006. Improving traditional-conventional medicine collaboration: perspectives from Cameroonian traditional practitioners. *Nordic Journal of African Studies* 15(1): 1-15.

IndexMundi, 2010 report on Cameroon Inflation Rate (Consumption prices) and Country Comparison Unemployment Rate.

Jua, N.B. 1991. Cameroon: jump-starting an economic crisis. *Africa Insight* 21(3): 162-170.

Konings, P., 2006. Bendskin drivers in Douala's New Bell neighborhood: masters of the road and the city, in Konings, P. & Foeken, D., eds., *Crisis and Creativity: Exploring the Wealth of the African Neighborhood.* Leiden – Boston: Brill, pp. 46-65.

Konings, P., 1996. The post-colonial state and economic and political reforms in Cameroon', in Fernandez Jilberto, A.E. & Mommen, A., eds, *Liberalization in the Developing World: Institutional and Economic Changes in Latin America, Africa, and Asia.* London – New York: Routledge, pp. 244-265.

Lantum, D., 1978. *The Pros and Cons of Traditional Medicine in Cameroon.* Yaounde: UCHS.

Lantum, D., 1985. *Traditional Medicine of Cameroon: The Case of Bui Division.* Yaounde: P.H. Unit.

Lantum, D., 2007. The place of policy in applied health care and special reference to African traditional medicine. *ATPS Special Paper Series,* no. 31.

Malaquais, D., 2001. Arts de feyre au Cameroun. *Politique Africaine* 82: 101-118.

Malaquais, D., 2002. Blood money, a Douala chronicle, in Ntone, E. & Edgar, P., eds., *African Cities Reader.* Cape Town: African Centre for Cities, University of Cape Town, pp. 137-149.

Ndjio, B., 2006. Intimate strangers: neighbourhood, autochthony and the politics of belonging, in Konings, P. & Foeken, D., eds., *Crisis and Creativity: Exploring the Wealth of the African Neighborhood.* Leiden: Brill, pp. 66-87.

Niger-Thomas, M., 2000. *Buying Futures: The Upsurge of Female Entrepreneurial Crossing the Formal/informal Divide in South West Cameroon.* Leiden: University of Leiden, Research School CNWS.

Njimanted, G.F., 2006. Growth and flexibility of government tax revenue: the Cameroon experience. *Journal of the Cameroon Academy of Science* 6(2): 127-135.

Stratégie Sectorielle de Santé: Analyse Situationelle du Secteur Santé au Cameroun. Yaounde: MPH, 2002.

Talougang, J. & Krieger, M., 1998. *African State and Society in the 1990s: Cameroon's Political Crossroads.* Boulder, Co.: Westview Press.

Toussaint, H. (undated), *Working to Help the Sick in West Africa and Beyond.* The Réseau YES-Benin academic paper.

WHO, 2001. *Legal status of traditional medicine and complementary/alternative medicine: A Worldwide Review* (WHO, Geneva), pp. 5-40.

WHO Media Centre, 2003. *Traditional Medicine.* Fact Sheet no. 134.

Taking Africaness and African Law Seriously in South African Law Schools: some conceptual challenges[1]

Francis B. Nyamnjoh

One of the challenges facing the South African state and higher education institutions is reconciling in the curriculum the competing and often conflicting values that in recent history shaped the different legal perspectives and realities of 'citizens' (the free, recognized, represented and entitled minority white population) and 'subjects' (mostly the unfree, invisible, dispossessed, disenfranchised majority black population) of the apartheid era. Formerly the white minority of apartheid South Africa prescribed and enforced what was good for them and imposed on the majority black population legal regimes informed by largely distorted and frozen colonial inventions of African 'traditions', often invented to suit the ambitions of dominance of colonial/apartheid South Africa. This legacy of controversy partly explains current needs to take Africaness and African law seriously. Post-apartheid transformation necessitates curricular reform and this is urgent because the newly enfranchised majority black population is critical of continued subjection by remaining laws of an era that denied them humanity. To take Africaness and African law seriously, two important series of questions should be addressed: a) about what 'African identity' and what it means for people in post-apartheid South Africa; and b) about what it is to be 'indigenous'. To define the indigenous simply as those who were there first and are still there, and so have rights to their lands, or even as those particular groups who were left on the margins of development, or whose cultures and ways of life are subject to discrimination, contempt, and threat, etc. is to invite inquiry about the reality of internal and external migration and the politico-economic, cultural, and historical factors that have configured competing articulations of being indigenous. This rich and

[1] An earlier version on this chapter was presented as a keynote address at a conference on Africanisation of Law Curricula in South Africa, held at the University of South Africa (UNISA) College of Law, 28-29 September 2009, Pretoria.

complex patchwork appeals to a sort of flexible indigeneity, to which South Africa, like neighbouring Botswana can attest historically. The history of (South) Africa demonstrates flexible modes of belonging that make it difficult to claim identities in essentialist terms. The challenge for the evolving legal system in South Africa is how to embrace these complexities, and have the law curriculum reflect the depths and diversity of experiences of South Africans. This is especially challenging, given the tendency for the law to prefer clarity over ambiguity. Meaningful cultural, political, economic, and legal recognition and representation can be negotiated for individuals and groups, to account for conviviality and accommodation and to counter the diminishing circles of inclusion imposed by race, ethnicity, class, gender, and geography, and a 'new' law curriculum should reflect the variety of cultural understandings of the meaning of human dignity that can be found in the multiple cultural 'traditions' of the South African 'Rainbow Nation'.

Introduction

One of the challenges facing the South African state and higher education institutions is that of reconciling in the curriculum the competing and often conflicting values that shaped the different legal perspectives and realities of citizens (the free, recognised, represented and entitled minority white population) and subjects (prominent among whom the unfree, invisible, dispossessed, disenfranchised, and bantustanised majority black population) of the apartheid era. Like with the masters and the free of ancient Greece, the political, cultural and economic white minority of apartheid South Africa prescribed and enforced legally only what was good for them and their interests. They also prescribed and imposed on the majority black population legal regimes informed by distorted and frozen colonial inventions of African cultures and traditions. Naturally such traditions, invented to suit the ambitions of dominance of colonial and apartheid South Africa, were controversial and perhaps explain current preoccupations with taking Africaness and African law seriously (Ntlama & Ndima 2009). Those subjugated by apartheid could not do much in their subjugation to influence curricula, so it is quite understandable that post-apartheid transformation should include curricular reform, as what is taught informs what is practiced (Gutto 2006). It is also urgent because the newly enfranchised majority black population is critical of continued subjection by unpopular laws of an era that denied them humanity. And it is only by recognizing the place of all and sundry that South Africa can come fully into its potential, for its people, and for the continent.

The colonial and apartheid inventions of cultures and traditions meant the silencing of more indigenous consensual approaches and variants of legal values informed by prevalent notions of personhood and social action such as *Ubuntu* (Nkondo 2007; Thomas 2008). In this regard, Mahmood Mamdani's (1996, 1998, 2000) distinction between 'citizen' and 'subject' and between 'culture talk' and 'rights talk' are useful analytical starting points. Starting points because, if we are to remain faithful to the lives of ordinary people and their infinite capacity to negotiate and navigate the various identity margins in their lives, there is little to suggest that people live their lives neatly as citizens on the one hand and as subjects on the other (Werbner 2004). In the same way, nothing prevents individuals and communities from embracing and eventually celebrating and aggressively defending imposed identities or 'invented traditions' (Ranger 1984). Concerning the latter point, John Comaroff and Jean Comaroff (2009) are quite instructive on the commodification and corporatisation of ethnicity and cultural identities in South Africa and globally.

Often in law the tendency is to consider society as a homogenous unit and to seek to justify laws with the need to protect the individual or the society from each other. As Montesquieu put it in his 1748 *Spirit of Laws*, the individual must be checked to ensure that he or she does not pursue selfish interests to the detriment of the collective interest. He argued that society needs laws of morality to keep the individual in check. Legislators must, through political and civil laws, confine the individual to his or her duties and responsibilities to society, lest they forget the importance of interdependence and conviviality. He added that respecting a common set of values makes sense to the extent that there is justice, and that justice can only be possible if everyone recognises that his freedom ends where another's begins. In the case of South Africa, a multiracial, multiethnic and multicultural society with a past of tense, bloody and highly unequal racialised and ethnicised relationships, it makes sense to extend the function of the law to include intermediary groups (racial, ethnic, cultural, religious, etc.) that mediate the relationship between the individual and the state. A multicultural, multiethnic and multiracial society needs to protect itself not only against the selfish interests of individuals, but also against the selfish interests of racial, ethnic and cultural entities or communities, making it clear to them that their freedoms end where those of others begin. To do this meaningfully, the law and thus law curricula must be reformed to reflect the interests and value systems not only of each and every South African as an individual, but also of South Africans belonging to cultural, ethnic and racial collectivities that shape their thinking, outlook and action within the South African state as a system of interconnected hierarchies of power relations.

It is only in this way that law can ensure that the quest for the successful functioning of post-apartheid South Africa is not merely a ploy to continue serving and servicing the interests of a powerful and only marginally reconfigured elite few to the disadvantage of the majority as individuals and also as groups. Nothing else quite makes sense in post-apartheid South Africa than to seek group restitution and reparations for those who were dispossessed and disenfranchised as a group, and not merely as individuals. The conversation towards legal representation for collectivities recommended here should be pursued concurrently with individual rights. In other words, the prospect of democracy being simultaneously an individual and a group right and aspiration must be taken seriously in rethinking law curricula in post-apartheid South Africa.

Africanity in Post-apartheid South Africa

To put on a solid foundation efforts to take Africaness and African law seriously, there is need to answer two important questions not in abstraction or with prescriptions, but as informed by the lived experiences of actual people within a particular socio-political and historical context. The first of these questions is: What is it to be African? What does it mean to be African in post-apartheid South Africa? Who qualifies to claim Africa? Who doesn't, and why? Is being African or claiming Africa an attribute of race and skin colour (black, white, yellow), birth (umbilical cord, birth certificates, identity cards, passports), geography (physical spaces, home village), history (encounters), culture (prescriptive specificities), economics (availability and affordability, wealth and deprivation), sociology (social configurations and action, inclusion and exclusion), psychology (mindsets), philosophy (worldviews), politics (power relations), or collective memory (shared experiences and aspirations), to name just a few of the many possibilities that present themselves? Or a process through which a world – that is not rigidly geographical, racial or cultural – is constructed and represented? Is football and Bafana Bafana (or Castle Beer) more African in the South African context than Rugby and the Springboks (or braai)? Is Rondebosch in Cape Town less African and therefore less deserving of Africaness than Langa, Khayelitsha and Gugulethu? Is Hillbrow in Johannesburg less South African than Sandton, because it happens to have been taken over by the *Makwerekwere*?

These questions have deep roots in debates about ethnicity, citizenship and identity, and in the definition of rights, entitlements, duties, and responsibilities. The answers to them define and confine privileges and advantages under the law. If we are not careful, of the many that are called only a few shall be chosen. The

God of religion might be for all and sundry, but that by no means implies that the privileged few shall bend over backwards to accommodate those at the margins of identity or those at the margins of current legal frameworks. By ensuring that belonging is articulated around the logic of exclusion, we guarantee that only those who truly matter shall be elected to our ever diminishing circles of inclusion.

That said, these questions are, of course, not uniquely South African. Indeed, similar issues have been debated with considerable passion in other parts of the continent and the world both historically and currently, and contestations around them have also been played out in violent ethnic confrontations, civil wars, and inter-state conflicts. While they may seem straightforward to answer, the questions have been rendered much more complex by the dynamic interplay of race, ethnicity, gender, geography and religion in the structuring and exercise of power and opportunity. Precisely for this reason, the questions cannot be addressed in the abstract. An investigation of the real lives of ordinary South Africans, and even of the elite few who are ever so keen to talk left and act right and to champion difference and dichotomies, would show determined efforts and ongoing processes at building identity bridges in their lives than is often recognised or acknowledged.

How one grapples with these questions and with Africaness is not only situationally determined but is also a function of how selective one is with regard to various indicators, like race, ethnicity, gender, etc. Some individuals and communities on the continent and elsewhere might claim Africaness or have it imposed upon them for various personal, collective, historical and political reasons. It is not always straightforward to say which claims may be legitimate and why, especially as identity is not only how one sees oneself but also how one is seen, categorised and related to by others, particularly where the absorption of new populations is involved. This is all the more so as identities are themselves always in mutation, shaped as they are by changing historical contexts and circumstances, such as internal and international migrations and shifts in social power relations.

It is, however, safe to say that to most ordinary people in South African townships, ghettoes and villages, Africaness is more than just a birth certificate, an identity card, or a passport – documents that many of them may not have, even as others coming from elsewhere and waving the flag of Africaness may have all these documents and more. For the ordinary person, to be African in South Africa is not simply to be labelled or merely defined as such. It is to be a social actor/actress enmeshed in a particular context that has been and continues to be shaped by a unique history marked, among other dynamics, by power relations informed by interconnected local and global hierarchies of humanity and personhood, as well as unequal encounters and misrepresentations often informed by the arrogance and ignorance of the economically and politically powerful who take the liberty to arrogate cultural superiority to themselves. For the masses of South Africans, Africaness is above all a lived reality, one constantly shaped and reshaped (*socially produced*) by their toil and sweat, even as they struggle to live in dignity and to transform their societies progressively. For these South Africans, the fact of their Africaness is neither in question nor a question. And the least they would expect from concerned legislators and legal scholars is to refrain from adding to their burdens in the name of a socially and culturally disembedded and ahistorical legal scholarship and practice that trivialises their collective experiences and memories.

Being indigenous

The second important question is: What is it to be indigenous? As I have had occasion to argue elsewhere (Nyamnjoh 2007a), to define indigenous peoples simply as those who "were there first and are still there, and so have rights to their lands" (Maybury-Lewis 2005), or even as those "particular groups who have been left on the margins of development", "are perceived negatively by dominating mainstream development paradigms", "whose cultures and ways of life are subject to discrimination and contempt", and "whose very existence is under threat of extinction", a definition adopted by the African Commission's Working Group of Experts on Indigenous Populations/Communities (ACHPR & IWGIA 2005: 87-97), is to incite inquiry about the reality of internal and external migration and the political, cultural, economic, and historical factors that have configured competing articulations of being indigenous. Although such strategic essentialism may be understandable and indeed useful in the pursuit of common ambitions of dominance or in redressing injustices collectively experienced as a colonized or subjected people (and Black South Africa is an excellent case in point), it hardly provides for theorizing pre- and postcolonial identities as complex, negotiated, relational and dynamic experiences that respond to and feed from local and global interconnecting hierarchies (Hall 2010), shaped by processes with which there are neither permanent winners nor permanent losers. Qualifying to be considered 'authentic' or 'bona fide' is a function of the way race, geography, culture, class, and gender define and prescribe, include and exclude. These hierarchies of humanity assume different forms depending on encounters, power relations, and prevalent notions of personhood, agency, and community. Africa offers fascinating examples of how the term *indigenous* was employed in the service of colonizing forces, of how colonially created or re-imagined ethnicities have had recourse to indigeneity in their struggles against colonialism, and of how groups vying for resources and power amongst themselves have deployed competing claims to indigeneity in relation to one another. The work of Piet Konings on identity politics, civil society movements and liberation struggles, especially in Anglophone Cameroon and by Anglophone Cameroonians, is particularly instructive on this theme of contested indigeneity and belonging (Konings 2009, 2010, 2011; Konings & Nyamnjoh 2003).

In Africa, the meaning of 'indigenous' has thus varied tremendously. Communities large and small have both accepted and contested arbitrary colonial and postcolonial administrative boundaries and the dynamics of dispossession. Failing to achieve the idealized 'nation-state' and relatively weak vis-à-vis global forces, governments have often sought to capitalise on the contradictory and complementary dimensions of civic, ethnic, and cultural citizenships. In this context, being indigenous socio-anthropologically is much more than merely claiming to be or being regarded as the first. Colonial and apartheid regimes of divide-and-rule created and imposed a proliferation of 'native identities' circumscribed by arbitrary physical and cultural geographies. They made distinctions between colonized 'natives' and colonizing Europeans but also between 'native citizens' and 'native settlers' among ethnic communities within the same colony. In this context, to be called 'indigenous' meant to be primitive, which became a perfect justification for the colonial 'mission civilisatrice,' for dispossession and confinement to officially designated tribal territories, homelands or Bantustans, usually in callous disregard for the histories of relationships and interconnections forged with excluded others, and the differences and tensions even among the included. In all, being indigenous was for the majority colonized 'native' population to be shunted to the margins in socio-economic and juridico-political terms. These dynamics of classification and rule conceived of the 'natives' through frozen ideas of culture and imagined traditions applied under 'decentralized despotisms' in rural areas, while the town and city were reserved for the minority colonial settler population and their purportedly 'modernising,' 'cultured' and 'detribalised' African servants and support staff (Mamdani 1996, 1998). Even then, the colonial and apartheid authorities made it extremely difficult for their African servants and support staff to feel at home away from home, thus driving even the most reluctant of them to look back to their home villages for solidarity and sustenance, when they would have preferred permanent integration as bona fide townsmen and townswomen (Mayer 1971; Bank 2011).

If this negative history still shapes the highly critical stance of African intellectuals and nationalists toward all nebulous claims of autochthony, it has also, quite paradoxically, tended to render invisible the everyday reality of postcolonial Africans (including those same intellectuals and nationalists) as straddlers of civic, ethnic, and cultural citizenships on the one hand and multiple global and local cosmopolitan identities on the other. For example, being Zulu and participating in various Zulu cultural beliefs and practices to promote and preserve and evolve 'the Zulu nation' does by no means contradict one's African National Congress (ANC) membership and identity as a cosmopolitan South African citizen who is a frequent flyer and a soccer-loving, Pentecostal Law Professor of international renown living in Sandton, Johannesburg and cherishing flashy French and Italian designer suits and shoes, big Breitling watches and gold, diamond-studded rings, and the choicest wines while animating a newspaper column on western art and being creative and innovative in his appropriation of technologies such as fancy cars, the internet (Facebook, Twitter, etc.) and the mobile devices (Blackberry, i-phone, i-pad, etc.). It is with this in mind that Fiona Forde (2011), in her *An Inconvenient Youth*, draws on Chimamanda Ngozi Adichie's (2009) caution against 'the single story', to argue that Julius Malema, president of the ANC Youth League until his destitution in February 2012 for disciplinary reasons, is a far more complex person than the one-dimensional, caricatured media portrayals of him that both his supporters and detractors would suggest.

With growing uncertainties and realizations of the inadequacies of bounded citizenship and its illusions of autonomy, rigid and highly exclusionary affirmations of being indigenous have become obsessive among majority and minority communities alike within various states in Africa. Current clamours for cultural renaissance, Ubuntu and Africaness amongst the majority black victims of apartheid South Africa could be understood within this framework, and especially given the surging economic downturns and ever diminishing possibilities for the rights and entitlements promised all and sundry under the post-apartheid constitution.

Notwithstanding such uncertainties and insecurities, seeking rigid or bounded indigeneity or Africaness in the 21st century, however justifiable, is an exercise to be undertaken with extreme care. For one thing, most of the archival documentation, maps and anthropological literature available is quite problematic, in that it was produced to service and facilitate colonial administration, rather than advance disinterested scholarship. In other words, although all traditions and identities are imagined or invented, what we run the risk of using as evidence, in our claims of Africaness and African Law, is material made available by the very colonial and apartheid regimes whose authority to define and confine we are contesting.

A good case in point comes from neighbouring Botswana. In the year 2000 when I was still teaching at the University of Botswana, a judgement was made that generated much heated debate. In a ruling on a case of adultery, Mr E.J.M. Showa, Assistant Customary Courts Commissioner, used *A Handbook of Tswana Law and Custom* (first published in 1938) by Isaac Schapera, a South African anthropologist, to overturn an earlier judgement "awarding eight head of cattle to Mrs Tshoganetso Ramoroka, who had sued Ms Gofhaone Bonno for destroying her marriage" (Mogale 2000: 8). Using Schapera's book, Commissioner Showa wrote:

> "I want to deal with the law in regard to cases of adultery in Customary Courts and I quote: 'Adultery on the part of the wife is held to be a more serious offence, and her husband has the right to claim damages from her paramour – a right which she cannot exercise against her husband's concubine. It is recognised that a man is inclined to be promiscuous: monna pôô ga a agelwe lesaka, goes the saying: 'A man, like a bull, cannot be confined in a kraal.'"

Women and women's organisations were reportedly 'highly offended' by the ruling. As an anthropologist, Schapera, informed largely by a male-dominated 'native' hierarchy, researched into Tswana law and custom, and his findings were eventually compiled into a handbook for the then Bechuanaland Protectorate Administration. At the time of the compilation, he might have argued that the benefits of his research far outweighed the risks to his Tswana subjects. If anything, he was doing them a favour by putting them on the scientific and cultural maps of the world. But as Mamdani has argued, most so-called customary laws of Africa today were largely inventions by native male collaborators (often chiefs) of the colonial project, and seldom a reflection of how individuals and groups actually related to one another within a given 'tribe' – another invention in many regards. The "colonial powers presumed an implicit and unchanging consensus over the customary," which might explain why they turned to the leadership of each tribe (the chief) "to enforce their notion of custom as law" and also "assured them backup support from colonial institutions – and direct force, if need be – in the event they encountered opposition or defiance" (Mamdani 1996: 109-137). Thus, even if Schapera were to claim to have been impartial and sensitive to the predicaments of his research subjects at the time of his research, the women, who over half a century later were to be victimised by his 1938 handbook as the 'authority' on Tswana law and custom, would have challenged him for not having been impartial and sensitive enough. This raises the difficult question of the extent to which it is possible to be objective yet sensitive to social relations, which are inherently power relations, even in and among groups that qualify as poor and/or marginalized.

Though certain colonial anthropological texts are problematic, we cannot afford to throw the baby out with the bathwater of colonial anthropology (Nyamnjoh 2011). No creativity, imagination or invention, however insensitive to the predicament of those it seeks to represent or caricature, is undertaken entirely in a void. It suffices to approach these texts with the critical mindedness necessary to sift out what is relevant to cultural renaissance and a more representative legal framework in post-apartheid South Africa. In this connection, John Comaroff has done some very fascinating legal anthropology on various aspects of Tswana institutions and society both in Botswana and South Africa, since the early 1970s. In his study of laws regulating chieftaincy or marriage, John Comaroff privileges the ethnographic description of social action over prescription, statements of principles or declarations of intentions. He is very critical of others who, in their attempts to theorise on these very same institutions, focus analysis "almost exclusively upon institutional and constitutional arrangements," thus assuming "the classical dichotomy between ascription and achievement" and taking "as given that stated rules should actually determine the careers of actors in the public arena" (Comaroff 1978: 1, 1981). His insights on how the post-apartheid constitution is acted out by judges and South African citizens could be a useful guide in developing conviviality between text and practice in the way courses are designed and taught in South African law schools. Equally instructive are his and Jean Comaroff's insights on violence, crime and the primacy of disorder in postcolonial contexts, despite an apparent fixation on legalities (Comaroff & Comaroff 2006). This would entail a multidisciplinary approach involving legal practitioners and academics of law and society from disciplines such as law, sociology, anthropology, history, and political science.

A territorially confined Africanity?

Similar to what Piet Konings (2009, 2010, 2011) and others have documented of Cameroon, the current fascination with indigeneity amongst South African nationals is paralleled by increased awareness and distinction between 'locals' and 'foreigners' or 'insiders' and 'outsiders' with the emphasis on opportunities and economic entitlements. Apart from official measures to restrict access to citizenship by foreigners from Africa north of the Limpopo (who are often derogatorily categorised as *Makwerekwere*), public attitudes even amongst South African blacks towards foreigners seeking Africaness are generally hardening (Mpe 2001;

Nyamnjoh 2006, 2010; Pillay *et al.* 2008; Sharp 2008; Sichone 2008; Peberdy 2009; Neocosmos 2010; Landau 2011). Yet the very same South Africans eagerly and triumphantly point to *Ubuntu* and the generosity and hospitality it inspires towards foreigners and strangers (Ramose 1999). It is true that the accelerated mobility and economic downturns of the 21st century have come with ever increasing feelings of insecurity and uncertainties, but scapegoating strangers and foreigners is hardly in tune with the spirit of Ubuntu, especially as there is no reason to assume that all problems would be solved once outsiders are out of the way. Or that the social production of outsiders would cease with the elimination of the current category of outsiders. As Piet Konings' work (2009, 2010, 2011) on neoliberal bandwagonism and statehood in Africa suggests, the real causes and solutions to present day predicaments lie elsewhere.

Ubuntu and Africaness are thus useful only to the extent that we do not attempt to limit their breadth for instrumental reasons. There is no objective reason whatsoever why we should assume that Ubuntu and Africaness should start and end with us or with some other specific South African community. Any such assumption is problematic, especially as the very same philosophies of personhood and agency that inform the current call for Ubuntu and Africaness are present in other parts of Africa and beyond. These shared values have withstood the test of colonialism, apartheid and neoliberalism. Indeed, these marginalized yet resilient beliefs, institutions, customs, and outlooks documented by anthropologists and historians (however controversial) demonstrate the fact and force of ideas of personhood and agency – that compete with those embedded in the practice of liberal democracy focused on individual rights – and demonstrate the profundity of the ways of life inspired by such outlooks.

Need to reconcile ethnicity and citizenship

In Cameroon (Konings 2009, 2010, 2011; Konings & Nyamnjoh 2003), there is tension between ethnicity and citizenship, in the way identity and belonging are claimed and denied. It is a tension noticeable throughout Africa (Mamdani 1996, 2009; Salih & Markakis 1998; Geschiere 2009; Geschiere & Nyamnjoh 2000; Englund & Nyamnjoh 2004). Given dreams of modernity and fascination with the nation-state by African elites (Comaroff & Comaroff 1993, 1999; Deutsch et al. 2002), I can very well understand why South Africans would be totally flabbergasted by what I am suggesting, but let's take a closer look at what the pursuit of the modern nation-state has delivered in concrete terms in Africa. Post-independence nation-building has meant the privileging of large-scale over small-scale indigeneity, and, paradoxically, the agency of the autonomy-seeking right-bearing individual over the domesticated agency of groups, communities and societies (Nyamnjoh 2002). The quest for congruence between culture and polity has resulted in the undue essentialisation and oppression or celebration of identities while overlooking ongoing contradictions, contestations, and clamours for rights and entitlements by marginalised collectivities (Nyamnjoh 2005; Konings & Nyamnjoh 2003; Konings 2009, 2010, 2011).

As the pursuit of nation-building increasingly fails to justify the sacrifices made in its name, individuals and communities become more vociferous about the inequalities such sacrifices have engendered or exacerbated (Englund and Nyamnjoh 2004). The upsurge in calls for *Ubuntu* and Africaness (Ramose 1999; Mbembe 2006; Nkondo 2007; Thomas 2008; Ntlama & Ndima 2009; Ndlovu-Gatsheni 2009) and the commodification of ethnicity in South Africa (Comaroff and Comaroff 2009) speak for the continuous relevance of group and cultural solidarities in the face of the uncertainties of neoliberal possibilities. 'Decentralised despotism' constructed or appropriated by the colonial state is being drawn on in post-apartheid South Africa fight against inherited discrimination or to protect a heritage of privileges (Mamdani 1996, 1998, 2009). South Africans, even the most modernized, seem reluctant to be identified solely as nationals. They seem rather reluctant to let go of the problematic racially informed lexicon of the apartheid era (whites, Africans, coloured, Asians). Few of them are just content with being South Africans in a simple, straightforward civic sense. Nobody, it would appear, is exclusively cosmopolitan or exclusively indigenous, as everyone negotiates both almost effortlessly and unconsciously. That cultural citizenship remains of utmost importance to South African elites, regardless of their subscription to the 'modern' civic regime of rights, is further evidenced by the widespread reluctance to sacrifice their ethnic and cultural identities. Despite hundreds of years of interethnic marriages and relationships, the patriarchal customs of cultural communities have ensured the illusion of ethnic purity by stubbornly adhering to narrowly defined traditions of descent. This juridico-political or structural rigidity emphasizes cultural essentialism despite a reality of flexible indigeneity (Sharp 2006; Boonzaier & Spiegel 2008).

Liberal democracy, especially as exported to Africa, has not been too keen to acknowledge and provide adequately for such social nuances in its articulation of citizenship (Nyamnjoh 2005). Yet in South Africa as well as other parts of the continent not only does indigeneity matter, struggles for cultural rights are rife and include cases of disenfranchised majorities seeking redress against a state controlled by a minority. Liberal democracy promises political, economic, and cultural enrichment for all but is able to provide it only for a few, and in uncertain ways (Konings 2009, 2010, 2011). Its rhetoric of opening up, of cosmopolitanism and of abundance is sharply contradicted by the structural reality of closures and rigid indigeneity, when most of its disciples are within and between cultural communities and states. Winner-takes-all politics has tended to downplay the reality of migratory flows that challenge rigid claims of indigeneity, while blindly yielding to the dictates of those powerful enough to override even the legitimate claims (Sharp 2008; Peberdy 2009; Neocosmos 2010; Landau 2011).

Flexible indigeneity and flexible citizenship

Indigeneity is a process subject to renegotiation, as rising expectations by individuals and groups evolve. Political, cultural, historical, and economic realities determine what form and meaning the articulation of indigeneity assumes in any given context. Individuals and communities may be entitled to rights, but who actually enjoys rights does not merely depend on what individuals and groups may wish or are entitled to under the law, by birth, or in a universal declaration of one kind or another. Increasingly and quite paradoxically in South Africa and elsewhere, globalization and the accelerated flow of capital, goods, electronic information and migration is exacerbating insecurities, uncertainties and anxieties, bringing about an even greater obsession with autochthony, and the building or reactualisation of rigid indigeneity.

Productively addressing surging uncertainties and anxieties is hardly to be accomplished through a narrow and abstract definition of indigeneity, much less in any politics of exclusion and difference within and between groups, indigenous or foreign. The answer is not simply to shift from a state-based to a more individual-based universal conception of citizenship, as some have suggested, because this fails to provide for the rights of collectivities, however construed. The answer to the impermanence of present-day achievements lies in incorporating 'outsiders' without stifling difference and in building of partnerships across those differences. The answer, in other words, is in a cosmopolitan life informed by allegiances to cultural meanings drawn from different sources in the rich repertoire of multiple, kaleidoscopic encounters by individuals and groups. Englund talks of cosmopolitanism, informed by relationships that stress 'a deterritorialised mode of belonging,' that makes it possible to feel at home away from home (Englund 2004). So that (a) 'home' isn't necessarily place – though it might be; and (b) increasingly one can feel 'at home', simultaneously, in many 'places'. I revisit this theme in the image of Cameroonian bushfallers as frontier people, who negotiate and navigate myriad places and spaces, challenging essentialisms, and imaging new futures (Nyamnjoh 2011).

This rich and complex patchwork goes beyond the rigid indigeneity implicit in the distinction between 'ethnic citizens' and 'ethnic settlers' – and appeals to a sort of flexible indigeneity, to which South Africa, like neighbouring Botswana (Nyamnjoh 2007a) can attest historically. Indeed, African communities are historically renowned for their mobility and their flexibility in indigeneity (de Bruijn, *et al.* 2001; MacGaffey 1995), a reality only enhanced by the arbitrary nature of colonial boundaries and a dominant neoliberal philosophy of life, agency, and responsibility that privileges profit over people. The history of South Africa demonstrates flexible modes of belonging that make it difficult to claim identities in essentialist terms. Over the years, the real sociology and anthropology of South Africa's constituent communities suggest far more contradiction, contestation, negotiation, interdependence and conviviality in the identities of ordinary people and communities than is often acknowledged or provided for politically, culturally or in scholarship. How will the evolving legal system in South Africa embrace these complexities? How will the law curriculum reflect the depths and diversity of experiences of South Africans? This is especially challenging, given the tendency for the law to prefer clarity over ambiguity, even while allowing for interpretation, which sometimes leads or can lead to (over?)simplifying complexity – the complexities and messiness of reality and of the everyday – to the detriment of justice. Indeed, 'law' and 'justice' are not always synonymous, as justice is usually in the eye of the beholder. However, it is worth bearing this challenge in mind, all the same.

The tendency especially in Africa has been for scholars to deemphasize small-scale 'ethnic' in favour of large-scale 'civic' citizenship, whose juridico-political basis is uncritically assumed to be more inclusive than the cultural basis of ethnic citizenship. The mistake has been to focus analysis almost exclusively on institutional and constitutional arrangements, thereby downplaying the hierarchies and relationships of inclusion and exclusion informed by race, ethnicity, class, gender, and geography that determine indigeneity in real terms. There has been too much focus on 'rights talk' and its 'emancipatory rhetoric' (Mamdani 2000; Englund & Nyamnjoh 2004; Englund 2006) and too little attention accorded to the contexts, meanings, and practices that make indigeneity possible for some but an aspiration relentlessly deferred for many. Multiculturalism (Taylor 1994, Kymlicka 1995) and the concept of cultural citizenship (Torres et al. 1999; Mercer 2002) have actually won themselves more disciples recently, not least from among scholars, who are no longer simply keen on juridico-political citizenship but also on claiming indigeneity over and beyond the essentialist identities the state has to offer.

The history of difficulty in implementing rigid notions of 'nation-state,' 'indigeneity' and 'citizenship' in Africa attests to the gross inadequacy of a narrow and inflexible juridico-political regime of rights and entitlements in a context where individuals and communities are questioning the western monopoly over 'freedom of imagination' and challenging themselves to think of 'new forms of the modern community' and 'new forms of the modern state' (Chatterjee 1993: 13). The challenge is clearly to hearken to the reality of Africans and their communities as they experiment with different configurations and seek broader, more flexible ways of understanding and relating to belonging. Meaningful cultural, political, economic, and legal recognition and representation can be negotiated for individuals and groups, to account for conviviality and accommodation and to counter the ever diminishing circles of inclusion imposed by race, ethnicity, class, gender, and geography.

The emphasis should be on the freedom of individuals and communities to negotiate inclusion, opt in or out, with flexibility of belonging in consonance with their realities as identity straddlers. Are there some cultural practices by groups marginalised under apartheid that could be drawn upon to complement the current orthodox legal regime and its fixation with the individual? I have heard of some minority religions in South Africa, whose 'laws' differ from Roman-Dutch and common law in regard to marriage and divorce – even while 'state' law is common to all. If those identifying with such religions were permitted to choose the system under which they wished to be married, with the knowledge that in the event of divorce they would be bound by their own marriage choice, then one would have a situation that respects both the individual and the collectivity. The law of the collectivity would have to be flexible and accommodating to the wishes of the broad spectrum of the social categories that continue to enrich it with their everyday enactment of the *habitus* that links them.

Such flexible indigeneity is incompatible with the prevalent illusion that the nation-state is the only political unit permitted to confer citizenship in the modern world (Nyamnjoh 2006, 2007b). Neither is it compatible with a regime of rights and entitlements narrowly focused on yet another chimera — 'the autonomous individual' (Comaroff and Comaroff 1999). Everywhere the price of perpetuating these illusions has been the proliferation of ultranationalism, chauvinism, racism, ethnicism, and xenophobia, which has radically repressed the fragmented, multinational, and heterogeneous cultural realities of most so-called nation-states. The tendency has been for indigeneity thus inspired to assume the stature of a giant compressor of, especially, cultural differences. Almost everywhere, this narrow model has cherished hierarchies based on race, ethnicity, class, gender, and geography that have tended to impose on perceived inferior others decisions made by those who see themselves as more authentic or more deserving of citizenship. Indigeneity that hails from such a celebration of insensitivities is clearly not a model for a future of increased mobility and increased claims for rights, recognition, and representation by individuals *and* collectivities.

Any reformed curriculum for law schools in South Africa would therefore not only seek to bring on board in a major and significant manner legal systems long trivialised, caricatured or ignored under colonialism and apartheid. It would also have to document and provide for ongoing tensions over entitlements, cultural 'purity,' and belonging and exclusion among ethnic groups in the new South Africa. The curriculum must provide as well for the fact that in Africa, where the nation-state project has been achieved more in rhetoric than in reality, indigeneity is claimed not only by 'first peoples' but by other ethnic communities (majorities and minorities) as well. These challenges should, I hope, be meaningfully resolved in favour of teaching and learning, and laws and practices of inclusion rather than regimes of exclusion, especially if the lawyers trained are to be relevant to the challenges of a 21st century characterised by flexible mobility seeking recognition for 'flexible indigeneity' and 'flexible citizenship.' Since the new South Africa recognizes and respects complexity, in my view, it would be good to include in a 'new' law curriculum the variety of cultural understandings of the meaning of human dignity that can be found in the multiple cultural 'traditions' in the South African 'Rainbow Nation'.

References

ACHPR and IWGIA, 2005. *Report of the African Commission's Working Group of Experts on Indigenous Populations/Communities*. Copenhagen: Transaction Publishers.

Adichie, C., 2009. The danger of a single story'. TED Conferences, www.ted.com/talks/lang/eng/chimamanda_adichie_the_danger_of_a_single_story.html, accessed 29 September 2011.

Bank, L., 2011. *Home Spaces, Street Styles: Contesting Power and Identity in a South African City*. London: Pluto.

Boonzaier, E. & Spiegel, A., 2008. 'Tradition', in: N. Shepherd & S. Robins, eds, *New South African Keywords*, pp. 195-208. Johannesburg: Jacana.

Chatterjee, P., 1993. *The Nation and Its Fragments: Colonial and Postcolonial Histories*. Princeton: Princeton University Press.

Comaroff, J. & Comaroff, J.L., eds, 1993. *Modernity and its Malcontents: Ritual and Power in Postcolonial Africa*. Chicago: University of Chicago Press.

Comaroff, J. & Comaroff, J.L., eds, 1999. *Civil Society and the Political Imagination in Africa: Critical Perspectives*. Chicago: University of Chicago Press.

Comaroff, J., & Comaroff, J.L., eds, 2006. *Law and Disorder in the Postcolony*. Chicago: University of Chicago Press.

Comaroff, J.L., 1978. Rules and rulers: political processes in a Tswana chiefdom. *Man* (N.S.) 13(1): 1-20.

Comaroff, J.L., 1981. The management of marriage in a Tswana chiefdom, in: Krige, E.J., & Comaroff, J.L., eds, *Essays on African Marriage in Southern Africa*, pp. 29-49. Cape Town/Johannesburg: Juta.

Comaroff, J.L., & Comaroff, J. 2009. *Ethnicity, Inc.* Scottsville: University of KwaZulu-Natal Press.

De Bruijn, M., van Dijk, R., & Foeken, D., eds, 2001. *Mobile Africa: Changing Patterns of Movement in Africa and Beyond*. Leiden: Brill.

Deutsch, J-G., Probst, P. & Schmidt, H., eds, 2002. *African Modernities*. Oxford: James Currey.

Englund, H., 2004. Cosmopolitanism and the devil in Malawi. *Ethnos* 69(3): 293-316.

Englund, H. & Nyamnjoh, F.B., eds, 2004. *Rights and the Politics of Recognition in Africa*. London: Zed Books.

Forde, F., 2011. *An Inconvenient Youth: Julius Malema and the 'New' ANC*. Johannesburg: Picador Africa.

Geschiere, P., 2009. *The Perils of Belonging: Autochthony, Citizenship, and Exclusion in Africa and Europe*. Chicago: University of Chicago Press.

Geschiere, P. & Nyamnjoh, F.B., 2000. Capitalism and autochthony: the seesaw of mobility and belonging. *Public Culture* 2000 12(2): 423-452.

Gutto, S.B.O., 2006. Towards a new paradigm for Pan-African knowledge production and application in the context of the African Renaissance. *International Journal of African Renaissance Studies* 1(20): 306-323.

Hall, S., 2010. Foreword, in: H. Anheier & Y.R. Isar, eds, *The Cultures and Globalization Series: Cultural Expression, Creativity & Innovation*, pp. ix-xii. Los Angeles: Sage.

Konings, P., 2009. *Neoliberal Bandwagonism: Civil Society and the Politics of Belonging in Anglophone Cameroon*. Bamenda-Leiden: Langaa-ASC.

Konings, P., 2010. *Crisis and Neoliberal Reforms in Africa: Civil Society and*

Agro-Industry in Anglophone Cameroon's Plantation Economy. Bamenda-Leiden: Langaa-ASC.

Konings, P., 2011. *The Politics of Neoliberal Reforms in Africa: State and Civil Society in Cameroon*. Bamenda-Leiden: Langaa-ASC.

Konings, P. & Nyamnjoh, F.B., 2003. Negotiating an Anglophone Identity: A Study of the Politics of Recognition and Representation in Cameroon, Leiden: Brill.

Kymlicka, W., ed., 1995. *The Rights of Minority Cultures*. Oxford: Oxford University Press.

Landau, L.B., 2011. *Exorcising the Demons Within: Xenophobia, Violence and Statecraft in Contemporary South Africa*. Johannesburg: Wits University Press.

MacGaffey, W., 1995. Kongo identity, 1483–1993. *South Atlantic Quarterly* 94(4): 1025–1037.

Mamdani, M., 1996. *Citizen and Subject: Contemporary Africa and the Legacy of Late Colonialism*. Cape Town: David Philip.

Mamdani, M., 1998. *When Does a Settler Become a Native? Reflections of the Colonial Roots of Citizenship in Equatorial and South Africa*, Text of Inaugural Lecture as A.C. Jordon Professor of African Studies, University of Cape Town, 13 May, New Series no. 208 (http://hrp.bard.edu/resource_pdfs/mamdani.settler.pdf).

Mamdani, M., ed., 2000. *Beyond Rights Talk and Culture Talk*. Cape Town: David Philip.

Mamdani, M., 2009. African intellectuals and identity: overcoming the political legacy of colonialism, in: William Gumede & Leslie Dikeni, eds, *The Poverty of Ideas: South African Democracy and the Retreat of Intellectuals*, pp. 122-142. Johannesburg: Jacana.

Maybury-Lewis, D., 2005. Defining indigenous, *Cultural Survival Quarterly* 29(1). (http://www.culturalsurvival.org/publications/cultural-survival-quarterly/none/defining-indigenous).

Mayer, Ph., 1971. *Townsmen or Tribesmen: Conservatism and the Process of Urbanization in a South African City*. Cape Town: Oxford University Press.

Mbembe, A., 2006. South Africa's second coming: the Nongqawuse syndrome', *Open Democracy*, 15 June. (http://www.opendemocracy.net/content/articles/PDF/3649.pdf).

Mercer, C., 2002. *Towards Cultural Citizenship: Tools for Cultural Policy and Development*. Stockholm: The Bank of Sweden Tercentenary Foundation.

Mogale, T., 2000. Women highly offended by "A Man is a Bull" ruling, in: *The Botswana Gazette*, Wednesday, 29 March, p. 8.

Mpe, P. 2001. *Welcome to Our Hillbrow*. Pietermaritzburg: University of Natal Press.

Ndlovu-Gatsheni, S.J., 2009. Africa for Africans or Africa for "natives" only? "New nationalism" and nativism in Zimbabwe and South Africa. *Africa Spectrum* 44(1): 61-78.

Neocosmos, M., 2010. *From 'Foreign Natives' to 'Native Foreigners': Explaining Xenophobia in Post-apartheid South Africa: Citizenship and Nationalism, Identity and Politics*. Dakar: CODESRIA.

Nkondo, G.M., 2007. Ubuntu as national policy in South Africa: a conceptual framework. *International Journal of African Renaissance Studies* 2(1): 88-100.

Ntlama, N. & Ndima, D.D., 2009. The significance of South Africa's Traditional Courts Bill to the challenge of promoting African traditional justice systems. *International Journal of African Renaissance Studies* 4(1): 6-30.

Nyamnjoh, F.B., 2002. "A child is one person's only in the womb": domestication, agency and subjectivity in the Cameroonian Grassfields, in: R. Werbner, ed., *Postcolonial Subjectivities in Africa*, pp. 111-138. London: Zed Books.

Nyamnjoh, F.B., 2005. *Africa's Media, Democracy and the Politics of Belonging*. London: Zed Books.

Nyamnjoh, F.B., 2006.*Insiders and Outsiders: Citizenship and Xenophobia in Contemporary Southern Africa*. London: CODESRIA/Zed Books.

Nyamnjoh, F.B., 2007a. Ever diminishing circles: the paradoxes of belonging in Botswana, in: Starn, O., & de la Cadena, M., eds, *Indigenous Experience Today*, pp. 305-331. Oxford: Berg.

Nyamnjoh, F.B., 2007b. From bounded to flexible citizenship: lessons from Africa. *Citizenship Studies* 11(1): 73-82.

Nyamnjoh, F.B., 2010. Racism, ethnicity and the media in Africa: reflections inspired by studies of xenophobia in Cameroon and South Africa. *Africa Spectrum* 45(1): 57-94.

Nyamnjoh, F.B., 2011. Cameroonian bushfalling: negotiation of identity and belonging in fiction and ethnography'. *American Ethnologist* 38(4): 701-713.

Peberdy, S., 2009. *Selecting Immigrants: National Identity and South Africa's Immigration Policies 1910-2008*. Johannesburg: Wits University Press.

Pillay, S., Barolsky, V., Naidoo, V., Mohlakoana, N., & Hadland, A., 2008. *Citizenship, Violence and Xenophobia in South Africa: Perceptions from*

South African Communities, South Africa Human Sciences Research Council (HSRC) report.

Ramose, M.B., 1999. *African Philosophy Through Ubuntu*. Harare: Mond Books.

Ranger, T., 1984. The invention of tradition in colonial Africa, in: E. Hobsbawm & T. Ranger eds, *The Invention of Tradition*, pp. 211-262. Cambridge: Cambridge University Press.

Salih, M.M.A. & Markakis, J., eds, 1998. *Ethnicity and the State in Eastern Africa*. Uppsala: Nordiska Afrikainstitutet.

Schapera, I., 1994. *A Handbook of Tswana Law and Custom: Compiled for the Bechuanaland Protectorate Administration*. Hamburg: International African Institute/Lit Verlag.

Sharp, J., 2006. The end of culture? Some directions for anthropology at the University of Pretoria. *Anthropology Southern Africa* 29 (1 & 2): 17-23.

Sharp, J., 2008. "Fortress SA": xenophobic violence in South Africa. *Anthropology Today* 24(4): 1-3.

Sichone, O., 2008. Xenophobia and xenophilia in South Africa: African migrants in Cape Town, in: Werbner, P., ed., *Anthropology and the New Cosmopolitanism: Rooted, Feminist and Vernacular Perspectives*, pp. 309-332. Oxford: Berg.

Taylor, C., 1994. *Multiculturalism: Examining the Politics of Recognition*. Princeton: Princeton University Press.

Thomas, C.G., 2008. *Ubuntu*. The missing link in the rights discourse in post-apartheid transformation in South Africa. *International Journal of African Renaissance Studies* 3(2): 39-62.

Torres, R.D., Miron, L.F. & Inda, J.X., eds, 1999. *Race, Identify and Citizenship: A Reader*. Oxford: Wiley-Blackwell.

Werbner, R., 2004. *Reasonable Radicals and Citizenship in Botswana: The Public Anthropology of Kalanga Elites*. Bloomington: Indiana University Press.

Football in Cameroon: its origins, politics and sorcery

Paul Nchoji Nkwi

The growth and popularity of football in Cameroon has been exponential since its first participation in the 1982 World Cup, emerging without a defeat. Cameroon's representation at World Cups has also been consistent: 1982, 1990, 1994, 1998 2002 and 2010. Although it failed to appear in 2004, its participation in 2010 in South Africa confirmed its standing as a major football nation. Implanted in Cameroon during the colonial period largely through missionary schools, football did not gain importance until the 1970s when Cameroon for the first time organized the African Nations Cup resulting in an abysmal failure on the part of Cameroon to capture the cup on its own soil. Furthermore, the impact created by the 1982 participation in the World Cup would place Cameroon on the World Football Map and dragged politicians into the fray to exploit it to the fullest. Indeed, the national team, the Indomitable Lions, did not even touch a tenth of the over 250 'ethnic groups' in Cameroon but there has been a dominance of players from the Bassa, Beti, Bamileke and Douala ethnic groups. The performance of some of these players was often lifted to the level of 'sorcery' and 'witchcraft'. Before the 1982 World Cup, rumours had it that the Peruvian team had hired witch doctors to protect their players from the sorcery of the Cameroon team. Whether these stories are true or false, they indeed sometimes feed into the gossip that animates all football matches of great importance. Caught up in the euphoria of the popularity of the sport, government has fully exploited a sport animated by players whose genius is largely nurtured in the shanty towns of the big cities rather than government policy of providing a quality football infrastructure. Although the football federation moved football into a professional league, the state is still a major player because the so-called professional teams still rely on the state to provide the basic sport infrastructure. Often, it is the money that the state and state officials are interested in which often drives players of the national team to openly disagree with football officials who enrich themselves at the expense of players. Embezzlement of funds is notorious. Funds destined for players have often disap-

peared into the pockets of officials between two airports. The recent refusal of the national team, captained by Samuel Eto'o, to play a friendly match with Algeria in December 2011, was just the tip of an iceberg.

Introduction

Since the 1980s football has been one of the most popular sports in Cameroon, and one that often galvanizes the psyche of the nation. The sport is the most celebrated in the country and takes precedence over any other sport, be it handball, basket-ball, tennis, swimming, rugby, boxing, racing, or karate. Indeed, football has acquired the name of 'king sport', to the extent that some refer to it as a 'religion'. Its importance in Cameroon seems to be comparable with the game's place in Brazil, one of the leading football nations in the world, because in both countries football seems to take central public stage at critical moments. The fans of the national team that constitute the core faithful appear during matches in various paraphernalia highlighting the love for, dedication to and adoration of the team. Some fans even carry 'magical' items and consult the gods before matches, thus lifting the game to a mystical level. In Cameroon, a 'highly indebted poor country' (HIPC)[1], football serves often as a unifying factor in moments of frustration for millions of people whose rulers seem to be unable to deal with the effects of poverty they have contributed to create over the last three decades.

Since the 1980s, football has also ceased to be considered as merely a game in Cameroon. As in other countries, it offers lucrative employment to some, and an activity on the same level as other professions (teaching, masonry, driving, etc.).

The 1980s were marked by a transformation of the national team, the Lions,[2] due to its remarkable performances at the international and regional level.[3] Since then, government, youths, sponsors and even musicians have taken a growing interest. In the daily life of Cameroonians football has now assumed not only a sportive, but also political, economic and mystical status.

In this essay, I will discuss the origins of the sport in Cameroon and its societal and 'developmental' impact. I will also assess the national team and its major achievements, the ethnic background of the principal players, the management of football at the political level, the relation between football and sorcery, football as a professional business, and the future of football in Cameroon.

1 World Bank classification of poor countries. Though very rich in natural resources, it is yet poor and highly indebted.

2 See: www.camlions.com.

3 Cf. http://fr.wikipedia.org/wiki/\%C3\%89quipe_du_Cameroun_de_football.

Origins of football in Cameroon

The modern history of football as a sport goes back to 1863, with the founding of rugby and football associations in Britain. Football was already played in Cameroon by the 1920s, and organized teams were formed during the 1930s in Douala and Yaoundé — though they were often the preserve of the elite (cf. Clignet & Stark 1974; Tsanga 1969). After independence in 1960, football became widely practiced, leaving the schoolyards and spilling into the streets and open spaces.

The Cameroonian Football Federation (FECAFOOT)[4] was created just prior to independence, and the Federation joined FIFA in 1962 and the Confédération Africaine de Football (CAF) in 1963. Thanks to these affiliations, Cameroon's national team and clubs have participated regularly in different competitions organized by these organizations. While FIFA organizes the World Cup every four years, CAF organizes the African Cup of Nations (CAN) biannually. Cameroon first participated in the CAN in 1970. In 1972 Cameroon hosted the event and there were high hopes for the national team. In preparation for hosting the African Cup of Nations, Cameroon, under the auspices of then President Ahmadou Ahidjo, Cameroon constructed two stadiums: the Omnisports stadium (the Ahmadou Ahidjo Stadium) and the Unification Stadium in Douala, to celebrate the renaming of the country (which was formed from the French and English Cameroons) as the United Republic of Cameroon.[5]

The elimination of Cameroon by Congo in the 1972 semi-finals came as a shock to Cameroonians[6] and as a setback to the development of football in the country. For the past 40 years Cameroon, despite its performances at the international level, has been unable to organize a single African Nations Cup (CAN). The political acrimony that followed in 1972 led to the sacking of the Minister of Youth and Sports and other sport officials. This slowed down the momentum but also left the clubs to develop their skills without political interference. Ten years later, in 1982, the national team participated for the first time in the FIFA World Cup tournament, held in Spain, against the background of the dramatic poor performance of the Zaire national team during the previous World Cup. Its

4 See: www.fecafootonline.com.

5 In 1984 the country was renamed as simply the Republic of Cameroon.

6 Ahidjo was President when Cameroon was eliminated from the 1972 CAN. He took drastic measures, e.g., by sacking the Minister of Youths and Sports, and virtually had most of the culprits arrested and punished. The Cameroon Football Federation was reorganized, and since then Cameroon has never hosted the great event even though they have won the CAF cup at least four times.

exit in the first round of the 1982 Cup but without a defeat raised the stakes of football in Cameroon. The success of the national football team at this first major international outing would lead to nationwide celebrations and Cameroon earning respect for itself and for Africa.

The development of the national team

The Cameroonian Football Federation (FECAFOOT) organizes football events under the auspices of the Ministry of Sports and Physical Education (formerly the Ministry of Youth and Sports). The national team was baptized the "Indomitable Lions" in 1972, soon after hosting the CAN for the first time. And if Cameroon football is known today across Africa and the rest of the world, it is primarily thanks to the Lions, who performed extremely well in many major world tournaments since 1972. The team's record of participation in international competitions is shown in Table 1.

Table 1: Participation of Cameroon in African and World competitions, 1982-2012

Table 1: Participation of Cameroon in African and World competitions, 1982-2012

Competitions	Years
World Cup	1982, 1990, 1994, 1998, 2002
African Cup of Nations	1972, 1984, 1986, 1988, 1990, 1992, 1994, 1996, 1998, 2000, 2002, 2004, 2006, 2008, 2010
Union of Central African States (UDEAC) Cup	1984, 1986, 1987, 1988, 1989, 1990, 2003
Olympic Games	2000
Confederation Cup	2003

The participation of Cameroon in all these events occurred in a remarkable manner. With regard to the World Cup, two appearances in particular made a significant impact. In 1982, Cameroon returned home undefeated from the World Cup in Spain after playing some of the best teams in the world such as Italy, Poland and Peru. Furthermore, in 1990, Cameroon's performance went beyond all expectations, as the Indomitable Lions reached the quarter-finals, a feat which no African team had up to that point attained. The Cameroonian team beat the Argentinean team, the holders of the World Cup title, and the team with the best football player of the world at the time, Diego Maradona. Thanks to this performance, the overall number of African countries participating in the World Cup rose from three to five. FIFA was definitely impressed with the growth and quality of football on the African continent.

Besides these appearances in the World Cup, Cameroon won the African Nations Cup four times and became Olympic champions at the Sydney Olympic Games in 2000 after beating such great teams as Brazil and Spain. Table 2 below shows the performances of Cameroon at the international level.

Table 2: Competitions won by the Indomitable Lions of Cameroon

Competitions	Year
African Cup of Nations	1984, 1988, 2000, 2002
Olympic Games in Australia	2000
UDEAC or CEMAC Cup	1984, 1986, 1987, 1989, 2003, 2005
LG Tournament	2011

In addition to these victories at the international level, Cameroon was a finalist in the African Cup of Nations in 1986 in Egypt and in 2008 in Ghana and also a finalist in the UDEAC Cup in 1988 and 1990, as well as in the FIFA Confederations Cup in 2003.

These results earned Cameroon the title of the best African football side of the 20th century, as confirmed by FIFA and by CAF rankings. These performances also opened the doors of all Europeans clubs to Cameroonian footballers. In recent years, many Cameroonians have played, and still do, in great clubs such as Real Madrid, Barcelona, Chelsea, Inter Milan, etc., and earn fabulous sums of money. The presence of such great players who have many times proven their remarkable talents made Cameroon known all over Africa and everywhere in the world where people love football.

It is amazing to note that the Lions were eliminated from the 2012 African Cup of Nations by a very good Senegalese team: the Terragan Lions of Senegal qualified for the 2012 African Cup of Nations by knocking out Cameroon. It was thus eliminated from the competition already during the group stage, leaving the competition without a single point. Organized jointly by Gabon and Equatorial Guinea, the 2012 edition of CAN attracted fans who travelled from Cameroon to witness the matches live. When Senegal was later eliminated during the group stages, Cameroon fans saw this as a sign or bad omen cast on the Lions of Senegal by the Cameroon gods for having eliminated the Indomitable Lions. The fact that the cup was won by Zambia after eliminating one of the best teams on the continent, the Ivorian 'Elephants', added a new twist to that victory. It did not only demonstrate the growth of football on the continent, for many it also showed how the invisible ones or the *ancestors* of Zambian football inspired the Zambian players. The finals of the 2012 African Nations Cup were played in Gabon, the country in which the entire Zambian national team had perished after their plane crashed on the shores of Libreville, heading for the African Cup of nations in 2002 (which Cameroon won). Ten years later, a new breed of Zambian players, was able to lift the African Nations Cup, in the same city where their ancestors perished.

Ethnicity and football in Cameroon

Ethnicity in Cameroon football is interesting and complex. Cameroon has over 200 ethno-linguistic groups, but only a few have representatives on the national team. The names of great players who helped Cameroon win several competitions mentioned above are indicative: Milla, Abega, Kundé, Mbida, Mboma, Nkono, Bell, Omam, Kana, Mbou, Mfede, Eto'o. Most of them are from the cities of Yaoundé and Douala, where a large number of smaller, formal and informal stadiums allow youngsters to practice and perfect their skills. As shown in Table 3, the Bassa players are in the majority and the Beti, who are at their best in the midfield, constitute another dominant group.

Table 3: Some names of great players and their ethnic origin

Names of players	Ethnic affiliation
Milla, Mboma, Bell, Kunde, Omam, Kana, Mbou, Eto'o, Ebwele, Ekeke, Mbom, Njolea, Njea, Womé, Song	Bassa
Abega, Manga Onguené, Mbida, Mfede, Onana Eloudou, Nkono, Foé	Beti
Ndjonkek, Ndjitap, Wobo, Kameni	Bamiléké
Mbape Lepe, Ebongue, Douala	Douala

When they get to the national team, however, they are no longer Bassa, Beti, Bamiléké, or Douala. They are simply 'Indomitable Lions' and defend the honour and colours of Cameroon. It can therefore be said that in Cameroon football constitutes a tool for the consolidation of national unity (cf. Ntonfo 1994; Vidacs 1999).

Of the many football clubs in Cameroon, the most well known are *Canon Sportif* of Yaoundé, *Tonnerre Kalara Club* of Yaoundé, *Union of Douala* and *Racing Club* of Bafoussam. Over the years the major clubs have built a strong fan base, won cups in various national and regional competitions, developed an infrastructure and organized a strong human resource base. Indeed, these major clubs are located primarily in three provinces: Centre, Littoral and West. In the Centre and Littoral Provinces, the practice of football is facilitated by the availability of good infrastructure. In Douala and Yaoundé there are many more stadiums than in the other towns. In addition, the many unemployed young people living in these urban areas have turned to football to forget their frustrations or practice football in the hope they can make a mark and find their fortune as players abroad. As noted, in Cameroon football has thus not only remained a sporting activity but also become an emerging professional domain for socio-economic mobility.

The situation in West Province is rather interesting in this respect. Until recently, young people in the province did not look upon football as a possible income-generating activity. This province has over the years produced a rich elite and young people are often encouraged to engage in the informal economic sector. However, since the economic crisis of the late 1980s, football as a tool for survival developed quickly among the young people of the Bamileke ethnic group, whose elite is probably the richest in Cameroon. Since the mid-1990s, the Bamileke ethnic group has dominated in the first division in terms of both the number of teams and their organizational capacity. New football clubs have emerged at the provincial level as well as at the level of divisions and sub-divisions and even in villages. The West Province has more teams in the first division of the national football championship than any other province in Cameroon. Five teams from the West have become constants in the first division: *Fovu* of Baham, *Sable* of Batié, *Aigle* of Dschang, *Unisport* of Bafang, and *Stade* of Bandjoun. These are the prominent contenders for the championship in Cameroon, thanks to the dynamism and financial strength that the elite of this ethnic group has. Indeed, football has now become an enterprise requiring huge investments (salaries of players, facilities, transportation, equipment, etc). In fact, it is acknowledged that the Bamileke are the great financial and economic actors of Cameroon because of their alleged spirit of saving and their credit capacity (cf. Warnier 1993; Dongmo 1981; Tabapssi 1999). During the economic crisis that occurred between 1987 and 1990, a crisis whose effects are still being felt today (with its corollaries like poverty, unemployment, misery, etc.), many Bamileke continued to exercise their economic activities without any problem and with liquidity. With the help of their financial skills the Bamileke developed football into a marketable commodity, just as they developed other forms of enterprise (cf. Nkwi & Vidacs 1997). For example, the best known football schools in Cameroon (e.g., the *Kadji Football Academy*) are owned and run by the rich elite of the Bamileke ethnic group. Although the championship in Cameroon turned professional in 2012, it remains to a large extent at the amateur level due to lack of sufficient financing to sustain the clubs. It is only the national team that benefits from the attention of government and of some national and international sponsors (PUMA, Orange, MTN, PMUC, etc.).

Football and politics

The honour football has brought to Cameroon without any deliberate government sports policy has given football a political dimension. The president of the Republic of Cameroon, Mr. Paul Biya, asserted in a speech in 1988 that "*there is no minor sport, no major sport and neither are there any reserved sports*", but despite his efforts to place all sports on the same level the state appears to support and facilitate football to the detriment of other sports. One may ask why football is being given such a privileged position by the state.

Cameroon has been in an economic crisis since 1987; a crisis characterized by bad governance, corruption, embezzlement of public funds and aggravated by massive unemployment, poverty and social misery. This situation created tensions between the government and the people, conditions in which football became the '*opium of the people*'. The state used football victories to diffuse the tensions and make people forget their daily problems. Every victory of the *Indomitable Lions* is draped in state ceremonies with elaborate protocol that often involves the Lions making a victory tour through the capital from the airport to the Presidential Palace, there to be received by the Head of State. Other sports teams do not usually benefit from the same attention of the state authorities. There is no doubt that in Cameroon football has taken on a political dimension. Despite the enormous economic problems, people are often fascinated and enthralled by football and this diverts their attention from those critical problems of unemployment and other social problems (cf. Nkwi & Vidacs 1997).

Cameroonians are not happy with the way their country is being run. For the past three decades, Biya rule has brought only massive unemployment, economic misery, repression, widespread corruption and high levels of poverty. When the Lions perform well at the international level, the captivating nature of football usually galvanizes the nation, and Biya rides on the victories of the national team. Let us use a recent example to illustrate how football can be used and misused, and how these tactics do not always succeed.

On the day that Cameroon defeated Ghana and blocked them from reaching the finals of the 2008 African Cup of Nations, the state authorities in Yaoundé increased the price of fuel. The choice of that day was in conformity with the usual tactics that the state has used – that is, acting while the people are caught up in football frenzy. The authorities seemed to have thought that in their euphoria from the victory of the Lions over the Ghanaians, Cameroonians would swallow the bitter pill, as they had often done before. This time they were mistaken. The strike that paralysed the national capital Yaoundé and the economic capital Douala seemed to have taken the authorities by surprise.

The president of the workers' syndicate informed the government well in advance of a strike by all taxi and transport operators planned to start on Monday 25 February 2008. The syndicates had called on the government to lower the price of fuel to its earlier level as well as to redress other social ills. They expected that this would happen before February 25. But nothing at all was done. The government thought that if there was any strike action, it would not last for more than a day, as had been the case in the past. On February 25 the strike started. Nearly all the major towns of Cameroon were paralysed and business came to a standstill.

By Tuesday 26 February 2008, towns such as Yaoundé, Douala, Buea, Limbe, Bamenda, Bafoussam, Dschang, Bafang, Kumbo, Mutengene, and Foumban were in full gear in the strike. The Northern part of the country (Garoua, Maroua, Ngaoundéré) remained strategically aloof due to the fact that their fuel came from Nigeria for a much lower price.

The government expected that the taxi drivers would simply stay home and wait for its reaction to their demands. This was not the case. In all these towns similar actions could be observed: looting, intimidation, burning of old tyres along the public highways, destruction of public and private property. Most of those involved in such acts were youths who defied bullets, claiming that *a corpse cannot be afraid of bullets*. Such actions were met with furious reactions from the forces of law and order, resulting in the death of several citizens.

By the end of Tuesday at about 11:30 p.m. the results of the negotiations between government and the syndicates were published. Petrol prices were reduced, but that did not send people back to work. Instead, the strike increased in intensity. In most towns, schools, shops, markets and offices were all closed down. In Yaoundé, government offices were deserted by civil servants. The forces of law and order began to patrol the streets in Yaoundé with the objective of suppressing any further disturbances. Apparently, the ruling party, caught unawares, was confused and began to blame the opposition parties for instigating the troubles and for manipulating the youth. When rumours began to circulate on the impending speech of the Head of State, many hoped he would say the inevitable: that "...he will not run for president in 2011"[7]. Prior to the strike, the President of the Republic had announced that he was ready to modify the constitution and run for another term of office. According to polls conducted by the newspaper *Le Messager*, 87% of Cameroonians were opposed to Paul Biya staying in power beyond his current mandate. When he addressed the nation on February 28, he vowed to suppress the strike by any means and accused the opposition parties of fomenting the troubles. On Friday 29 February Yaoundé was like a war zone, with soldiers patrolling the streets and forcing shop owners to open their shops. As noted by many people at the time, Yaoundé was not *breathing any more* but *choking*. In the heat of political upheavals of the 1990s in Cameroon, President Biya asserted, in another speech on national radio and TV, that: "As long as *Yaoundé breathes, Cameroon is alive*." In 2008 the popular euphoria caused by the victory of the Lions in the CAN 2008 over Ghana melted away so fast that the state could no more play its little tricks on the people of Cameroon and keep the political capital in a coma.

Indeed, before the national team had left for Ghana, every member of the team was given 17 million CFA ($34,000), and promised 83 million francs each ($166,000) if the national team won. In other words, the state was ready to spend almost two billion CFA (one million US dollars). Although people were happy that the Lions were performing well at the 2008 CAN, many questioned these expenses at a moment when the government was refusing to increase the salaries of civil servants. It was apparent that the performance of the team was more important to the politicians than the general welfare of the people.

This government *largesse* can be explained by the fact that it is football that seems to have given government some credibility abroad. Non-Cameroonians often even seem to confuse the good health of Cameroonian football with the health of the Cameroonian state to the point that the state is given credit and favours by donor countries on several fronts: development assistance, political support, invitations to important world events, and provision of posts in international institutions (FIFA, the United Nations, African Development Bank, etc.). It is in this sense that the re-election of President Paul Biya is very often recognized at the international level, despite the fact that Cameroon is known for recurring massive electoral fraud (also in the 2011 presidential elections[8]), including the manipulation of electoral registers by state officials.

Indeed, football has had some impact on other sectors of the economy, and on

7 On October 9, 2011, Presidential elections were organized and Biya as usual, won, amidst claims of massive fraud.

8 See BBC news message, 'Cameroon election: SDF accuse Paul Biya's CPDM of fraud', 10 October 2011 (at: http://www.bbc.co.uk/news/world-africa-15238067).

culture. People often watch the African Cup of Nations or the World Cup matches in bars, restaurants and other places of leisure – to the great benefit of the economic operators. In addition, players like Eto'o, Mboma, and Foé have participated in the publicity billboards of phone companies or in fundraising efforts for the poor under the aegis of such international institutions as UNICEF.

At the cultural level, football has contributed to the marketing of the image of Cameroon abroad. During international competitions the Ministry of Culture works closely with the Ministry of Sports and Physical Education to bring Cameroonian dance troupes, comedians, musicians and other artists to entertain the fans. These entertainers accompany the Lions and play the role of cheerleaders and supporters of the national team, and the state covers the costs. This has certainly marketed the image of Cameroon especially abroad.

In addition, football is an instrument in general economic development, as businessmen accompany the players during major sports events to help create new business opportunities and attract new foreign investments. However, the state has not established a long-term plan to take advantage of and enhance the gains made during such international sports competitions. In addition to being one of the great football nations in Africa, we also saw that Cameroon acquired another notoriety – that of being one of the most corrupt countries on earth.[9]

Football and sorcery

It is difficult to establish a clear relationship between football and sorcery. In fact, sorcery is generally conducted and practiced in obscurity, without witnesses, and is seen and elevated to the manipulation of spiritual forces. Ethically, sorcery falls in the domain of '*unbecoming acts*', and it is used as an unorthodox means to achieve ultimate goals. Even when players and other football practitioners are said to integrate it into the practice of football, it is difficult to show its existence and effects.

Despite this, some Cameroonians believe that magic and sorcery are also at the service of football. Indeed, Cameroon has had players of great skills and reputation such as Milla, Nkono, Bell, Eto'o, etc. But some people still think that the performance of these players *must* be linked to the power of their *marabouts*. Among the fans, it is said that every time Roger Milla took a shot at the goal, goalkeepers saw two balls. Rumor also had it that the goal Omam Biyick scored

9 According to Transparency International's corruption perception index rating of 2008, Cameroon was in 144th place (of the total of 182). In 2011 it was in 134th place (See: www.transparency.org).

during the opening match of the 1990 World Cup against Argentina 'was prepared by a *marabout*'. Thomas Nkono, according to popular belief, always placed a magical spider-web in the goal to prevent strikers from scoring goals. This spider-web was mystical and was given to him by a *marabout* of the Yambassa ethnic group. Joseph Antoine Bell, one of the goalkeepers of the Lions, was said to be a great Rosicrucian, whose link to this sect increased his capacity to obtain victory by stopping strikers from scoring. These rumors lead the public to believe that sorcery and mysticism enhanced the performance of players who have become famous at home and abroad.

Some football fans believe that every team in Cameroon, including the national team, has its own *marabout*. Tonnere Kalara Club had at one point an albino *marabout* who was present in the stadium every time the team played. His aim was to contribute with mystical powers to the success of his team. Geschiere (1995), who observed the phenomenon of sorcery in the East Province of Cameroon, shows how football and sorcery evolved together. He describes a football match that took place in Abong-Bang between Union of Abong-Bang and another team of the same province. The victory of Union was synonymous with the promotion of the divisional officer of the same town to a high government rank. During the match, rumours began to circulate that the goalkeeper of the other team was carrying some *tree barks* and *gris-gris*, which would prevent the strikers of Union of Abong-Bang from scoring goals. However, the wife of the divisional officer reputedly entered the field during the match and 'took off the *gris-gris*' that the goalkeeper was wearing. It was after this incident that *Union* of Abong-Bang was able to win the match and the divisional officer of Abong-Bang was later promoted. Some sources assert further that the political elite organize yearly football competitions with the aim of becoming famous, or of being elected Member of Parliament or mayors of their towns (cf. Sarro 1999; Schatzberg 2006).

Although the skills of the players largely explain their performances and achievement, it is often difficult to convince some Cameroon football fans that victories can be won without the use of sorcery or witchcraft. Some fans show up at matches dressed in paraphernalia that suggests their belief in the power of sorcery. Fans of some Europeans clubs dress in ways that suggest to African fans that mysterious forces are at play in football. The fact that some players are reluctant to dismiss the rumors fuels the fans' belief in the prevalence of sorcery.

Developments towards the professionalisation of football in Cameroon

The championship in Cameroon was organized on an amateur basis until 2012. During the period prior to professionalization, clubs of the Cameroonian Football Federation (FECAFOOT) were largely supported financially by the presidents of clubs and a few influential lovers of the sport. Among the social evils of the Cameroonian system are institutionalized corruption, lack of funds and good infrastructure (stadiums and training facilities). These have affected the quality of football to such an extent that clubs like *Canon*, *Cottonsport*, *Tonnère*, *Union*, and *Racing* do no longer produce the quality results on the African scene as they used to do before. Promising, talented players migrate to Europe, North Africa and the Middle East because most of the clubs they play for at home were unable to provide decent salaries or special allowances.

In Cameroon, the stadiums are built and maintained by the Cameroon state and the poor state and shape of the infrastructure reflect the kind of governance in place. The facilities are not even sufficient for the growing number of young people taking football seriously. The three sports stadiums of Yaoundé, Douala, and Garoua were built several decades ago under the first president, Ahmadou Ahidjo, and these have often been left to deteriorate. President Paul Biya and his government paid very little attention to infrastructural development but have exploited to the fullest the victories the national team has brought home. For more than 25 years, the virus of corruption and embezzlement has destroyed the potential of a vibrant football future. Instead of constructing new stadiums, government officials have built palaces with the funds generated by the participation of the national team in different international competitions.[10] One Minister of Youth and Sports is said to have made a fortune after Cameroon's participation in the 2002 World Cup in Japan and South Korea and he constructed a palace in one of the Yaoundé suburbs. During the 1994 World Cup in the USA, another Minister was given funds for players, but he arrived in the USA without the money. The Lions went on strike, requesting the payment of their allowances. The Minister never produced the money. However, as always, funds were eventually obtained from other sources to keep the Lions quiet and continue their participation.

Recently Samuel Eto'o was suspended for 15 matches with the Lions for refusing to play a friendly match with Algeria. This refusal was over the failure of the managers of Cameroon football to pay the allowances allotted for partic-

[10] Government officials who have managed football in Cameroon during the 30 years of Biya's stranglehold on Cameroon are among the richest people in Cameroon, whose investment in real estate is no public secret.

ipation. It was on 12 December 2011 that the homologation and discipline of FECAFOOT suspended Eto'o, captain of the Lions for 15 matches. The news was received with bitterness by most diehard fans and the general public. As captain, Eto'o had indeed consulted players who refused to play a friendly match with the Algerian national team for obvious reasons: failure to pay dues for the matches. After all, this was not the first time officials were failing to live up to their obligations. When the Lions, after the brilliant LG tournament in Marrakech, were to travel to Algiers to play the friendly match, they had been told the allowances would be paid on arrival. Knowing what the Cameroon football officials are, the players through Eto'o demanded the allowances beforehand. That was done, but without result, and so the match never took place. The Algerian Football Federation inflicted a one million dollar fine on the Cameroon Football Federation. In its meeting of December 12, both Eto'o and the vice-captain Eyong Tarkang as well as Assou Ekotto were punished. The harsh sanction on Eto'o was based on the accusation that he had incited his teammates. Eyong Takang is quoted as having said this: "... the players will not come to that meeting because they know what you (officials) are going to say. The captain (Eto'o) has said we will not go to Algiers" (FECAFOOT Report 2011). Despite negotiations with the players, football officials and the Ministry responsible for sports, the Lions refused, and never played the friendly match. It was apparent from the attitude of the players that the football officials used them to make promises which were never fulfilled to the letter. In the debate over the allowances, the Ministry of Sport and Physical Education refused to assume any responsibilities for the payment.

The uneasy relationship between the Ministry of Sports and Physical Education and FECAFOOT has further contributed to the lack of development of football in Cameroon. Usually the quarrel is over the management of resources or financial benefits that are derived from the organization football matches. The rivalry over the management of funds earmarked for football makes the further development of the sport nearly impossible. Cameroon as a football nation has lost its pride. The failure of the Lions to qualify for the 2010 World Cup in Germany and the poor performances of Cameroonian teams on the African scene dented the reputation of the national team, even though some of the great stars of European football leagues still are Cameroonians. The poor performance of the Lions has gradually taken away their capacity to strike fear in the hearts of their adversaries. Cameroonians could not believe that their national team was not going to 2012 CAN festival when the Lions were eliminated by the Senegalese team.

The performances of Cameroonian players in European leagues still give young people something to dream of, that is, one day playing in Europe. Indeed, many football schools were created, giving rise to a lucrative business preparing young people for a future in football abroad. Many want to leave for the greener pastures in Europe. Conservative figures show that there are hundreds of Cameroonian players playing in the best leagues and clubs in Europe, North America, the Middle East and Asia. Their success abroad fascinates young Cameroonians faced with unemployment and poverty. Many therefore keep alive the ambition or dream to migrate and find a team that needs their talents. Indeed, it has an impact on local football clubs, when their best players are either leaving or are being traded off for money by owners of national clubs.

The emergence of football education institutions has had two effects. Firstly, it has provided a formal network for the preparation of young people for a professional football career. The major objective of these schools has been to train young talents and find interested clubs for them. Secondly, the existence of these schools has led many young boys to abandon their formal education and concentrate fully on the acquisition of football skills in the hope that they will, in the very near future, find a team abroad willing to take them. Having abandoned their formal education and failing to find a European club to take them can be very frustrating, and sometimes can lead them to join gangs and other socially problematic groups. The riots of February 2008 in major cities of Cameroon were probably in part the venting of that frustration. In fact, even thousands of young men and women with formal education (secondary schools and universities) cannot find jobs. Finding jobs usually means bribing government officials who control the web of systematic corruption built over a 25-year period of strategic mismanagement of the rich resources of the Cameroon nation.

The creation of the professional league in Cameroon in 2011, known as LIFPROC,[11] is not just meant to be a lucrative enterprise. The real issue is how football can lifted to such a level if the clubs still have to depend on the state to provide the basic infrastructure. How can amateur football transform into professional football without appropriate training facilities (stadiums), or a visible and appropriate headquarters with transparent administrative machinery? How can these elite clubs transform overnight into a truly professional business enterprise? Indeed, the professional league (LIFPROC) officially started on 14 January 2012 in Douala, with the presentation of its logo (LFPC) and its sponsor, MTN-Cameroon. For the historical record, the first professional match was between *Union of Douala* and *Tiko United*, a match with about 8,000 spectators that was retransmitted live from the Reunification Stadium.

[11] Ligue Professionnel de Football du Cameroun.

Conclusion

Football in Cameroon is an activity that has ascended to the status of a religion. The 'high priests' of this religion are the members of FECAFOOT, whose rites and rituals are often incomprehensible to the altar servers, the players, because the real meat of the celebration, the flows of money that come with it, is often shrouded in secrecy. The worshippers, the fans, who pay for the services, are often a negligible quantity and relegated to the background and silenced, but still remain an important component of the religion.

Cameroon has lived through great moments of football between 1982 and 2002. In the last 25 years, Cameroon has won historic victories on the African and world stage. It is thanks to these victories that Cameroon gained a name internationally. But unfortunately the policy framework of football in Cameroon has not been consonant with the top achievements of the national team. It is not even seen as a scandal that Cameroon, with its acquired football reputation, does not have stadiums up to standards, or is not capable of organizing international tournaments. Nor has the country been able to organize a single African Nations Cup for more than three decades. The future of football in Cameroon seems to be compromised, and if nothing is done by policy makers Cameroon may go further through a dry spell in its football history. Its absence in the 2012 CAN football tournament was a pointer. Some observers have asserted that Cameroonian football is sick and that the search for appropriate, efficient and lasting solutions by Cameroon officials is now imperative.

References

Baller, S. & M. Saavedra eds, 2010. Les terrains politiques du football, special issue of *Politique Africaine* 118: 5-141.

Clignet, R. & M. Stark, 1974. Modernisation and football in Cameroun. *Journal of Modern African Studies* 12(3): 409-421.

Commission Fédérale d'Homologation et de Discipline de la Fédération Camerounaise de Football: décision no. 28 fcf/cfhd/2011 affaire: fecafoot December 2011.

Dongmo, J.-L., 1981. *Le Dynamisme Bamiléké. La Maîtrise de l'Espace Agraire.* Yaoundé: Édition Clé.

Geschiere, P., 1995. *Sorcellerie et Politique en Afrique*. Paris: Karthala.

Nkwi, P.N. & B. Vidacs, 1997, Football: politics and power in Cameroon. In: G. Armstrong & R. Giulianotti, eds, *Entering the Field: New Perspectives on World Football*. Oxford: Berg.

Ntchapda, P. Arnaud, Cameroun: La Ligue de football professionnel entre en jeu. *Le Jour,* 16 Janvier 2012.

Ntonfo, A., 1994. Ethnie et sport au Cameroun. In: *Ethnie et Développement National. Actes du Colloque de Yaoundé 1993*. Yaoundé: Éditions du Crac.

Sarro, R., 1999. Football et mobilisation identitaire: la 'réinvention des traditions' par les jeunes Baga de Guinée. *Politique Africaine* 74: 153-161.

Schatzberg, M.G., 2006. Soccer, science, and sorcery: causation and African football. *Afrika Spektrum* 41(3): 351-369.

Tabapssi, Famndié Timothée, 1999. *Le Modèle Migratoire Bamiléké (Cameroun) et sa Crise Actuelle: Perspectives Économique et Culturelle*. Leiden: CNWS Research School of Asian, African and Amerindian Studies, Leiden University.

Tchoussi, Emile Zola Ndé, 2012. Affaire Samuel Eto'o: La Fifa demande des explications à la Fecafoot, *Cameroon Tribune*, 23 January 2012.

Tsanga, S., 1969. *Le Football Camerounais. Des Origines à l'Indépendance*. Yaoundé: n.p.

Vidacs, B., 1999. Football in Cameroon: a vehicle for the expansion and contraction of identity. *Culture, Sport, Society* 2(3): 100-117.

Warnier, J.P., 1993. *L'Esprit d'Entreprise au Cameroun*. Paris: Karthala.

Sagacity spirit and ghetto ethic: Feymania and new African entrepreneurship

Basile Ndjio

Since the early 1990s, young successful confidence tricksters and transnational swindlers, commonly characterized in Cameroon as feymen, have become emblematic figures of African economic adventurers and subversive 'criminal' entrepreneurs who transcend national boundaries and operate both in Africa and the West. Through what the public opinion in this country generally refers to as feymania – a practice which involves business fraud, financial deception and confidence trick,- many of these formerly disenfranchised urban youths have managed to gain access to wealth from which they were previously excluded by the corrupt and clientelist regime of president Biya. In this paper, we argue that, unlike what some analysts have maintained about criminal or unlawful business practices in Cameroon, the propagation of feymania-related activities in this country is less the result of the growing process of criminalization of the Cameroonian state, than the logical consequence of the pervasiveness in this country of what we have called 'sagacity spirit' and 'ghetto ethos'. By these expressions, we mean a way of life which makes an apology of a culture of resourcefulness and inventiveness, as well as it promotes unethical values and immoral principles. Then, it is this philosophy of the poor, which provides ideological and moral supports to young Cameroonians who are involved in the practice of feymania and other forms of unlawful activities encouraging the propagation of new modes of African entrepreneurship. Moreover, I maintain that without the prevalence of this underlying ethos in Cameroon, the practice of feymania would not have flourished in the country to the point of now having invaded all spheres of life in Cameroonian society.

Introduction

This contribution is an homage to a gifted and passionate researcher whose scholarship has been marked by a constant emphasis on the inventive spirit of marginalised Africans, and their exceptional ability not only to adapt to modern changes, but also to invent new opportunities for enrichment in contexts of economic austerity and structural adjustment measures, and above all, of dwindling of prebends that in the past enabled postcolonial leaders to maintain the social balance and political order. For example, in a fascinating study on marginalised youths of New-Bell in Douala, the economic capital of Cameroon, Piet Konings observed that since the start of the economic meltdown in the late 1980s, most young men and women from this poverty-stricken neighbourhood have been trying to survive 'by engaging in legal activities such as petty trade and production, and/or various illegal activities such as prostitution, smuggling', etc (Konings 2006: 47).

A particular case is the *feymen,*[1] as Cameroonians generally call young successful confidence tricksters, transnational swindlers and other shady 'businessmen'. They have become role models for many youngsters. Through what has since the early 1990s been popularized in Cameroon as *feymania* – practices which involve confidence tricks, money doubling, business frauds, financial deceptions and swindling – many of these young 'criminal' entrepreneurs, who mostly originate from underprivileged social backgrounds, manage to accumulate immense fortunes. This has enabled some of them to wear flashy clothes, drive fancy cars, live in impressive mansions in gentrified residential areas of Douala and Yaounde (the political capital), or to patronize music bands or football clubs in their home town or native village (Malaquais 2001; Ndjio 2001, 2006). Like the notorious Nigerian '419' email scammers (cf. Apter 1999: 267-307; Glickman 2005: 460-89; Smith 2001: 803-26) or the famous Congolese *mikilistes* and *bana Luanda* (see De Boeck 1998: 777-809; MacGaffey & Banzenguissa-Ganga 2000), *feymen* are iconic figures of economic adventurers, and especially subversive 'criminal' entrepreneurs who do not content themselves with only downplaying the importance of the postcolonial state as an inescapable centre of production and distribution of riches. They also aspire to free themselves from state paternalism.

[1] Although *feymania* is mostly a male-dominated activity, there is however a small number of active *feywomen* who usually make use of their charms to bait some naïve western and Arab dupes. Some of these cunning female tricksters often work together with their male partners who are often their boyfriends or close relatives. See the case discussed elsewhere (in Ndjio 2012, chapter IV).

Feymania appears more and more as the embodiment of a growing economy of hoodwinking, fraud and trickery, which today enables many marginalised urban youths in sub-Saharan Africa at large to gain access to financial and material resources from which they were previously excluded in the formal economy.

In addition, since the early 1990s these unorthodox economic practices have become the epitome of forms of African entrepreneurship that generally give priority to what Geschiere & Konings (1993: 7) euphemistically call 'alternative modes of accumulation', which in themselves challenge the officially sanctioned modes of wealth creation in postcolonial Africa. In fact, *feymania* may be called the archetype of what John Flemming, former chief economist of the European Bank for Reconstruction and Development, once referred to as 'mafia capitalism' (Flemming 1995: 45-56), based on the effort to create riches by appealing to techniques that contravene national and international laws, rules and conventions regarding economic activities. By 'mafia capitalism', we mean here any economic practice that not only transgresses such conventional business ethics but also disregards moral values and ethical principles. The concept of mafia capitalism also accounts for any business enterprise that connives with immoral values and deceptive ethics.

The present study, based on ethnographic research conducted between 2001 and 2005 and some shorter subsequent work in Cameroon and in some European countries (France, Great Britain, Germany and the Netherlands), is the prolongation of my previous reflections on the moral economy of swindle and deceit that yields 'unconventional' and 'unethical' modes of wealth production in which underprivileged urban youths in Africa at large, and particularly in Cameroon, are playing a crucial role (Ndjio 2001, 2006, 2012a and b). The aim of this study is less to make an ethical evaluation of the behaviour of African economic agents than to attempt to shed light on the precepts, dogmas and systems of values that inform the actions, attitudes and conducts of those who, in Cameroon, are engaged in *feymania*-related business and other forms of unlawful activities encouraging the propagation of new modes of African entrepreneurship, which more and more espouse the style and logic of 'adventure' or 'mafia' capitalism.

The main argument of this chapter is that contrary to the criminologist approach which tends to relate the expansion of *feymania*-related activities in Cameroon to the growth of criminal enterprises at the very heart of the Cameroonian postcolonial state (see Bayart *et al.* 1999; Hibou 1999: 70-113, 2004, Malaquais 2001), it is what the local popular urban parlance generally refers to as *esprit de sagacité* ('sagacity spirit') and *éthique du ghetto* ('ghetto ethic'), which has been providing philosophical, ideological and 'moral' support to Cameroonian cunning urban tricksters and other 'businessmen' whose ethical maxim seems to be: 'Dishonesty is our best policy.' In more general, these notions of 'sagacity spirit' and 'ghetto ethic', which are generally associated with the behaviour of the urban poor, makes reference to all manoeuvres, tactics, schemes, (dirty) tricks and strategies enabling these marginalized groups to get round internal and external constraints. In the popular understanding, these pervasive terms usually refer to attitude and behaviour determined either by cleverness, inventiveness and cunningness, or rather guided by trickery, recklessness and dishonesty. Thus, in this contribution we define these notions of 'sagacity spirit' and 'ghetto ethic' as both a philosophy and a morale that promotes the culture of resourcefulness, ingenuity and adaptability, as well as exalt attitudes like unscrupulousness, and double-dealing.

Moreover, I maintain that without the prevalence of this underlying ethos in Cameroon, the practice of *feymania* would not have flourished in the country to the point that it has now invaded all spheres of life in Cameroonian society.

This chapter also seeks to give insights into the ambivalent attitude of the Cameroonian government towards these 'unorthodox' and 'amoral' economical practices and those who perform them. I will show, for example, that, confronted with the upsurge of subversive modes of enrichment mainly developed outside the state framework, Cameroonian officials produced a series of moralizing discourses that criminalized *feymania*-related practices and depicted *feymen* as smooth criminals, white-collar bandits or unscrupulous swindlers who feared neither God nor man. At the same time, successful *feymen* who accepted the 'dance of collaboration' (Rush 1990) with the ruling CPDM (Cameroon People's Democratic Movement) regime, or allowed themselves to be 'captured' by state power, were praised by government officials as 'young, dynamic entrepreneurs'.

A brief history of *feymania* entrepreneurship

One of the unexpected consequences of the protracted economic crisis that many African countries have been experiencing since the late 1980s, and their marginalisation in the world economy, is incontestably the emergence of new modes of capitalization of wealth that encourage new economic behaviour, shape a new art of entrepreneurship, and especially prepare the ground for what can be provisionally called 'African capitalism', whose complexity is not yet very well understood by social scientists (Ellis & MacGaffey 1996: 19-41; MacGaffey 1994: 189-204). What particularly marks out this 'new African entrepreneurship' is less the fact that it essentially lives on fraud, prevarication and other fraudulent practices, than the fact that it clutters itself very little with ethical values and moral principles. Another critical characteristic of these non-conventional forms of economic conduct is that they dissolve the difference between criminal behaviour and legitimate profit-seeking, between normal economic activities and vulgar criminal practices, as well as turning African entrepreneurs into immoral economic agents who seem to be essentially driven by 'ruthless acquisition, bound to no ethical norms whatever,' as Max Weber (1958: 71) would say. This is what many students of African entrepreneurship have observed among the new generation of African businessmen and entrepreneurs who are notorious for their passion for shady business, dirty tricks, fraud and smuggling, and especially their inclination for taking an unfair advantage of their business partners' trust (Bayart 1994; Hibou 1999: 70-113; MacGaffey 1987, 1994: 189-204; MacGaffey & Bazenguissa-Ganga 2000; Ndjio 2002a and b; Warnier 1993, 1994: 175-201). For example, in an interesting article about what he called '*La "bigarrure" des patrons Camerounais*' (variegation of Cameroonian patrons), the French anthropologist Jean-Pierre Warnier (1994: 175-201) showed that the actions of many of them were informed by unethical principles and immoral values such as deception, unscrupulousness, hypocrisy and duplicity.

In Cameroon, popular imagination generally characterizes these patterns of unconventional economic conduct as *feymania*. In general, this concept refers to wealth acquired by occult means, and especially to unlawful business practices that make use of embezzlement, corruption, money-doubling, wheeling-dealing, sophisticated business frauds and financial deceptions (Bayart 2004: 93-104; Malaquais 2001; Ndjio 2001; Séraphin 2000). The word '*feymania*' also accounts for an immoral personal demeanour which implies deceit, trickery and dishonesty (Ndjio 2006). As suggested, the notion accounts for fantastic forms of wealth creation, which are officially unsanctioned because they derive from business activities or economic practices which contravene conventional norms and moral values, and especially circumvent official economic regulatory channels. While the word '*feymen*' is indistinctly associated with nouveaux riches, wheeler-dealers or racketeers (*affairistes*), swindlers or tricksters (*frappeurs*), and more importantly with rich *sorcerers* (*mokoagne men*).

As alluded to earlier, he concept *feymania* was popularised in the early 1990s as a result of the emergence of a group of successful young conmen and tricky businessmen who came to be known by the public as *feymen*. At that time, when people spoke of *feymania*, they generally referred to the 'ability to attain wealth through witchcraft, trickery and devilish intelligence (and not through violence),' as Hibou (2004: 7) has explained.

In the discussions on the social origins of this new form of African entrepreneurship, some analysts have linked its emergence to the double process of privatisation and criminalisation of the Cameroonian state, and to the informalisation of the local economy (Bayart 2004: 93-104; Bayart *et al.* 1999; Hibou 1999: 69-113, 2004; Malaquais 2001, Roitman 2005). Others relate it rather to the social and economic marginalisation of the youth in the country (Courade 2000; Jua 2003: 12-36). Though we sympathize with some of these explanations about the political, economic and social conditions that prompted the rise of the economy of swindle and trickery in Cameroon, we, however, believe that they have played only a very mediated role in this process. That is why we offer a proposition that insists more on historical contingencies. More explicitly, our argument is that the figures of subversive urban tricksters and deceitful businessmen emerged in the early 1990s at a particular moment in the history of postcolonial Cameroon: firstly, the predicament of modernity in sub-Saharan Africa at large, and particularly its manifestation in Cameroon. This crisis of the modernist project is epitomized in this country by the demise of the welfare state that formerly positioned itself as a major actor in the production and distribution of wealth (cf. Ndjio 2009).

Secondly, the propagation in Cameroon, as in many other African countries, of *feymania*-related activities and other modes of 'mafia capitalism' should be understood in relation to the effort of many marginalised Africans at large to 'reinvent' the global capitalist system. By 'reinvention of capitalism' – an expression taken from J-F. Bayart (1994) – I do not only mean the remodelling of its rationality and logic, but also the questioning of the ethical codes, principles and laws that govern economic activities and commercial transactions at both the local and the international level. This process also implies a corruption of its conventional norms and systems of values. In a forthcoming study on this African 'reinvention' of neoliberal capitalism (cf Ndjio 2012b), we will show for example that one of the schemes developed by young African 'criminal' entrepreneurs consists in converting global capitalism into a global economy of crime, swindle and fraud. Another manoeuvre involves the denaturalization of the global capitalist system into what Comaroff and Comaroff (1999: 279-301, 2000: 291-343) have coined the 'occult economies.'

Sagacity spirit

Whether they carry out their swindling operations at home or abroad, the behaviour and attitude of most of cunning urban tricksters are influenced by a shared ethos, the most noticeable aspect of which is what many Cameroonians refer to as *esprit macro* (the 'cretin spirit') or the *esprit de sagacité* ('sagacity spirit'). These pervasive notions make reference not only to representations and beliefs that people who live on the margins of 'modern' and affluent society have in common. They also account for actions and tactics that enable marginalized urban youths from Douala and Yaounde (political capital of Cameroon) escape poverty and destitution. As witnessed during my fieldwork among local *feymen* and their counterparts who resided in Paris or London, the sagacity spirit goes along with the culture of trickery, inventiveness, and informality, or with what one of our informants once called *l'art de la débrouillardise* (the art of resourcefulness).

The life history of Yomes (a pseudonym), a young successful *feyman* who was forced to flee his home country in 1998 after a confidence trick he played on both a top ranking officer in the army and a wealthy local businessman connected to the CPDM ruling party, is instructive in more than one respect. I came to know Yomes in 1997, when I was still involved in the gambling business. Like many of the *nouveaux riches* from Yaounde, this young *feyman* was one of the regular customers of the *Café du Boulevard*, a smart café and gambling house of which I was the assistant manager. This exclusive resort was not only the recommended place for many successful trickster businessmen and racketeers who wanted to dramatise their importance or display their wealth. It was also the hub for the exchange of news and gossips about both local *feymen* and their fellows who resided in other cities of the country and even abroad. Like many *feymen*, especially those who were the first to get involved in *feymania*-related practices in the early 1990s, Yomes came from a destitute family who lived in Madagascar, a popular neighbourhood in Yaounde. At twelve, he found himself fatherless, and by the time he was fifteen, the then teenager was forced to give up his studies after two consecutive failures to get admission to the government secondary school. As his mother, who was a petty merchant from Mokolo market, did not have enough money to enrol him in a private secondary school, the would-be *feyman* turned street vendor. In the beginning, he started selling cigarettes, sweets and handkerchiefs on the streets of Yaounde, especially at the Carrefour Warda junction and the Post Office roundabout, thanks to the little start-up capital he received from his mother (FCFA 5,000). In the end, when this trade was no longer profitable because the market had reached saturation point as a result of the involvement of many young street vendors in the same business, he switched to the selling of peanuts and aubergines during the holiday period, and then to the trade of school stationary at the start of the academic year. As I learned from one of Yomes's close relatives, in order to support his younger siblings and his now disabled mother, he had to walk throughout the whole city in the sun and rain with his goods on his head. This flexibility and entrepreneurial spirit allowed him to accumulate some money in less than two years of activities. He later used his capital to invest in the toy business. He got his goods from Chinese and Pakistani wholesale merchants from the Yaounde central market and the commercial avenue. His business was doing pretty well until the day the local police and city council agents, who were operating in the wake of the government 'cleaning campaign,' confiscated his merchandise and that of other street vendors without pressing charges. With no connections to administrative authorities, and having no money to bribe the state agents who live off the extortion of street vendors and petty traders from the market, he had no choice but to abandon his goods to them. But this setback did not deter the young man's project.

So, in search for a more meaningful life, the would-be *feyman*, with one *nangaboko* (street child) he befriended during his hard times, developed a number of new strategies enabling them to make a little money for subsistence purposes. One of the tactics they resorted to was to engage in petty thievery and larceny. For example, Yomes and his cronies used to pick the pockets of passers-by, or to pinch things from shops by hiding them under their trousers or shirts. These stolen items were later resold to other street vendors or to casual customers. Another strategy involved the practice of beggary. Having noticed that only elderly beggars, women with babies and especially the handicapped aroused people's compassion, the two cunning *nangaboko* decided to feign all sorts of disabilities. They drew their inspiration from a French B-movie titled, *Chacal* (jackal), in which the main character who was hired by a French extremist group to assassinate the General de Gaulle, faked his identity in order to escape the police's notice. As Yomes confided in me the day two beggars asked us money in the *Café du Boulevard* where we were playing billiard:

> Do you know why I was generous with these two beggars? It is because they reminded me of the time when I was a *nangaboko* too… I had a friend of mine who is presently in the *front* (swindling operation) in Indonesia. Together with him, I used to extort some money from naïve passers-by, by passing myself off as a disabled person. Our initiator was the main character of the *Chacal* movie. Did you watch that film? (I nodded my head). So, like *Chacal*, we made people believe that we were either blind, deaf, dumb or disabled war veterans, or that we had a stammer.

For example, at the Rond Point de la Poste, which is the most important junctions in the city, they used to pass themselves off as refugees from Chad or Liberia, who were victims of war in their country. To encourage people to be generous with them, they walked by limping, or they hid one of their feet or arms in their clothes, so as to give the impression that they were dismembered:

My friend 'Chacal' had even made himself an artificial limb which evidenced his disability. That is why he was named after the actor of the *Chacal* movie. At the Carrefour Warda, we rather faked blindness by embalming our eyes with *mentholatum* (a popular mentholated ointment imported from Nigeria), or by turning our eyelids inside out. In seeing us performing, you would swear to it that we were really blind [. . .]. In general, I was the blind man and my friend 'Chacal' was my guide, because I performed better than he did. Although I was 'blind,' I always had my eyes on 'Chacal,' because I knew that a little lapse of concentration on my part was enough for him to '*frapper*' (deceive) me.

They liked to target people who drove expensive cars, especially foreigners who were more generous than the locals. That is why they chose to establish their *front* at the Carrefour Warda:

This place was a strategic point, for there were always traffic jams because of police check points and traffic lights that regularly obliged drivers to stop here. In addition, most of well-off people who lived in affluent neighbourhoods in the Capital passed by this junction. Sometimes, when we did not make enough money to meet our needs, we acted as sick men who needed some financial assistance to buy their medicine. To dispel any doubt, we would present people with forged medical books or prescriptions. All these strategies enabled us to make more money than real beggars, and even than those who had a formal job.

It is the same sagacity spirit that informs the actions of the present Cameroonian confidence tricksters and hustlers who essentially live off confidence tricks, financial deceptions and other fraudulent schemes, the common practice of which is the so-called 'multiplication of banknotes' and the 'black money scam.' In *feymania*-related practices, the sagacity spirit finds its expression through what Garas, a notorious *feyman* who pretends to be one of the initiators of *feymania* in Cameroon,[2] once called '*l'art de la composition*' (the art of muddle or deception)'. This means, the skill of getting money from some naïve and avaricious businessmen or politicians by trapping them into signing over major assets, or in arousing from them the strong belief that the trickster has magical powers to increase their capital. As he explained in one local newspaper,[3]

I met a prosperous Greek businessman in Istanbul and told him that I could make him become very rich, if he agreed to going into business with me. I explained to him that I

2 See *L'Action*, no. 202, 28 November 2000; *Le Messager*, 08 July 2001.

3 Cf. *Le Messager*, no. 1212, 10 May 2001: 8.

could produce US million $ notes. To prove him that I could make it, I produced some copies of US $ 200 notes. He took them and went to many banks to check. A few hours later, he came back and told me that all the notes were genuine. The man was now convinced of my technique. He agreed to be my business partner. I ended up getting US $ 500,000 from him and disappeared.

It is through such deceptions that people who are attracted by the lure of effortless earnings are deprived of their fortunes and left completely broken. There are many stories in Cameroon about some entrepreneurs or state officials who have been hoodwinked by some unscrupulous tricksters. For example in October 2000, one of the most satirical newspapers in Cameroon, *Le Messager Popoli,* echoed the rumour about a senior official at the Presidency from whom a group of young *feymen* extorted 150 million FCFA (more than U$ 300,000). Other local newspapers, which reported the same story, named several ministers and top-ranking officers in the police and army among the victims of a large-scale swindle organized by these young conmen who had succeeded in cheating more than 2000 Cameroonians.[4] To achieve their coup, the tricksters set up a fictitious financial institution,[5] which was allegedly involved in financial speculations at the stock exchange and had fixed ties with some well-known issuing houses in Switzerland and Italy.[6] The scheme consisted of convincing people to take a share or invest their money in this financial house, with the prospect of drawing substantial profits from the monthly extra-dividend (between 12% and 18%) that was promised to the investors.[7] Enticed with promises to gain money in little time, many Cameroonians (mostly senior bureaucrats) withdrew their capital from a number of banks and *tontines* (mutual credit associations), and invested it in the *Leadership Academy*, without knowing that they were lured into a trap. Before these naïve savers realized that they had been cheated, initiators of this artful fraud had already run off towards Europe. It was reported that one of the leaders of the fictitious financial institu-

4 See *L'Action*, 28 November 2000; *La Nouvelle Expression*, 23 April 2001; *Mutations*, 12 July 2001.

5 This institution had different names: International Financial Association (IFA); *Leadership Academy, SA*.

6 The (monthly) rate of interest, estimated at 15% of the investment, was so attractive and alluring because it was three times higher than what local banks generally offer (yearly) to their clients (between 4,5% and 5%).

7 Those who invested at least FCFA 20 million (managers) supposedly received between 15% and 20% of their holdings; assistant-managers (under FCFA 20 million) were expecting at least 15% of their investments; dealers (under FCFA 10 million) received between 10% and 15% of their assets.

tion, who was caught at Douala international airport with his briefcase full of cash, bribed the police officers with FCFA 8 million in order to free himself.

This large-scale fraud recalls the confidence tricks that the gang of Donatien Koagne, the most notorious Cameroonian *feyman*, played on many Kenyan top-ranking officials and high-profile businessmen between 1994 and 1995, and which finally urged the local authorities to restrict the entry of Cameroonian nationals to their country. As one official at the Jomo Kenyatta international airport explained to a group of unfortunate Cameroonian journalists who were declared *persona non grata* in Kenya:

> Since the coup that Donatien Koagne pulled off here in 1994, the presence of a Cameroonian national now arouses a great fear among many Kenyans. He had taken advantage of the former head of state's trust. They were much closed. President Arap Moi considered him his trustworthy friend. Donatien Koagne spent much of his time here in Nairobi. I knew that because at that time, I was already posted to the Jomo Kenyatta international airport. In 1994, at the height of the economic depression when the state was cash strapped, he fooled the head of state into believing that he could multiply the public treasury. Put at ease, President Arap Moi accepted his proposal, and summoned a cabinet meeting. In the end, a huge amount of money that was collected from public saving banks and other state-controlled companies was put at the *feyman*'s disposal. I saw him leaving the country with several tin trunks full of bank notes. But this money has never come back to Kenya. Like Donatien Koagne, many other Cameroonian nationals were engaged in confidence tricks, or in drug trafficking and armed robbery in many cities of Kenya. These criminal activities finally urged Kenyan authorities to ban Cameroonian nationals from entering to the country (my translation).[8]

It was not the first time that Cameroonian swindlers deceived the local elites or extorted foreign officials and businessmen. Indeed, according to some French newspapers,[9], between 1992-1995, they succeeded in extracting more than 15 billion FCFA from Mobutu Sese Seko, the former Zairean President, 40 billion FCFA from Blaise Compaoré, the President of Burkina Faso, and 20 billion FCFA from the former Togolese strong man, Gnassimbé Eyadema. The same misfortune happened in 1994 to some Equatorial Guinean top-ranking officials who had been hoodwinked by three Cameroonian swindlers. These con artists promised to help Obiang Nguema's government to bail out the state coffer, but succeeded in emptying the public treasury, and then disappeared, as their counterparts did with Moi's government in Kenya (see *Le Messager,* 17 March 1999). In reaction to this deception, the Equatorial Guinean authorities arrested and expelled from their country

8 Cf. *Mutations*, 21 October 2004: 3.

9 Cf. *Libération*, 14 November 1998, and *Le Canard Enchaîné*, 27 April 1997.

more than one thousand Cameroonians who were living there.[10] Since *feymen*'s spectacular coups in this country, the relationships between the Equatorial Guinea and Cameroon have become strained. For Equatorial Guinean officials often accuse their Cameroonian counterparts of being lax with *feymen* and other Cameroonian criminal entrepreneurs who generally find refuge in their home country.[11]

What all these stories reveal is not only the feats achieved by these young conmen who seem to have found a 'magical' way of getting money without effort, but also show the ability of these professional crooks to arouse from their victims an entire trust and assurance that they can make them become richer in little time. These recent years in Cameroon, there have been a lot of speculations in the local media about the *feymen*'s skill at swindling their victims with sometimes unbelievable ease.[12] The idea has been advanced that these confidence tricksters cheat their victims because they are *bon tchatcheurs* (smooth talkers) who master the art of 'composition' (muddle), *eksi* (manipulation) and *verbage* (persuasion), to use the local urban vernacular expressions. However, I believe that the success of the *feymen* also comes from the fact that they almost always succeed in engaging their (prospective) victims into utterly *believing* in 'magical deals,' which generally lead the dupe(s) nicely into magical tricks. The tricksters always entrap their (prospective) victims in a fool's bargain which resembles a kind of tricky game in which one party strongly believes that to win or achieve his objectives (accruing his capital), he must put all his confidence in the other party who has all the reasons to be smart or to take unfair advantage of his partner's trust: the *mougou* (dupe or prospective victim) always trusts his cunning associate who *has made him believe* that he (*feyman*) has a trick of producing money, or of turning whitewashed sheets of paper into real bank notes. In the perspective of increasing his capital, the *feymen*'s victim is ready to empty his safe, even to mortgage all his assets for the benefit of a partner whose sole intention is to deceive him. While the con man knows that to swindle his victim he needs to 'game' him, as *feymen* usually say. Many young Cameroonian tricksters I have spoken with translate the art of *game* as the ability either to trick the *mougou* into doing what the swindler wants or expects, or to mistake the dupe with false promises that the *feyman* cannot keep. Some of my informants rather associate the 'art of game' with the art of simulacrum and affectation, since the con artists generally conceal from their victims their underhand plan or malevolent intention: swindling the dupes.

---

[10] Several African and western businessmen who fell into the trap of these cunning tricksters (Cf. Malaquais 2001).

[11] *Jeune Afrique L'Intelligent*, 18 May 2000: 8;*Le Messager*, 16 August 2000: 3.

[12] *L'Action*, 28 November 2000: 5-6, *Le Messager*, 16 November 1996.

Indeed, to succeed, a *feyman* needs to wear a mask of appearance enabling him to flout his identity, cover his real activities or hide his real project. To be convincing, he must pretend to be not what he is really, but someone else; that is, an honest businessman or an expert who *knows* how to produce bank notes, and even a good man (benefactor) who just wants to help his fellow to gain some money, and not a vulgar crook or a smooth criminal who only lusts after his victim's money. The purpose of this simulacrum or *dédoublement* (split personality) is of course to make the *mougou* trust him, so that he can easily take him in. But by 'gaming' or playing with his victim who naively believes in him, a *feyman* mischievously sets little value on the dupe's trust he does not share (breach of trust). That is why 'the art of game', as much as the art of *feymania* implies both the policy of distrust and disloyalty, even dishonesty. The logic of trust or *confiance* that most of the *feymen*'s victims naïvely share is counterbalanced strongly by the logic of distrust, which defines the real *modus operandi* of the *feymen* (cf. Ndjio 2002b).

Ghetto ethic

The actions of *feymen* are also driven by what I call *ghetto ethic*. It is this ethic that helps understand why Cameroonian international swindlers who, as noted earlier, originate for the most part from poor families, generally pay lip service to moral principles and ethic values. The 'ghetto ethic' is an analytical concept I use here to describe the principles and values that structure the life and social imaginary of the large majority of Cameroonians, particularly the masses of destitute urban dwellers who live in concentric zones of poverty and misery of New Bell and Bépanda in Douala, and Madagascar and Nkongkana in Yaounde. But I do not mean that this ethic is reducible to the worldview of 'the wretched of the earth', who live in a state of destitution. The tendency of the parasitic bureaucratic elites who are a past master at misappropriating the state resources, misleading international organizations, siphoning the public funds or embezzling international aid, or the Cameroonian businessmen – alluded to earlier – who for the most part have made fiscal fraud, tax evasion, smuggling and contraband their favourite game, is a strong reminder that the ruling classes' demeanour is also influenced by this ghetto ethic. If there is anything in this country that evidences what Mbembe (2001: 102-43) calls the 'logics of connivance and familiarity' which, according to him, inform the relationships between the postcolonial elites and the masses, it will be this ghetto ethic. It can be said that it is because Cameroonians share this ethos, regardless of their social and cultural backgrounds, and their political and religious affiliations that they participate at different levels in the process of criminalization of the state in Cameroon.

The notion of 'ghetto ethic' refers to an ethic that exalts behaviour such as an independent-minded spirit, a tendency to resist to any form of institutions and authorities, an inclination to disregard any administrative laws and regulations, unscrupulousness, recklessness, and dishonesty (cf. Courade 2000; Konings 2006: 46-65). More precisely, the ghetto subject is generally viewed by members of the elite classes as well as the masses as a 'wicked' subject who has the morals of an alley cat, for he/she considers that necessity knows no law. In the ghettos of New Bell and Madagascar where some attitudes such as honour, virtue, goodness and honesty are regarded as a *luxe* that the poor cannot afford, many people strongly believe that only a fool or naïve (*broutman*) or a mischievous person who has the ulterior motives (*arrière-pensées*) can be 'honest in a country where everybody is dishonest,' as one of my informants once put it (Ndjio 2002b). If integrity, righteousness, virtue and morality are generally associated in these spaces of crime and deprivation with foulness *(brout na sick)*, or are suspected of hiding deceitful behaviour or an underhand scheme, it is because the locals are always inclined to deceive each other, to tell lies, to be unfaithful to their own precept, to break their word or split their personality. For example, a man or a woman who has squandered his/her meagre wage or household budget on slot machines or the PMUC (betting on horse races) will make his/her partner believe that he/she pickpockets have stolen his/her purse. A husband who is supposed to be at work, will encounter in a brothel his wife who should be doing her shopping. A staunch opposition militant will turn an enthusiastic sympathiser of the ruling CPDM party during election campaigns because he/she can get some clothes or bank notes from the barons of this party (see Hansen 2000). A girl will feign to be pregnant in order to get some money from her stingy lover. No wonder that a character that local populations admire the most in a movie is generally the *méchant* (ugly or bad man) or the *truand* (trickster). The folk are also attracted by movies which deal with deceit, trickery, infidelity, duplicity and treason, like the Hollywood movie, *True Lies* – translated by Cameroonians as the *caméléon* (chameleon) – which enjoyed a great success in the popular neighbourhoods of Douala and Yaounde. For many people could easily recognise themselves in the main characters' chameleon-life.

The ghetto ethic is also expressed through the locals' bad habit of playing confidence tricks on their neighbours, or of making the most of any situation that they face. For instance, you will buy a bottle of wine or champagne, or new clothes in the market just to find out once at home that the cunning merchant has mischievously sold you a bottle full with soap-water or rags. If you go to a local bazaar to get a loaf of bread for your breakfast, you are likely to be given a stale (*pain rassis*) by the seller who will do his best to persuade you that your loaf has only been affected by damp. If you are a foreign tourist, and you decide to change your currency into the local FCFA in one of street *bureaux de change* of the Avenue Kennedy in Yaounde or the Boulevard de la République in Douala, you run the risk of discovering in your bundle of FCFA several forged bank notes that were slyly mixed up with genuine notes, so as to mislead the dupe that you have become. Or that the cunning money-dealer has not put enough notes into the pack that was handed over to you, or has mischievously inserted in the bundle smaller denominations than the ones bargained for. If you are vigilant enough to discover that you have been foxed, and then decide to claim your money back, the con artist will tell you that you are a dishonest person, and will likely shout 'Stop, thief!'

Any disaster or misfortune that affects the country, the region or the neighbourhood is seen above all as an opportunity to earn money. For example, when a catastrophe occurs somewhere, people will pass themselves off as disaster victims at the expense of real victims, just to get aid from the state or international organisations, even if they live far afield from the disaster area. For example, on 14 February 1997 some residents of Sam-Effoulam, a popular neighbourhood in Yaounde, allegedly derailed a tanker that transported petrol destined for the *Société Camerounaise de Dépots Pétroliers*, a parastatal company (cf. *La Nouvelle Expression*, 16 February 1997). As usual, this 'accident' offered the locals who crowed on the accident spot the opportunity to siphon the petrol that escaped from the tanks, and that would be resold later to car users. But the merrymaking turned into a tragedy when in his eagerness to make the most of this unexpected godsend as well, one of the looters inadvertently threw a cigarette end on the ground, thus causing a huge explosion that killed more than 200 people and wounded several hundreds. Word had it that all the victims were autochthons from that neighbourhood, because the *allogènes* residents had allegedly been expelled already from the accident scene by the former, on the grounds that the accident occurred on their 'soil' (see Geschiere and Nyamnjoh 2000: 423-52). But when the government decided to offer bereaved families 200,000 FCFA (more than U$ 400) for each corpse, Cameroonians from different ethnic groups and neighbouring towns ostentatiously mourned for people with whom they had no connections, just because they wanted to get their share of the state's money. At the Yaounde military base where the corpses were displayed, it was pathetic to see all these men and women jostling, squabbling or exchanging blows for a cadaver that would enable them to earn 200,000 FCFA. Some cunning people rather found it less laborious to collect corpses that destitute families often abandon in municipal mortuaries, and then went and trade them with corrupt state agents. To facilitate their transactions, some of them even took care to burn their 'cadavers' so as to make them look like the burned victims of the Sam-Effoulam catastrophe. A man even prided himself on having 'collected' five corpses, which brought him in one million FCFA. One can understand why the newspaper *Le Messager* (21 February 1997) talked of 'cadavers that make other people's fortune'.

All these examples show that the belief, behaviour and attitude of the marginalized groups in Cameroon are largely inspired by what Nantang Jua (2003: 26-27) coins as 'beat-the-system mentality,' which, according to him, has been erected in this country as the norm. It is this ethos that leads many second-class citizens to hold for true that 'hustling is not stealing' (*débrouiller n'est pas voler*). For example, those who steal, pillage or misappropriate state funds are generally considered *débrouillards* (= resourceful people) by their entourage, and not thieves, poachers or plunderers. If they happen to distribute their ill-gotten money to their village fellows or kinsmen, they will be viewed as good people. It is the same ethic that prompts the people to consider that in a context marked by what the popular imagination calls *guéme* (economic crisis) and *foirage* (lack of money or being cash-strapped), 'Any means will do, provided that it helps you earn money' ('*Tous les moyens sont bons, pourvu que cela t'aide à gagner de l'argent*'), as one *feyman* from the Nkoulouloum market in Douala, once phrased it. This means that, in their attempt to cope with austerity and uncertainty that impinge on their lives, people will resort to occultism, prostitution, swindle, seizure, banditry, and other illegal or unlawful practices that enable them to give themselves and their families a better life (see Trani 2000; Malaquais 2001; Jua, *ibid.*; Roitman 2005). Even tragedy and misfortune that affect a particular community or the whole country, as discussed above, will be turned into a means of accumulation.

There is no denying that this ghetto ethic provided an ideological infrastructure to young men who in the early 1990s initiated the practice of *feymania* in Cameroon. Because the international swindler who swindles naïve local or foreign businessmen and bankers, by fooling them into believing that he is able to turn a blank paper into a dollar or euro, is driven by the same ideology that urges the cunning merchant or street vendor of Douala and Yaounde to deceive his/her customers, by selling fake items to them, the bureaucrat who siphons the public funds or the profaner who strips the dead of their assets. Both of them are the products of a society where ill-gotten fortune thrives, or where 'money has no odour,' as Cameroonians generally say. For example, in response to a group of

Cameroonian journalists who asked him why *Kenyan* customs officers generally considered Cameroonians dishonest people, or suspected them of being potential tricksters, one Nairobi-based Cameroonian *feyman* who was on his way to Dubai for a swindling operation in the Persian Gulf, had these words:

> To tell the truth, I understand why Kenyans generally distrust us. We Cameroonians are all *frappeurs* (swindlers), even when we are still in our mother's womb. We are all guided by the *esprit de sagacité*. We are people *sans foi ni loi* (fearing neither God nor man). With Cameroonians, the rule is *pas d'erreur* (no mistake), because if you trust a Cameroonian, it is at your own risk. Even you my fellow countrymen, if you are fool enough to trust me, I will not hesitate to *frapper* (deceive) you and run away. I personally live on people's naiveté. Presently, I am going to the *front* in the Persian Gulf, and I hope to find there some *mougous* on whom I will play a confidence trick, and run back home.[13]

The same ghetto ethic influenced the actions and behaviours of the *feymen* I encountered in the course of my fieldwork in Cameroon and in Paris and London. This was the case of the group of young *feymen* from Paris with whom I spent more than two months (June-August 2002). Although most of them have been living in the French capital for at least six years (some of them even had a French citizenship), and may rightly consider themselves 'Parisians,' the ghetto mentality of New Bell and Madagascar, the two neighbourhoods from which most of them originated, continued to dominate their way of life. Some attitudes described early, such as hypocrisy, treason, mischief and deception, were widespread within this group. There was a general tendency among these people not only to take unfair advantage of their business partners' trust, but also to deceive even their close friends. Relationships among friends or associates were always fraught with double-dealing and duplicity even if in public people generally displayed a strong sense of honour, honesty, solidarity, friendship, attachment and harmony that masked the fact that they were much more fair-weather friends than real friends. Treacherous attitudes prevailed among these young people when it came to money matters, especially to sharing the spoils. For example, one day I had an appointment with Dave, one of the *feymen* I worked with. When I reached his house, I found him hotly arguing over the phone with one of his friends. The argument was so tense that he ended it by abruptly hanging up the phone. My host, who visibly had lost his temper, explained to me that the man he had just quarrelled with was one of his friends and business associates, who was trying to *rouler* (diddle) in a tricky business that they put up together with their other cronies, and that earned them 450,000 euros. The trickster who was entrusted with the mission to collect

[13] Cf. *Mutations*, 21 October 2004: 5.

the money from their *mougou* (an Arab businessman) fooled his accomplices into believing that he only received 200,000 euros from their victim. It was the revelation of another conman to whom their cunning associate disclosed his secret that alerted the five disgruntled tricksters to the fact that their friend had foxed them. I also learnt from Dave that Guiff, another member of the *feyman* gang I worked with, was arrested and sent to prison in Spain together with four of his cronies, because one of their accomplices betrayed them to the Spanish police in order to keep all the money that they got from their monkey business.

Let us now focus our attention to the way the Cameroonian state deals with the *feymania* mode of wealth accumulation.

Feymania and the state in Cameroon

Confronted in the early 1990s with the emergence of young successful criminal 'entrepreneurs' who mostly came from regions of the country that were generally associated with the opposition movement, the ruling CPDM regime initially adopted a sceptical attitude towards *feymania*-related practices and those who were involved in then. Until 1996 (when the Cameroonian government decided to make *feymen* the spearhead of the economic revival, see below), *feymen* were regularly portrayed by pro-government media as professional crooks connected to syndicates of organized crime.[14] One government official described *feymen* as 'rascals and white collar criminals who not only distract the Cameroonian youth from the noble objectives assigned to them by President Biya, but also tarnish the image of the country abroad' (cf. *L'Action*, 12 November 1995; see also Mono Djana 1999, 1997). As a result of this negative perception of *feymen*, a number of them, especially the most successful among them, permanently endured police harassment. Garas, the notorious *feyman* quoted earlier, revealed in *Le Messager* (10 May 2001: 8) how upon their return to Cameroon after a fruitful swindling operation abroad, *feymen* were often stripped of their assets by customs officials, or taken into custody. In 1993 for example, Donatien Koagne, alias the 'King of Cameroon', was kept in custody for several days at the headquarters of the Douala *Police Judiciaire* (= detective division of the police) for involvement in criminal activities (see also Malaquais 2001: 31).

Several reasons justified the government's rigorous policy towards the *feymen*. The first reason was the independent-mindedness of many prominent international swindlers towards state authority and their inclination to downplay the importance of the postcolonial state in the production of riches. Indeed, contrary to the

[14] See *Le Patriote*, 25 May 1996; *L'Action*, 2 June 1996.

older generation of businessmen whose business interests were closely connected (and still are) with that of the 'bureaucratic bourgeoisie' (Bayart 1993: 95; see also Joseph 1977), a great number of *feymen* who came from the underprivileged classes initially kept a distance from state officials and politicians with whom they shared no social background, and much less cultural affiliation. In addition, in their accumulative projects, many of these 'criminal' businessmen tended to give priority to what I referred earlier as 'alternative modes of accumulation', outside the formal circuits of the national economy. So, by capitalizing their riches outside the state framework, and by affirming their autonomy vis-à-vis the political and administrative powers, *feymen* rather opted for competition with the dominant groups instead of collaboration. It meant that from the very beginning, this new independent class of successful 'criminal' entrepreneurs refused to be *responsible* businessmen, who like the former financial elites relied on the magnanimity and goodwill of the men in power. Instead, *feymen* asserted themselves as the *truands* (tricksters), who considered the bourgeoisie class above all as a dupe that had to be swindled.

So, as the *truands*, the newly emerging group of *feymen*, in the early 1990s symbolised the 'figures of ruse and intelligence' (Hibou 1999: 69-114), who slyly challenged the felonious and brutal state. They were people who contested the social order that excluded them from a share in the national resources. Rejecting the social arrangements that kept them away from access to wealth, not only did these young people manage to get out of the desperate conditions they were living in; they also invented their own mode of enrichment. Some subsequently tried to better their lives by engaging in unlawful activities or tricky businesses which have been described by Vwakyanakazi (1982: 98), as an 'act of rebellion against the political and economic systems, and the dominant groups'.[15] While in their effort to get access to wealth, others rather took the liberty of cheating members of the ruling classes or their close relatives, who later came to symbolize what is known in the *feymen*' s milieu as *gros pigeon* (big or naïve sucker). As discussed earlier, the *gros pigeons* also included foreign heads of state or wealthy businessmen who were hungry enough for a quick buck. Between 1994 and 1999, the practice of *feymania* seemed to be abridged to the art of deceiving these big suckers, or of extorting money from those who '... *rendent définitivement plus pauvres les Camerounais*',[16] as the popular Cameroonian singer Lapiro de Mbanga points out.

Secondly, successful *feymen* also had a propensity to contest the bureaucratic

15 Quoted by MacGaffey 1987: 49.

16 Making Cameroonians become definitely poorer.

elites' lavish lifestyles, and their display of grandeur and wealth. They did it, by driving cars, wearing clothes or constructing houses which were fancier, more expensive or extravagant than those of the ruling classes. Some prosperous professional swindlers were insolent and disrespectful enough to deprive the *big men* of their young mistresses, outstrip them in the purchase of houses, or make a fool of them. In other respect, the efforts of these *nouveaux riches* to gain reputation and status on the basis of richness, and their ability to command deference and respect from others as a result of that wealth, directly or indirectly challenged the established system of hierarchy that generally accorded status to holders of political power, or to those who are closely linked to them. Thirdly, a number of Beti elites from the Cameroonian forest region, who hold the political power in Cameroon since 1982, perceived *feymania*-related practices which at that time were largely dominated by young Bamileke from the Grassfields region of Cameroon, as another Bamileke scheme to assert their economic domination over other ethnic groups.[17] Moreover, as these practices were developed by the disaffected youth of Yaounde, Douala and Bafoussam who used to lead the *ghost town operations* (general strikes) in the early 1990s, many CPDM barons tended to associate *feymania*-related practices with new forms of resistance against the ruling CPDM regime after the controversial 1992 presidential elections, and the failure of the opposition movement to unseat Paul Biya, the incumbent president.[18] As one ruling party's sympathizer wrote in *Le Patriote*, a pro-government newspaper:[19]

> Failing to overthrow the Biya regime through the *ghost town operation*, riots, demonstrations, slanders and lies, the enemies of the nation are now trying through *feymania*-related practices and criminal activities, not only to spread disorder and disturbance throughout the country, but also to sabotage the government's effort to fight criminality and corruption in the country.

The *nouveaux riches*' habit of challenging the established system which conditioned the different modes of access to wealth and to invert to their own advantage particular configurations of power, wealth and hierarchy that characterized Cameroonian postcolonial society finally led the CPDM government to associate

---

17 It should be underlined that a large majority of Cameroonian businessmen and entrepreneurs come from the Bamileke ethnic group, which largely has control over a number of key activities (trade, small and medium-size industries). See Dongmo (1981); Warnier (1993).

18 This new form of struggle in which the subordinate groups were engaged, embodied the shift from an overt practice of indiscipline and subversion that was the main characteristic of the previous model of dissidence, to what J. Scott (1990) would have termed 'a hidden transcript of resistance'. See also Mbembe (2001: 147); Ndjio (2005: 265-94).

19 See *Le Patriote*, 23 April 1998: 1.

feymania-related practices with the opposition movement. Likewise, *feymen* were generally cast in the role of the villains and criminals, or considered dangerous *opposants* (political opponents) that needed to be disciplined by all means.

But the overwhelming economic and political crisis of the early 1990s finally compelled the Cameroon authorities to change their negative perception of *feymen*. Moreover, this distressing situation urged them to establish clientelist relationships with successful professional tricksters and conmen. This was justified by the fact that the Cameroonian government saw in their illicit fortune a means to bail out the national economy that was cash strapped, and especially to curb the impact of the devastating 'ghost town operation' (Malaquais 2001: 10-17).

The first calming gesture that Cameroonian officials manifested towards the former 'bad boys' occurred in April-May 1994, when they largely relied on some wealthy *feymen* to finance the participation of the *Indomitable Lions* (the national football team) to the World Cup in the United States. The Biya regime expected the success of the national football team at the World Cup to embellish its scornful image, but lacked financial means for achieving its project. For at that time, Cameroon was on the verge of financial paralysis because of a pervasive economic and political crisis. Cash money had to be found urgently and by all means in order to support the famous national football team, which was often presented by official propaganda as the crucible of the national unity, and the pride of all Cameroonians, regardless of their ethnic, regional or political affiliations. State authorities thus encouraged some well-off *feymen* to participate in the mediatised *Opération Coup de Coeur* (a charity operation) that Cameroonian officials organised between April and May 1994 to collect funds for the *Indomitable Lions*. Apparently, notorious conmen who largely contributed to the success of this operation were suddenly no longer considered government's *opposants* or professional swindlers, even if some barons of the ruling CPDM party were concerned by the fact that the *feymen*'s wealth might also be used to back the opposition, notably the Social Democratic Front party.

Some government officials took advantage of the *Opération Coup de Coeur* that publicly convened the officialdom and the *feymen* community to reinforce the already existing clientelistic relations with some notorious professional swindlers. This was the case of the late Jean Fochivé, who allegedly became the godfather of number of criminal entrepreneurs in the country (see *Le Messager*, 20 November 1998). The close connections that linked him with the gang of the famous Donatien Koagne perfectly exemplified the intimate relationship that was created after May 1994 between the ruling class and some successful *feymen*. In the article mentioned earlier, the editor in chief of the Cameroonian newspaper *Le Front In-*

dépendant disclosed how between 1994 and 1995 Mr. Fochivé regularly assigned members of security forces to escort Donatien Koagne and his lieutenants each time they came back from the *front* abroad. In addition, he used to send his battalion of tricksters all over the world, in search of what the newspaper called *effort de guerre*.[20]

However, the major change in the governmental policy toward the *feymen* came about in 1996, when receipts and tax revenues[21] generated by these *nouveaux riches* helped the Cameroonian state to keep its finances afloat despite the suspension of international aid (cf. Courade 2000; Jaerts *et al.* 2000). By investing their money in various activities (car trade, gambling industry, building, clothing trade, banks, transport, etc.) successful tricksters and con men became for the Biya regime an important link in the process of 'economic revival' in Cameroon. The state's dependence on these 'criminal' entrepreneurs to revitalize the local economy or to counteract the opposition in their native region sometimes compelled Cameroonian authorities to turn a blind eye to their illegal or criminal activities, as long as these prosperous racketeers would not ally with the opposition movement. Because of this *realpolitik*, officials who were overtly opposed to the government's amenability towards the *nouveaux riches* were ostracised or dismissed. For example, in February 1996 Mr. Douala Moutome, then Minister of Justice and well-known for his distrust of *feymen*,[22] was removed from the government following his courageous decision to put in detention Jean-Pierre Sa'ah (who at that time was the most notorious *feyman* in Cameroon). Due to his strong connections with some officials at the Presidency, this notorious con artist was set free, and even allowed a 'medical evacuation' to France.[23]

'Jean-Pierre Sa'ah's affair,' as the newspaper *Aurore Plus* (24 June 2003: 4) called it, evidenced the interest that the Biya regime paid to successful *feymen*, who were now presented by state officials or public media as 'dynamic young Cameroonian businessmen' that the country was proud of; they were praised for their financial skills and their entrepreneurial spirit. Some of these racketeers were even welcomed with the red carpet treatment by Cameroonian authorities. For example, in July 1996 Simon Achidi Achu, the former Prime Minister, with

---

20 See *Le Front Indépendant*, 26 June 2003: 11.

21 Some local newspapers talked about between FCFA 180 and 200 billion that was invested in the local economy by *feymen*. See the article,' *Les feymen au secours de l' économie camerounaise*' (*Feymen* help the Cameroonian economy) in *Le Messager*, 14 June 1996: 5-6.

22 In an interview he granted in 1995 to *Cameroon Tribune*, the pro-governmental newspaper, Mr. Douala Moutome described *feymen* as 'bent businessmen, experts on tricky business who fear neither God nor man.' See *Cameroon Tribune*, 15 November 1995: 6.

23 See *Le Front Indépendant*, 26 June 2003: 11.

great pomp received a group of local, well-known *feymen* who were member of the newly created *feymen* association commonly known as ASOJHAC (Association of Young Cameroonian Businessmen). During this reception, extensively commented upon by the local media, he described these professional crooks and wheeler-dealers as 'successful businessmen whose dynamism and entrepreneurship spirit could inspire many young Cameroonians'.[24]

Conclusion

This study has shown that whether they are localizing or globalizing *feymen*, the *jeunes hommes d'affaires* (young business operators), as Cameroonian con men, racketeers and wheeler-dealers like to be called, share almost the same social imaginary and systems of values which form the 'Cameroonian ideology' or 'way of thinking.' Like many of their fellow countrymen, *feymen* are the heirs of the dogmas and principles which profess that hustling is not stealing, and that in the time of economic crisis, cash strapping and uncertainty any means will do, provided that it helps you earn money. This pervasive ideology also holds for true that, 'it is dishonest to be honest in a country where everybody is dishonest,' or that only the 'end justifies the means.' What I have referred to as the 'sagacity spirit' and the 'ghetto ethic' are two of the most salient aspects of these shared values that urge many Cameroonian swindlers, adventure capitalists and tricky businessmen not only to adopt the morals of an alley-cat, but also to erect dishonesty, double-dealing, fraud, cunningness and trickery as the norm. It is only by acknowledging these underlying attitudes and convictions (i.e., sagacity spirit and ghetto ethic) that we can have a better understanding, not only of the cunning and devious behaviour of young urban tricksters and Cameroonian patrons, but also of the subversive character of these unorthodox economic practices popularly known in Cameroon as *feymania*, and more importantly their transgression of basic ethical values and moral principles.

In other respects, this research on young Cameroonian urban tricksters and dubious entrepreneurs shows how important it is to follow an often neglected lead in existing studies of anthropologists and political scientists, who mainly analyse the expansion of outlaw business enterprises and unregulated economic activities in sub-Saharan Africa in relation to the informalization of economies and societies, to the patrimonialization and criminalization of the state, or to the 'political instrumentalization of disorder' (Chabal & Daloz 1999). Though most of

[24] See the *Cameroon Tribune*, 12 May 1996.

these analysts do acknowledge the global background of such developments, in their empirical explorations they do not insist enough on the extraverted dimension of African criminal entrepreneurship. That is why it was important to highlight here this particular aspect of both *feymania*-related activities and advance fee scams – often labelled 'West African organised crime' by Western criminologists –, particularly their close connections with the West. For example, in my previous work (Ndjio 2006, especially Chapter VI), the inquiry into the ramifications of this African criminality to some Western countries led me to a surprising discovery that young West African criminal entrepreneurs, most notably Cameroonian transnational swindlers and confidence tricksters, often succeeded in *feymania*-related practices because of their ability to subvert the official mode of functioning of the so-called well-regulated and law-abiding Western societies. They flourished in unlawful economic activities because they were able to find niches of crime and contributed to turn these Western countries more into 'criminal states'. Clearly therefore, these crime activities have their impact on the West as well, making them truly global operations.

References

Apter, A., 1999. IBB=419: Nigerian democracy and the politics of illusion, in: J.L. Comaroff & J. Comaroff, eds,*Civil Society and the Political Imagination in Africa: Critical Perspectives*. Chicago: University of Chicago Press, pp. 267-307.

Bauman, Z., 1997. *Postmodernity and its Discontents*. Cambridge: Polity Press.

Bayart, J-F., 2004. Le crime transnational et la formation de L'État. *Politique Africaine* 93: 93-104.

Bayart, J-F., 1996. *L'Illusion Identitaire*. Paris: Fayard.

Bayart, J-F., 1993. *The State in Africa: the Politics of the Belly*. Trans. by Mary Harper. London – New York: Longman.

Bayart, J-F. ed., 1994. *La Réinvention du Capitalisme*. Paris: Karthala.

Bayart, J-F., S. Ellis & B. Hibou, 1999. *Criminalization of the State in Africa*. Oxford: James Currey.

Beauchamp, T. & N. Bowie, eds. 1992. *Ethical Theory and Business*. Englewood Cliffs, N. J.: Prentice Hall.

Brittan, S., 1995. Economics and ethics, in: S. Brittan & A. Hamlin, eds. *Market Capitalism and Moral Values*. Aldershot: Edward Elgar Publishing, pp. 1-23.

Brittan, S. & A. Hamlin, eds, 1995. *Market Capitalism and Moral Values*. Aldershot: Edward Elgar Publishing.

Chabal, P. & J-P. Daloz, 1999. *Africa Works: Disorder as Political Instrument*. Oxford – Bloomington: James Currey – Indiana University Press.

Comaroff, J., & Comaroff, J.L., 2000. Millennial capitalism: first thoughts on a second coming. *Public Culture* 12(2): 291-343.

Comaroff, J., & Comaroff, J.L., 1999. Occult economic and the violence of abstraction: notes from the South African postcolony. *American Ethnologist* 26(2): 279-301.

Courade, G., ed., 2000. *Le Désarroi Camerounais. L'Épreuve de l'Économie-monde*. Paris: Karthala.

De Boeck, F., 1998. Domesticating diamonds and dollars: identity, expenditure and sharing in Southwestern Zaire (1984-1997), in: B. Meyer & P. Geschiere, eds, *Development and Change,* special issue on 'Globalization and Identity: Dialectics of Flows and Closures', 29(4): 777-809.

De George, R., 1982. *Business Ethics*. New York: Macmillan.

Dongmo, L., 1981. *Le Dynamisme Bamileke (Cameroon)*. Yaounde: CEPER, vol. 2.

Ellis, S. & MacGaffey, J. 1996. Research on sub-Saharan Africa's unrecorded international trade: some methodological and conceptual problems. *African Studies Review* 32(2): 19-41.

Flemming, S.J., 1995. The ethics of unemployment and Mafia capitalism, in: S. Brittan & A. Hamlin, eds, *Market Capitalism and Moral Values*. Aldershot: Edward Elgar Publishing, pp. 45-56.

Foko, E., 2000. Gestion du risque et accumulation communautaire chez les Bamileke, in: G. Courade, ed., *Le Désarroi Camerounais. L'Épreuve de l'Économie-monde*. Paris: Karthala, pp. 177-190.

Geschiere, P. & Njamnjoh, F., 2000. Capitalism and autochthony: the seesaw of mobility and belonging. *Public Culture* 12(2): 423-452.

Geschiere, P. & Konings, P., eds, 1993. *Les Itinéraires d'Accumulation au Cameroun*. Paris: Karthala.

Glickman, H., 2005. The Nigerian '419' advance fee scams: prank or peril? *Canadian Journal of African Studies/Revue Canadienne d'Études Africaines* 39(3): 460-89.

Hansen, F., 2002. 'A chiefly political masquerade? Illusion games in local elections.' Paper presented at the Seminar on 'Terms of Trust', Leiden, 18-20 September.

Hibou, B., 1999. The 'social capital' of the state as an agent of deception, or the ruse of economy intelligence, in: Bayart J.-F., S. Ellis & B. Hibou, *Criminalization of the State in Africa*. James Currey: Oxford, pp. 69-113.

Hibou, B., ed., 2004. *Privatising the State*. Trans. Jonathan Derrick. London: Hurst & Co. – Paris: CERI.

Jaerts, J-J., *et al.*, 2000. *L'Économie Camerounaise: un Espoir Évanoui*. Paris: Karthala.

Joseph, R. 1977. *Radical Nationalism in Cameroon. Social Origins of the UPC Rebellion*. Oxford: Oxford University Press.

Jua, N.B., 2003. Differential responses to disappearing pathways: redefining possibility among Cameroon youths. *African Studies Review* 46(2): 12-36.

Konings, P., 2004. 'Bendskin' drivers in Douala's New Bell neighbourhood: masters of the road and the city, in: P. Konings & D. Foeken, eds, *Crisis and Creativity: Exploring the Wealth of the African Neighbourhood*. Leiden and Boston: Brill, pp. 46-65.

MacGaffey, J., 1987. *Entrepreneurs and Parasites: The Struggle for Indigenous Capitalism in Zaire*. Cambridge: Cambridge University Press.

MacGaffey, J., ed. 1991. *The Real Economy of Zaire. The Contribution of Smuggling and Other Unofficial Activities to National Wealth*. London: James Currey.

MacGaffey, J., 1994. State deterioration and capitalist development: the case of Zaire, in: B.J. Berman & C. Leyse, eds, *African Capitalists in African Development*. Boulder, Col.: Lynne Rienner, pp. 189-204.

MacGaffey, J., 1998. Creatively coping with crisis: entrepreneurs in the second economy of Zaire (the Democratic Republic of the Congo). In A. Spring & B.E. McDade, eds,*African Entrepreneurship: Theory and Reality*. Gainesville, Fl: University Press of Florida, pp. 37-50.

MacGaffey, J. & R. Bazenguissa-Ganga, 2000. *Congo-Paris: Transnational Traders on the Margins of the Law*. Oxford: James Currey.

Malaquais, D., 2001. *Anatomie d'une Arnaque: Feymen and Feymania au Cameroun*. Paris: CERI.

Mbembe, A., 2001, *On the Postcolony*. Berkeley – Los Angeles: University of California Press.

Mbembe, A., & J. Roitman, 1995. Figures of the subject in times of crisis. *Public Culture* 7(2): 323-52.

Miaffo, D. & J-P. Warnier, 1993. Accumulation et ethos de notabilité chez les Bamileke, in: P. Geschiere & P. Konings eds, *Itinéraires d'Accumulation au Cameroon*. Paris – Leiden: Karthala – ASC.

Ndjio, B., 2012a. Overcoming marginalization: young confidence tricksters from Cameroon and Nigeria, in Alcinda Honwana, ed., *African Youth: from Marginalization to Ctizenship* (forthcoming).

Ndjio, B., 2012b. *Magie et Enrichissement Illicit: Feymania au Cameroun*. Paris: Karthala/Sephis.

Ndjio, B., 2006. *Feymania*: *New Wealth, Magic Money and Power in Contemporary Cameroon*, Amsterdam: University of Amsterdam (PhD dissertation).

Ndjio, B., 2005. Carrefour de la joie: popular deconstruction of the African postcolonial public sphere. *Africa* 75(3): 265-94.

Ndjio, B., 2002a. '*Feymania:* A new way of imagining modernity in the contemporary Cameroon'. Paper presented during the Seminar on Africa. Leiden University 15 March.

Ndjio, B., 2002b. '*Feymania* in Cameroon: the politics of (dis)trust.' Paper presented during the international conference on 'Terms of Trust in Africa.' Leiden: CNWS, Ethnology Museum, ASSR: 18-20 September.

Ndjio, B., 2001. '*Feymania* in Cameroon: hidden ways of enrichment and alternative visions modernity.' Paper presented during the International conference on the 'Genealogies of modernity', organised by the ASSR/University of Amsterdam, 27-30 August.

Mono Djana, H., 1999. *Le Temps des Clarifications*. Yaounde: Liberté.

Mono Djana, H., 1997. *Les Proverbes de Paul Biya*. Yaounde: Carrefour.

Reidenbach, R. & D. Robin, 1989. *Ethics and Profits*. Englewood Cliffs, N.J.: Prentice Hall.

Roitman, J., 2005. *Fiscal Disobedience. Anthropology of Economic Regulation in Central Africa*. Princeton – Oxford: Princeton University Press.

Rush, J., 1990. *Opium to Java: Revenue Farming and Chinese Enterprise in Colonial Indonesia, 1860-1910*. Ithaca, NY: Cornell University Press.

Scott, J., 1990. *Domination and the Arts of Resistance. Hidden Transcripts*. New Haven – London: Yale University Press.

Sen, A., 1995. Moral codes and economic success, in: S. Brittan & A. Hamlin, eds, *Market Capitalism and Moral Values*. Aldershot: Edward Elgar Publishing, pp. 23-34.

Sen, A., 1987. *On Ethics and Economics*. Oxford: Blackwell.

Séraphin, G., 2000. *Vivre à Douala*: *L'Imaginaire et l'Action dans une Ville Africaine en Crise*. Paris: Karthala.

Smith, D.J., 2001. Ritual killing, 419, and fast wealth: inequality and the popular imagination in Southeastern Nigeria. *American Ethnologist* 28(4): 803-26.

Trani, J-F., 2000. Les jeunes et le travail à Douala: la galère de la deuxième génération après l'indépendance, in: G. Courade, ed., *Le Désarroi Camerounais. L'Épreuve de l'Économie-monde*. Paris: Karthala, pp. 153-176.

Vwakyanakazi, Mukohya, 1982. African Traders in Butembo, Eastem Zaïre

(1960-1980): a Case Study of Informal Entrepreneurship in a Cultural Context of Central Africa, Ph.D. Dissertation, University of Wisconsin, Madison.

Warnier, J-P., 1994. La bigarrure des patrons camerounais, in J-F. Bayart, ed., *La Réinvention du Capitalisme*. Paris: Karthala, pp. 175-201.

Warnier, J-P., 1993. *L'Esprit d'Entreprise au Cameroon*. Paris: Karthala.

Weber, M., 1958 [1920]. *The Protestant Ethic and the Spirit of Capitalism*. New York: Scribner's Press.

Examining the Architecture of Electoral Authoritarianism in Cameroon

Nantang Jua

Cameroon's transition to democracy in the 1990s, a result of elite pacting, was not consolidated. Instead, it mutated into electoral authoritarianism which allowed for limited forms of pluralism in civil society and multiparty elections. Though elections under this kind of regime are consistently flawed and manipulated, democratization is still a possible outcome in countries where they have been sufficiently institutionalized. That this has not been true in the case of Cameroon, it is argued in this chapter, is partially attributable to the absence of a stable and numerically viable opposition that can cooperate and coordinate effectively with 'civil society' and mobilize voters who already suffer from the redound effect of the possibility of change through voting with their hands rather than their feet. Not even Cameroon's high linkage with Western hegemonic states, notably France and the United States, has helped to promote democracy. Its (re)presentation as an 'island of peace' in an unstable region, and thus the need to insulate it from the 'neighborhood effect', has posed some policy dilemmas and analytical challenges for power elites that have captured policy making in the two states.

Introduction

L'État au Cameroun (Bayart 1979), a seminal work on the hegemonic state in postcolonial Africa, informed several studies of the state in other African countries, as well as a subsequent generic study by the same author, *L'État en Afrique* (1993). However, transition narratives that have been the staple of much recent political analysis of the 'third wave of democratization' in Africa have been predominantly large and comparative *N studies* that are relatively general both in aspiration and in their empirical grounding. In these small sample (within region) comparisons, Cameroon's political 'transition' has been labeled, *inter alia,* as flawed (Bratton & van de Walle 1994) or engendering only a patchy façade of an electoral regime (Lindberg 2006: 148).

However, Cameroon has also been a laboratory for studies in political transition using varying and varied conceptual approaches (see *inter alia*, Konings 2004, Takougang & Krieger 1998, Takougang 2003). Piet Konings has emerged as a leading *Cameroonianist*, though his work has focused primarily on the impact of Cameroon's sociological makeup – notably, the Anglophone/Francophone divide – on this process, deconstructing what has been termed the 'Anglophone problem'. A legitimate line of inquiry, it constitutes just one stroke of the brush on this broad canvas of civic disempowerment that seems to be the norm in Cameroon. Against this backdrop, the present chapter uses the model of 'electoral authoritarianism' as a conceptual framework to examine the 2007 legislative elections and the 2004 and 2011 Cameroon presidential elections. To this end, it analyzes recent electoral practices in Cameroon. Though a focus on electoral practices alone may be a thin understanding of democracy (Lindberg 2006: 21) and needs more context to evaluate it, it is important in so far as elections are the central arena of political struggle (Schedler 2006: 12).

Electoral authoritarian regimes allow for limited forms of pluralism in civil society and for multiparty elections, even if they seem to ratify the incumbents in power (Schedler 2006: 5). A preoccupation with 'culmination' outcomes (i.e., only the final outcomes) rather than 'comprehensive' outcomes that also take process into cognition[1] shows us the opacity that occurs mostly in the backstage of politics in the former (Schedler 2006: 17). Some measures, such as the enactment of discriminatory election laws and the banning of protest marches, benefit from the cover of law – invoking "the language of legality and public reason for their justification" (ibid.), and therefore the comfort of morality. Others are undercover activity or outright manipulation, like the alteration of electoral lists, the purchase and intimidation of voters, or the falsification of ballots on election day. Describing them as more decentralized activities ascribed to a myriad of public and private agents trying to do their job "without leaving public traces" (Schedler 2006: 9) seemingly absolves the state of superior responsibility, i.e., the doctrine that imputes to it responsibility for all malfeasance perpetrated by these elites or its failure to prevent them.[2] That the state has to be held to this standard is

1 See Amartya Sen (1999), *Development as Freedom*, New York: Anchor Books, p. 27.

2 Invoking this doctrine in the context of the genocide committed by the Janjaweed in Darfur, it has been argued that criminal responsibility inheres not only on this group but is also the responsibility of Sudanese authorities for failing to stop this. *Report of the International Commission of Inquiry on Darfur to the United Nations Secretary-General*, 25 January 2005, Geneva, pp. 36-37.

demonstrated by Juan Linz, who said that the breakdown of democratic processes is shaped not just by structural factors but also by the actions of 'relevant actors' and ultimately by 'the failure of leadership' (1978: 10-12).

By uncovering evidence of manipulation, pervasive and decisive in influencing electoral outcomes (Hartlyn & McCoy 2006: 42), carried out by 'relevant actors' with the (tacit) acquiescence of the state, this chapter seeks to "enter the hidden realm of authoritarian electioneering (that) constitutes an impenetrable black box (that) we can never almost whiten in its entirety" (Schedler 2006: 9). Though flawed and manipulated, the repetition of these electoral processes *can*, however, result in democratization (Lindberg 2009: 86). This is a possible outcome in countries where multiparty elections have been 'sufficiently institutionalized', that is, have convened at least four such presidential and four legislative elections during this period (Rakner & van de Walle 2009: 108). But multiparty election institutionalization, though a necessary condition, is not sufficient. The latter is contingent on the emergence of "a stable and numerically viable opposition (which) is a key requisite for horizontal accountability through legislative checks on executive power" (Rakner & van de Walle, 2009: 109) and can coordinate effectively, cooperate with civil society and mobilize voters by showing that electoral change (is) possible in the context of a vulnerable regime (Lindberg, 2009: 87). A constant struggle, it is rendered more difficult in contexts where the parliamentary opposition is insignificant and civil society organizations are weak (Alence, 2004: 177). Seemingly, Cameroon passes this litmus test, having convened Presidential elections in 1992, 1997, 2004 and 2011 and legislative elections in 1992, 1997, 2002 and 2007. But to what extent has the presence of the opposition enabled horizontal accountability rather than just a politics of presence?

Regime dynamics in electoral authoritarianism is also affected by external factors. In cases of high linkage [with....] Western or hegemonic states, "the density of economic, political, social, organizational and communication ties" and the leverage or the "vulnerability" of national governments to international pressure is high, as these governments can influence path dependence. As caveats, Steven Levitsky and Lucan Way (2006) have further posited that leverage is reduced "where there exist important competing issues or goals on Western political agendas" and the state has "access to political, economic and/or military support from an alternative regional power". It is the case, they argue, that vital assistance to autocracy in Cameroon from France, that has been a counter-hegemon in Africa, has enabled or reinforced authoritarian rule in that country (2006: 201). Konings uncritically accepts this 'realpolitik' thesis, advancing it as a justification for the ambivalent policy also of the United States toward the regime. Despite discontinuing the activities of the United States Development Agency (USAID) because of "the undemocratic political climate (that) did not permit aid to be utilized in the most judicious manner", the US continues to certify its democratic compliance (2004: 16), albeit that little evidence of change between then and 2011 was visible. Deconstruction of these hegemonic and counter-hegemonic states, I would argue, enables one to focus on the interests of power blocs that underlie the actual power institutionalized in these states (cf. Gramsci, in Castells 2004: 359). Plausibly, the capability of the Cameroonian electoral authoritarian regime to tap into some of these blocs or to graft itself onto these rhizomes that articulate policy begins to explain the ambivalence of US policy towards it.

Scripting Cameroon's democratic transition

The argument that Cameroon's so-called democratic transition was scripted by the ruling Cameroon People's Democratic Movement (CPDM) has been well rehearsed. After proclaiming 'no to imported models' and 'no to precipitated multipartyism', in the face of street protests, notably a ghost towns operation that exacerbated the state's financial crisis, the CPDM party-*cum*-regime realized that it had to "give up something in order not to lose everything" (Hirschmann 1965: 359). And so this hegemonic party reinvented itself; like a phoenix it was born again from its political ashes in 1990. Incumbency and claims to ontological superiority of its members, i.e., their monopoly over intelligence capital, provided it with an opportunity to seize control of the transition process. But more important were its ulterior motives. Only control of this transition could enable it redefine the terms of engagement, guaranteeing competition while not threatening its grip on and claims to power. Thus, it refused the call of the opposition for a sovereign national conference, the privileged site of collective political exorcism in the late 1980s-1990s in Africa. In lieu of this, it had summoned a tripartite conference in October 1991 where it accepted in principle the need for constitutional reform, the need for elections to ascertain the reconfiguration of the political landscape, while refusing the call for the creation of an independent electoral commission that was *sine qua non* for the participation of opposition parties in the process. But, perhaps realizing that money is a 'power resource' that helps in determining the range of strategic alternatives available to political actors (Przeworski 1991: 24), the regime corralled them by promising any political party participating the election 500 million francs CFA.

In conformity with the Tripartite Declaration, the first presidential elections of the transitional period were scheduled in October 1992, Paul Biya was the candidate of the CPDM, and his main rival was Ni John Fru Ndi of the Social Democratic Front (SDF) and a coalition of other opposition parties under the banner of the Union for Change. Control of the electoral process was assigned to the Ministry of Territorial Administration (MINAT) that had historically played this role in Cameroon. Arguably giving credence to Napoleon's thesis that "during a revolution whatever is ancient is the enemy", the Minister, Andze Tchoungui, convened a meeting of all provincial governors in September 2002, during which he insisted on *l'obligation du résultat*, i.e. the incumbent should win. Paul Biya had to win at least 60% of the votes cast in their province.[3] In effect, the regime was alive to Adam Przeworski's caution (1996: 6; 2000: 25) that mistakes sometimes occur in founding elections and the powers that be determined to make this a 'ritual of acclamation'. Because of this, the election was riddled with practices that compromised its freeness and fairness.

Arguably acknowledging this, the Chief Justice of the Supreme Court said in declaring the results that his hands were tied. In the 1992 elections Biya won 39.9% of the aggregate vote and Fru Ndi 35.9%. In passing a general verdict on the process, the US National Democratic Institute posited that Cameroon's electoral system was 'designed to fail'.[4] Arguably, attesting to the regime's lack of normative conviction of the superiority of liberal democracy as a mode of governance was its decision not to adopt the two-round majority system that is more favorable to presidential alternation and the nurturance of opposition parties, supposedly inspired by the French Fifth Republic. Rather, it was one of the few less democratic Francophone countries that opted for simple majority rules in presidential elections (Rakner & van de Walle 2009: 116).

It was in the wake of this election that political technologies that sustain electoral authoritarianism were honed. Paramount among them, and in compliance with the Tripartite Declaration, was a restructuring of the legal architecture designed to recognize Cameroon's politics of difference/belonging. Giving legal recognition to this in the preamble of the 1996 Constitution, scripted by the CPDM, the stipulation reads: "The state shall ensure the protection of minorities and shall preserve the rights of indigenous people in accordance with the law". No enforcement mechanism is provided, save for Article 57(3), providing that all chairpersons of Regional and Local government areas shall be indigenes and that the "bureau shall reflect the sociological components of the area". This constitutional fuzziness provided the regime with a "menu of manip-

3 Cited in letter of resignation (19 October 1992) from George Achu Mofor, Governor of the Eastern Province, to the President of the Republic.

4 National Democratic Institute (1993), *News Release*, 27 April.

ulation" (Schedler 2002) that serves as a risk avoidance strategy during elections, while underwriting the opposition parties' call for institutional reform that would end non-democratic restrictions. In this context, elections have become 'nested games' in "which strategic interaction *within* rules go hand in hand with strategic competition *over* rules" (Schedler 2006: 12-13).

Central to the struggle in this site of contestation has been the disagreement over the *plat de résistance* on the menu. In the view of the CDPM regime the Ministry of Territorial Administration (MINAT) could satisfy the hunger of all the political actors for free and fair elections – a claim that the opposition of course doubted *ab initio*. Using France as its referential horizon, MINAT argued that French administrators always performed this role adequately. Covered over in their submission is the fact that French administrators espouse *étatisme* as an organizational principle. Because of this political culture they have mutated into a 'universal class', in the Hegelian sense, sustaining the social order above fractious struggles in society. In the Cameroonian case, as part of *commandement*, they are beholden to the omnipotent regime-*cum*-state.[5] Furthermore, Cameroon, unlike other African countries, lacks a consensual code of conduct 'with sanctions to discourage breaches' for all stakeholders involved in the electoral process (Commonwealth Secretariat 2004: 20, 27). Absent these, civil servants in their 'conception of goods' have overwhelmingly privileged their vertical upward mobility concerns or survival over primary goods, which include, *inter alia,* rights and liberties (cf. Rawls 1971: 60-65). This skewed valuation fed the cynicism of the opposition. Even the promise of the Minister, Marafa Hamidou Yaya, prior to the 2004 Presidential elections that MINAT would "maintain neutrality and legality in the multiparty game, by putting in place within the time limit the various electoral commissions and providing them with the necessary logistical support for their functioning as well as procuring and distributing electoral material and documents in good time" (*Cameroon Tribune*, 5 February 2004, p. 4) did nothing to assuage their skepticism.

Against this backdrop, the opposition repeatedly insisted on the creation of an independent electoral commission. Their demand was echoed by international observers. In the wake of the 1997 Presidential elections, Commonwealth observers, for example, called for the creation of an 'impartial and autonomous institution' (Commonwealth Secretariat 2004: 14). In the face of overwhelming pressure, the Cameroonian government in December 2000 created the National Elections Observatory (NEO). Per Law No. 2000/016, amended by Law No 2003/015 of De-

[5] For details, see Mbembe 2001.

cember 2003, it was to be 'an independent body charged with supervising and controlling elections and referenda'. To this end it was mandated to monitor, report, and ensure compliance with the electoral law and 'to better promote a culture of accepting the verdict of the ballot box within political circles'. But the NEO did not live up to its mission. Exasperated, its coordinator for the North-West Province, adopting a Hegelian stance, posited that only 'divine intervention could bring about change among Cameroonians and ensure free elections.[6]

The Commonwealth, however, had a more rational explanation. Decrying the lack of sync between the ethic of conviction displayed (the government agreement to amend Law 2000/016) and the ethic of responsibility (its willingness to *implement* Law 2003/015), it noted:

> ... the law is not often implemented fully, even if it is at all, it is confusing. Key institutions which are supposed to exist do not exist. The Constitutional Council does not exist. The National Communications Council was dormant for six years. In many cases the law needs to be reviewed and amended. But while the discussion about changes are going on, it is critical that the existing law be implemented properly (2004: 44).

It is this concern that prompted the Council in the wake of the 2002 Municipal and Legislative elections to call for "the creation of an independent electoral commission responsible for all actions of the electoral process would command the confidence of all the interested parties" (Commonwealth Secretariat 2004: 14). Revealingly, while these criticisms were being made, the Cameroonian government was still vaunting the independence of the NEO.[7]

Continuous acrimony over an agreed-upon framework for elections – that even threatened social peace in the country – turned the gaze of the international community to Cameroon at a moment it was trying to reach the point that would enable it to benefit from Highly Indebted Poor Performance Countries (HIPPC) funds.[8] It was not surprising, therefore, that the National Episcopal Conference of the Catholic (CENC) Church, which had increasingly adopted liberation theology, en-

---

6 Cited in: http://www.leffortcamerounais.com/2007/07/high-time-for-d.html{\#}more.

7 See paper presented by Henri Eyebe Ayissi, Inspector General for Election Matter, Ministry of Territorial Administration and Decentralization, Cameroon, "Cameroon's Electoral System: Current Organization, New Challenges and Prospects" Conference of Commonwealth Chief Electoral Officers, New Delhi, February 24-26, 2005.

8 In effect, this was a "choice point", that is, a moment "in which the fortunes of the rulers and mass public vary inversely, activating citizens in way that require rulers to recalibrate electoral competitiveness (Mahoney, cited in William Case (2006), "Manipulative Skills: How Do rulers Control the Electoral Arena" in A. Schedler, ed., *Electoral Authoritarianism*, Boulder: Lynne Rienner, pp. 97-98.

tered the fray. Other civil society organizations, such as student, teacher and labor unions, though committed to liberalization, were more driven by group-specific agendas (Konings 2011). Sustained advocacy of democratization had been embraced principally by the churches, notably the Catholic Church, whose bishops issued several pastoral letters to this effect and which created Justice and Peace Committees across the country. Its implication in this process, even if by default, should not be seen as anomalous, as people in times of uncertainty tend to increasingly turn to spiritual leaders for moral frames in religious as well as secular matters (Gifford 1998).

Arguably, further enhancing the moral authority of the Church in popular consciousness was the deception with the SDF party as an agent of change. Abandoning the insurrectional strategy that had been its claim to fame – enabling Ni John Fru Ndi, its chairman, to be seen as *le président de la rue publique* rather than *république*, this party participated in the 1996 municipal and parliamentary elections. It won some seats in these state institutions, which it decided to take up on the pretext that it would open 'a new front against the regime'. But this decision sparked off polemics[9] in its ranks, as those who opted to stay in the trenches (re)presented this as taking a seat at the table with a view to participating in the 'politics of the belly'. This judgment looked prescient, as indeed the accusation that SDF parliamentarians were taking bribes (*gombo* in Cameroonian speak) became commonplace in public space. Not even its chairman J. Fru Ndi, who had been endowed with messianic qualities, was spared. Sani Alhadji, the estranged chairman of the SDF in the Central Province, accused him of using and (mis)appropriating most of the public subsidy of 456 million CFA francs meant to finance the party's participation in the 2002 elections: "He used most of the money to recover his twelve-month salary arrears and to buy two sports utility vehicles (SUVs) for private use, while allocating only a meager sum of 75.000 francs CFA to the constituencies for campaign purposes" (cited in Konings 2004: 17). In other words, this validated the *guarantismo* thesis, which says that there is an inverse relationship between the willingness of potential opponents of a regime to accept potential setbacks in democratic contestation and their access to specific

[9] Polemics, Foucault notes, is a powerful political model that "defines alliances, recruits partisans, united interests or opinions, represents a party, establishes the other as the enemy, an upholder of oppressed interests against which one must fight until the moment that this enemy is destroyed or either surrenders or disappears (1994), "The Care of the Self as a Practice of Freedom" in J. Bernauer & D. Rassmussen, eds, *The Final Foucault*, Cambridge, MA: MIT Press. In the case of the SDF, this is borne out by the fissiparous tendencies that emerged since it this moment (Konings 2004: 16-19).

guarantees offered by institutions (DiPalma 1990). Contributing gravitas to the perception of a pliant SDF, as complicit was Fru Ndi's unilateral decision to reverse the decision of its National Executive Committee to boycott state institutions in protest of the massive rigging that occurred during the elections (see Konings 2004: 18).

It is notable that these indictments were extensively carried by the alternative press, whose attitude toward the SDF had been one of *dramaturgiia*. This political technology involves the reshaping of politics as a highly choreographed event, the concoction of stories to shift political events in one's favor or to sell a particular politician or party.[10] Since the SDF had been a main beneficiary, their editorial shift was all the more remarkable. Ascertaining the press's contribution to the formation of a new consensus – turning this party into a damaged brand – that was inter-subjectively validated is difficult. But it kept the scandals alive. New ones, such as claims that Biya had paid for the medical evacuation of Fru Ndi's wife to Switzerland (where she died later), as well as paying for the costs of the burial, cropped up in quick succession.[11] Enigmatically if not revealingly, even the *Socialist Chronicle,* reputedly close to the party, also joined in the fray. Scandals, it has been argued, "... are struggles over symbolic power in which trust and reputation are at stake" (Thompson 2000: 244). And in the information age, symbolic power – i.e., the capacity to shape peoples' minds – is a fundamental source of power, and in this, scandal politics becomes a weapon of choice for the struggle (cf. Castells 2004: 396). As these scandals gained traction, the SDF was stripped of its symbolic power (Konings 2004: 305-306).

With the Church then left as the only credible driver for change, this institution finally made a proposal for a permanent independent body, endowed with the requisite administrative and financial autonomy, for running elections in Cameroon. The buy into this project from civil society, political parties as well as the diplomatic community, was immediate. It was against this backdrop that the Cameroonian government requested for the relevant document and initiated consultations with other stakeholders in the electoral process. Great was the surprise when it

---

[10] See Andrew Wilson (2007), "Virtual politics in the Soviet bloc" in *Open Democracy,* 17 July, p. 2. For the case of Cameroon, see Lyombe Eko (2004), "Hear all evil, see all evil, rail against all evil: *Le Messager* and the politics of resistance in Cameroon", in J. Mbaku & J.Takoungang, eds, *The Leadership Challenge in Africa: Cameroon under Paul Biya*, Trenton, NJ: Africa World Press.

[11] For another case in point, see the claim that Fru Ndi was given 500 million francs CFA by Biya so as scuttle the attempts of the opposition parties to form a coalition in the 2004 Presidential elections, cf. Xavier L. Deutchou, "Présidentielle 2004: Paul Biya a-t-il remis 500 millions à Fru Ndi?" *Mutations,* 22 février 2007.

introduced a bill in December 2006 to the National Assembly for the creation of *Elections Cameroun* (ELECAM), the independent body to oversee the electoral process. Reminiscent of previous bills, it was scripted by the state (party) and failed to recognize the fact that sovereignty belonged to the people. Notably, it empowered the President to appoint all members of ELECAM for a three-year period and renewable. Not only did this move help to attenuate democracy, it has actually contributed to the slide into one-party rule, as in Mozambique (Manning, 2010).

Disturbing also was a stipulation that ELECAM would function simultaneously with the NEO. Its Article 42(3) provided: while ELECAM is being created (a process envisaged to last between two and eighteen months), NEO and other state structures endowed with the competence to run elections shall continue to function.

Despite the difficulty in discerning intentionality, this smacked of dissemblance in popular consciousness. After all, in everyday life, it is said 'fool me once shame on you, and fool me twice shame on me'. The regime had already fooled the people once when it inserted a similar clause in the 1996 Constitution that it would be applied simultaneously with the 1972 Constitution. This strange legal architecture and the regime's failure to pass enabling legislation for the 1996 Constitution provided it with the cover of law, if not the comfort of morality, as it liberally applied articles from the old constitution. This disabled the 'codifying trust', which results "not only or even primarily from the codification of appropriate behavior in formal laws and regulation but from (shared) understandings of what is moral and appropriate behaviour" (Halpern 2005: 241). Against the backdrop, the British High Commissioner to Cameroon, Syd Maddicott, cautioned: "...the key to success of ELECAM will not be the letter of the law which will be finally promulgated but the political will of the government to make it work".[12]

From the foregoing, it is evident that the regime retained total control of the architecture of Cameroon's electoral process. But how does the edifice look from the inside? The 2005 Commission for Africa report (the *Blair Report*) proposed that an adequate gauge should be the 'sovereignty of people', and this required an investment in people as a mutual confidence building measure that would help reconnect people to the state.[13] To ascertain the extent to which a government realizes this, one has to look inside the electoral edifice. It should be free of any

---

[12] Cited in Yemti Ndienla (2007), "Cameroon: electoral body sparks debate", in *Ohmy News International*, at: http://english.ohmynews.com/articleview/article{_}view.asp?menu=cl.

[13] Commission for Africa (2005), *Our Common Interest: Report of the Commission for Africa*, March, at www.commissionforarfica.org.

structural flaws and actions of relevant political actors that would contribute to variations in the 'opportunity costs' of voting.

Electoral practices and outcomes in Cameroon

In October 2004 Cameroon held its third Presidential elections since transitioning to party democracy. Biya, the candidate from the CPDM, had been depicted shortly before the 2004 elections in *Africa Confidential* as "the most invisible President in Africa, who does not govern at all rather than badly, hanging above a society where it is permissive for everyone to take his share and leave the President alone. Everyone from the junior civil servant to the judge is preoccupied with rent seeking".[14] Despite this poor scorecard, he won with 70.92% of the votes in 2004. This performance proved that not even elite deal making that would have enabled the opposition to present a single candidate in this election would have made it a 'tipping game' (van de Walle 2006: 77). Biya's performance may constitute impressionistic evidence in chalking this up to a free fall in the popularity capital of the opposition. But this rush to judgement is tempered by the flies that were in the electoral ointment. The Commonwealth Observer group noted that the election process lacked the 'necessary credibility' (2004: 44), while CENC noted that "...the sovereignty of Cameroonians was in question (CENC 2005). But according to the President of the NEO that process had only lapses that were attributable to "dysfunctioning rather than fraud", while the official government paper *Cameroon Tribune* qualified the process as "regular and transparent" (14 October 2004, p. 8).

The next elections were held in July 2007. Undeterred by scant delegitimization of his regime as result of electoral contestation and its lack of performance towards attaining legitimation, Biya called on Cameroonians to give the CPDM a resounding victory in these parliamentary elections. In the 2002 parliamentary elections, this party had won 109 out of the 180 seats in the Assembly. Considering this as a slim majority, in a speech marking the official opening of the campaign Biya argued that only a clear majority would enable 'democratic consolidation' and 'give an impulse to the economy'. Thus, *contra* the claims of Lise Rakner and Nicolas van de Walle, this legislative election was not going to be a sideshow (2009: 112). Already ruffled by the Parliamentary investigations into corrupt practices by CPDM barons, initiated at the behest of the SDF Parliamentarians in 1999, the regime was bent on reversing its accountability deficits and

[14] Cited in *La Nouvelle Expression*, no. 1252, 21 April 2004.

promoting a veneer of democracy. But this was a choice point for Cameroonians, caused by a perception that corruption had metastasized among state functionaries. Between 1998 and 2004, the state lost 1,845 billion CFCA to this practice, an amount that was equivalent its 2002 budget (CONAC 2010: 21-22). Unlike in Ghana where this pervasivenesof corruption was a political liability and partially accounted for the defeat of the incumbent party (Gyimah-Boadi 2009), the CPDM won the election. The opposition's legitimacy was seriously dented by its penchant for mismanagement and scandals which it had portrayed as the hallmarks of the CPDM. A case in point was the SDF mayor of Andek who was accused by the District officer of administrative ineptness and converting the Council into a prebend.[15] So admittedly, while serving in local office for the opposition can be a boon, helping it build legitimacy as it participates in the distribution of resources for providing public goods (Rakner & van de Walle 2009: 118), it can also be a bane. Rent seeking, though micro-level behaviour, has negative macro-level implications. Exacerbating the repercussions of this perception of the opposition was its exclusion from the competitive clientelistic network, i.e., the opportunity to use state resources for patronage purposes. That District officers appointed by MINAT who are essentially peons of the CPDM have powers of oversight and veto over these councils denies the opposition the opportunity to distribute resources to its constituents and grow and sustain its support base, "both of which are indispensable when running for national office" (Rakner & van de Walle 2009: 117). Since this caused the opposition to suffer from a legitimacy deficit, the overwhelming consensus among Cameroonians that the CPDM would win the election. Surprising, however, was its wide margin of victory, which caused the chances of democratization by election to further recede. Table 1 shows the repartitioning of seats in the Assembly following this election.

As is evident from the discussion *supra*, this outcome cannot be chalked to the popularity of the CPDM. Rather it was pre-scripted. Fraud marred the whole process, leading the Embassies of the Netherlands, United Kingdom, and United States to observe in a joint communiqué that "... on the whole, these elections represent a missed opportunity for Cameroon" (16 August 2007). Contrary to this view, Marafa Yaya of MINAT claimed the absence of "... any major dysfunctioning susceptible of affecting its outcome. Minor incidents that were reported were quickly resolved. All dispositions for the verdict reflect the wishes of the electorate" (in *Cameroon Tribune,* 23 July 2007). This disagreement was signif-

---

[15] See Julius Fondong, "How the SDF can end its reverses and win all future elections", http: //weeklypost.tripod.com.

Table 1. Results of the 2007 parliamentary elections (Source: *Cameroon Tribune*, 23 July 2007)

Party	Number of Seats (180)
Cameroon People's Democratic Movement (RDPC)	153
Social Democratic Front (SDF)	16
National Union for Democracy and Progress (UNDP)	06
Cameroon Democratic Union (UDC)	04
Progressive Movement (MP)	01

icant for the United Nations Development Fund (UNDP): the United States and the Netherlands had sought make the elections credible by giving NGOs over 52 million francs CFA for a voter registration drive and for 'electoral governance'.[16] Not conceding either to the diplomatic community or to MINAT a monopoly over 'the protocols of pedigree' in this community of assessment (cf. Appadurai 2003: 11), only a careful examination of the whole electoral process could enable one to uncover the truth. Were the elections free and fair or did the regime benefit from a 'menu of manipulation'?

Analyzing the freeness and fairness of the 2007 parliamentary elections

Despite several population censuses, the last one conducted in November 2005, Cameroon's population is still not exactly known. According to estimates in 2007, its total population was 18 million. Using this as a base figure, the then American ambassador in Cameroon, Niels Marquardt, argued before the 2007 elections that their credibility would be in doubt if the electoral roll was less than eight million.[17] Figures always engender polemics in Cameroon. In the political grammar, this is referred to as *la guerre des chiffres*. Not surprising therefore, the opposition before the elections claimed that less than three million people had registered to vote. Ultimately, the MINAT claimed that five million people had registered

[16] See Yaouba Djaligue, "Inscriptions sur les listes électorales: Plus de 52 millions pour la sensibilisation", *Cameroun Tribune*, 2 April 2007.

[17] Cited in Ntemfac Ofege (2007), "It is time to walk away". Registration was like going through the eye of the needle. See: www.postwatchmagazine.com/files/time_to_walk_away1.pdf. In Yaounde where this process was supposedly easier, the American Ambassador complained that about a dozen of his Cameroonian staff was unable to go through this eye, albeit several attempts.

for the elections. This was just sparring; the real fight was over the number of people that actually voted. Marafat Yaya claimed that 62% of the electorate actually went to the polls.[18] The opposition put out a much lower figure, that was essentially corroborated by CENC when it noted the "... high voter apathy ... especially in urban centers where many failed to turn up in their different polling stations".[19] More damning was the claim of a United States diplomat that only 25% of the voters went to the polls.[20] Arguably, Cameroonians opted to vote with their feet rather than with their hands. Explaining this option, a student in the University of Yaounde noted: "We live in Cameroon and are aware of what happens. Why should I go to waste my time when I know that the results have already been fixed?"[21] Simply put, this was an admission that increasing opportunity costs of political participation had caused people to suffer from the redound effect. Prompting this increase was a sophisticated 'menu of manipulation'.

A cursory look at Cameroon's political grammar shows that it is replete with loaded concepts such as *village electoral* – which acknowledges that while people should be fully integrated in the place where they live, there is always *un autre chez soi* (another home area) – and *ethnofascisme*.[22] Foregrounding society's attempts to negotiate ethnic/tribal differences, they also feed off laws that acknowledge this perception. For example, Cameroon's Electoral Code (Law No. 91/020 of December 16, 1991), accepts the *autochtone/allogene* binary; its goal being to relegate opposition parties that have an ethnoregional basis to their home base. Specifically its Article 11 introduces differential entry costs to political participation. Unlike autochthones whose right to vote are uncircumscribed, allogenes are required to reside in the constituency in which they seek to vote for at least six months. Only after this can they be issued with a residence permit that enables them to register to vote (Jua 2001: 39-40). Issued by local administrators and chiefs, this was a Cameroonian rendition of *Staatsklugheitslehre* – that is Machiavelli's famous dictum that "princes should delegate to others the enforcement

18 See for example, François Bambou, "Comment le government organise la disaffection des électeurs" *La Nouvelle Expression*, 27 juillet 2007.

19 See: "Communique of the National Episcopal Conference on the July 22 elections in Cameroon".

20 Cf. www.leffortcamerounais.com/2007/08/us-embassy-disa,html{\#}more.

21 Cited in Jean-Bruno Tagne, "Elections: les jeunes boudent les listes électorales", in *Mutations,* 14 mars 2007.

22 For an explication of these concepts see, Gabriel Nlep in *La Nouvelle Expression*, special issue on "Minorités, autochtones, allogènes et démocratie", 1996: 18, and Mono Ndjana (1997), "Anti-plaidoyer pour les ethnies", in F. Eboussi Boulaga, ed., *La Démocratie à l'Épreuve du Tribalisme*. Yaounde: Friedrich Ebert Stiftung.

of unpopular measures and keep in their own hands the distribution of favors" (1961: 106). Administrators driven by *l'obligation du résultat* now used this law as a pretext for the wholesale disenfranchisement of people suspected of militating in Opposition parties. Whole neighborhoods or *quartiers* were disqualified because using an 'imaginative geography' that engendered and nurtured an intra-urban orientalism. In the Nylon neighborhood in Bafoussam, the chief refused to register Anglophones (CENC 2004: 28). Even this identity as a litmus test for disqualification is contingent as evidenced in the Anglophone part of the country. In the South-West Province, North-Westerners were asked to go and vote *chez soi*. Yet returning *chez soi* was no guarantee for voting, because on their arrival there they were told that they had to vote in their place of residence (Konings 2004: 14). Though correct, this argument does not interrogate the role of party identity in this disqualification process.

Similar to Harry Potter's 'sorting hat' used to allocate people to the various houses in the school of wizardry and which never fails, *allogènes* are sorted into *opposants* and *RDPCistes*. The latter, allowed to register and vote in their place of residence even in the absence of residence permits, can also return and vote *chez soi*. But for the former, their *terroir* (place of belonging) becomes their *territorium*, the place from which they are chased away during elections. Chased away during elections, they are bussed to their villages to vote. Arguably, this explains the provenance of electoral charters or bussing whereby people are transported to their *chez soi* to vote. Bussing, however, is not specific to Cameroon or the Third World. In the 2006 elections in the United States, for example, the Republican Party recruited homeless people from Philadelphia and paid them $100 each to pass out voter guides in Maryland, aimed at confusing black Democrats in that state to vote for the Governor Robert L. Ehrlich Jr. and U.S. Senate candidate Michael S. Steele, both Republicans.[23]

The commonality of bussing across various countries does not mean that it produces the same effect. In the United States it does not impact on the outcome of the process, and there is jurisprudence to show that bussing for electoral ends is punishable.[24] In Cameroon, it has been normalized, as evidenced by the use of the radio to convene people for this purpose. The implication of the opposition parties in this practice, notably the SDF,[25] shows that it has been banalized and is

23 See *Washington Post*, November 10, 2006, p. B01.

24 Eric Lipton & Ian Urbina, "In 5-year effort, scant evidence of voter fraud", at: www.nytimes.com/2007/0412/washington/12fraud.htmlpagewanted=3\&th\&emc=th.

25 See *Le Messager*, "Elections 2007: Des observateurs indépendents scrutent les causes de la débâcles de l'opposition", 25 July 2007.

now another site of contestation. As a result, the size of these electoral charters has grown phenomenally. For example, during the 2007 elections, about 2000 people were bussed in Bangangte and were lodged in hostels and entertained by musicians at night.[26] Remarkably, most of them were *allogènes* who could vote and vote several times. Its entrepreneurs are bold and scorn scandal, as attested by the threat of one of them to break the camera of a journalist if he filmed his charter. Neither are they deterred law, notably Articles 122 and 123 of the Penal Code, which provide for the punishment of voters who embark on fraudulent registration or take benefit from multiple registrations to vote several times. Such clauses do not serve as deterrent. Its normalization cannot be ascribed to the state as a lame Leviathan argument, but to political expediency or Nietzsche's 'will to power'. In other words, its focus was on cumulative outcomes.

Dissimulation which contributed to increasing the opportunity costs of voting was used to further deny the opposition a level playing field in some constituencies. People who succeeded in registering were unable to recover their voting cards because District Officers consciously hid them.[27] Going through this hurdle was not a guarantee that one could vote. It was commonplace to rotate the names of voters from precinct to precinct, moving them further away from their homes. And when handicapped, it was no use participating. Those pledging to vote for the CPDM did not face such pressure or constraints ...

Vote buying also pervaded the whole process. In one flagrant case, Cavayé Yéguié Djibril, the President of the National Assembly, promised the Presidents of precincts 300.000 francs CFA for the results to be skewed in favor of the CPDM, or 100.000 francs CFA to any precinct that voted 100% for the CPDM. That he made this declaration in the glare of television,[28] undeterred by its criminal aspects, is clear evidence of the non-level playing electoral field. Arguably, similar practices by the opposition might be pointed out in an argument to exonerate him. But more problematic was Djibril's implication in electoral heists in Tokombéré, using workers from the National Assembly that came to his village solely for this purpose.[29] Several other CPDM barons also deployed functionaries and resources for partisan purposes, despite the fact that this violated Article 40 of

---

26 See *ibid*.

27 As a case in point, the Divisional Officer for Mfoundi issued a communiqué on 15 July 2007 that voter cards had been available since 12 July 2007. Strangely, this was not the case when people went to this office.

28 See Christophe Mvondo, "Les evêques dénoncent Cavaye" in *La Nouvelle Expression*, 16 juillet 2007. Section 123 of the Criminal Code makes it a punishable offence to buy the vote of one or several electors by promising jobs to them in the public or private sector, gifts and other favors.

29 Cf. www.quotidienmutations.info/mutations/aout/1186389437.php.

Decree no. 94/199 of October 1994, which requires that civil servants be apolitical. Similarly, to promote free and fair elections, the Inter-Parliamentary Union prescribes that all states should "... ensure the separation of party and state and establish conditions for competition in legislative elections on an equitable basis". In its 2002 report, Transparency International attributed these abuses to a preoccupation among civil servants to protect their posts.[30]

Invariably, these malpractices elicited a myriad of complaints submitted to the Constitutional Court, which has jurisdiction over electoral disputes, including those from the opposition. But failure to comply with Article 49 of the 2004 Law on the Organization and Functioning of this court caused most of them to be rejected. It stipulates that all electoral petitions must bear the name of the petitioner and cannot be submitted by a political party. Invoking this proviso left the candidates in a legal conundrum. Most of their complaints were predicated on Article 47 on the Law, regulating the election of Members of Parliament and not requiring the detailed information as in the 2004 Law. In case of a conflict of laws, it is a principle of law that *specific* law overrides *general* law. But this principle was turned on its head. More disturbing was the variable treatment of these petitions by the Constitutional Court. Whereas it rejected requests from the opposition purportedly due to its failing to comply with Article 49 of the 2004 Law, those from the CPDM, with similar lapses, were admitted. Notable is the case of Eboumbou Patience from Wouri West constituency: her compliant, contrary to the law, was submitted by the CPDM, and her name was not cited in it.[31] Because of this variable legal logic, only five petitions for the cancellation of the election results were finally accepted.

The refusal to implement a recommendation of the National Vote Counting Commission (NVCC) canceling elections in Mayo Tsanaga also contributed to a decline in confidence in the CC. In one case in point, Mr. Elias Gondji, an outgoing CPDM MP who was standing for reelection, signed documents acknowledging his implication in the rectification, viz. falsification, of electoral results in precinct C at Boula. Admittedly, since this tampering did not impact on the overall outcome of the results in the constituency, the recommendation of the NVCC was disproportionate to the crime. But to the extent that is was meant to promote 'best practices', the goal of the recommendation was essentially pre-emptive.[32] Its

---

30 Cited in Valentin Simeon Zinga, "Le RDPC: la campagne illégale", *La Nouvelle Expression*, 18 juillet 2007.

31 *Le Messager*, "Fraude électorale: la gifle", 9 August 2007.

32 See Jean François Belibi, "Législatives 2007: La Cour Suprême sanctionne les fraudes du RDPC", in *Mutations*, 8 August 2007.

rejection by the Court only reaffirmed the perception in popular consciousness that the judiciary lacks independent agency, and is seen as a Trojan horse of the Executive. Article 38(3) of Cameroon's Constitution arrogates to the President the power to guarantee its independence as well as to appoint members of the bench and the legal department. It lacks basic guarantees, such as 'permanency in office', which US founding father A. Hamilton in *The Federalists Papers* argued was "... an indispensable ingredient in its constitution and in a great measure to the citadel of public justice and the public security". Denied "all possible care to enable it to defend itself against attack" (*The Federalists Papers* 1961: 465-466), it is subservient to the President. It is this relationship that largely explains the underdevelopment of electoral jurisprudence in Cameroon while discounting the social costs of political opportunism.

Information asymmetries caused by unequal access to public electronic media (radio and television, Internet) also compromised the fairness of the 2004 and 2007 elections. With a view to guaranteeing equity, Decree no. 92/030 of February 1992 provided that the time allocated to political parties in the media is to be proportionate to its representation. As a proviso, no party should have less than five minutes on television and less than ten minutes on radio daily during the campaign period. But the daily time accorded the parties by the Minister of Communications was: CPDM twenty minutes and ten minutes, SDF nineteen minutes and less than ten minutes and the National Union for Progress and Development (NUDP) seventeen minutes and less than ten minutes on television and radio respectively. Most of the other parties had six or seven minutes on radio and about three seconds on television. That is, besides the CPDM, SDF and NUDP, the total time given each of the other parties on national television for the two-week duration of the campaign was one minute twenty-four seconds! That was the equivalent of about a fifth of the time accorded to the CPDM each day. If access to the media is power, then denying them access disempowers them and contributes to their political irrelevance.

Exacerbating this inequity was the tendency to ban all political programs on private televisions during the elections. For example, 'Cartes sur tables', broadcast by STV, was suspended for the duration of the campaign.[33] Failing willing compliance, the state resorted to the use of symbolic violence, such as the threat to withdraw the licenses of media outlets. The overall goal is of course to prevent programs presenting another imaginary and therefore threatening the regime's monopoly control of 'truth production' space. That its truth is not 'really real' was

[33] See Decision No. 153/Mincom/Sg/Dag of 12 July 2007.

evident during the 2004 Presidential elections, when Cameroon Radio and Television (CRTV) on the even of the elections announced the withdrawal of Adamu Ndam Njoya, the candidate for a coalition of opposition parties running under the banner of the National Coordination for Reform and Reconstruction (Commonwealth Secretariat 2004: 30).

Given that similar harsh measures are not often imposed on the written press, it could be contended that the opposition could use this outlet to market its messages. But its effectiveness is constrained by two factors. It lacks the speed of the electronic media, and its access is limited to the literate. Not even the emergence of *Parlementaires débout*, people who read and interpret newspapers and other genres of political literature, can effectively reverse this prejudice.

The 2011 presidential elections

As indicated above, CPDM won an overwhelming majority, even if by foul, that Biya sought. *Contra* claims that this majority insulates the incumbent regime from political insecurity needed to enable it focus on the country's long term development prospects (cf. Alence, 2004: 166), it engendered political entropy in the transition process. Further eroding any powers this pliant institution had, its role now was reduced to rubber stamping Presidential initiatives. A disaffected CPDM legislator referred to it thus "more of a formality façade that conceals a stinking lethal mess, (whose) members, like maggots, feed without interval for fattening (*sic)*"[34] and arguably, maintaining Biya in power was the prime aim on its agenda.

To this end, the government submitted to it a bill amending some articles of the Constitution, specifically, Article 6.2 lifting presidential term limits that were currently fixed at two terms. Furthermore, Article 53.1 proposed that only the National Assembly and the Senate with a 4/5 vote can initiate high treason charges against the President, a power that was arrogated to the High Court of Justice in the 1996 Constitution. And as if to enable moral hazards, the proposed amendment to Article 53.3 gave the President immunity for acts committed in office, even after he leaves office. Gregoire Owona, the Assistant Secretary-General of the CPDM justified this thus: "Uncertainty is necessary in our system now".[35] Arguably, the latter was to preempt a rendition of what was happening to Frederick Chiluba, the Zambian President of who was being accused of misappropriating $46 million

34 mhttp://groups.yahoo.com/group/camnetwork/message/252461.

35 Conversation with Economic & Political officer, US Embassy, Yaounde, US Embassy, "Cameroon: Constitution revision moving forward": 08Yaounde346, 9 April 2008).

from the state.[36] Little wonder then that the amendments from a SDF parliamentarian who was a member of the Constitutional Laws Committee to cancel the proposed Article 6.2, adopt a two-round ballot for the Presidential elections, and maintain liability for unlawful acts committed by the president while in office were summarily rejected.[37]

Following the adoption of the governmental proposals *in toto*, the people were excluded from the process when the President ratified the amended constitution. People disempowerment hinged on a conviction that to avoid any show of force, as happened during the February 2008 in which scores were killed by soldiers, they will have to accept this as a *fait accompli*.[38] Thus, in this decision-making process in which people assessed their political strategies according to the alternatives feasible (Przeworski, 1991), the memory of the costs of state violence made exit or tolerance an acceptable option. Against this backdrop, Javier Puyol, the European Union Delegate was to caution against predicating the long-term stability of the country on a person rather than institutional basis: "It is important to make a difference between short term political stability imposed by security forces and the country where the people do not participate in decision-making."[39]

Arguably, the preoccupation with certainty also caused the government to introduce Bill no. 884/PJL/AN to amend and supplement certain provisions of the December 2006 creating ELECAM. Notable was Section 6.2, stripping it of the powers to "publish presidential, legislative and senatorial election trends". Purportedly, this was to align its provisions with Article 48(1) of the Constitution which stipulates "the Constitutional Court shall ensure the regularity of presidential elections, parliamentary election and referendum operations. It shall proclaim the results thereof". Furthermore, Section 40 provided that "state services shall collaborate with, and assist Elections' political impartiality" and ensure technical reliability of the mandate and structure of ELECAM, as was the practice in countries that were making some democratic advances such as Burkina Faso (Santiso & Loada, 2003:414). But this bill had a perverse effect. According to Marafa Hamidou Yaya, the Minister of Territorial Administration (MINAT), a revised version was the personal option of Paul Biya who had been presented with two options –

36 Remarkably, Chiluba also tried to revise the constitution to enable him stand for a third term to no avail. http://www.economist.com/node/14270119

37 Arguably, the intent behind these proposals was their nuisance value. In this Committee of twenty, there were only two opposition MPs and their CPDM counterparts were not narcissistic to vote in favor of these proposals, US Embassy, *op. cit.*

38 In *Ibid*.

39 See Tansa Musa, "Crackdown in Cameroon: Constitutional Amendment opposed", at http://africanpress.me/2008/02/24/crackdown-in-cameroon-constitution-amendment-oppossed.

one in which ELECAM would be independent and another in which it would share concurrent powers with MINAT.[40]

Undaunted by denunciations of this charade by the opposition and civil society as well as foreign countries committed to promoting democratic governance, the bill was passed into law. Plausibly, context provides a window to the intentions of the regime. Instructive was the case of Ivory Coast where full powers over the registration process led to trying to surreptitiously add some 465,000 'contentious ones' to the electoral lists.[41] Furthermore, it was also the IEC that declared Alassane Ouattara the winner of the November 2010 Presidential election in Ivory Coast. Political instability spread when the Constitutional Council reversed the result and declared Laurent Gbagbo, incumbent President as the winner. Because of the ensuing stalemate and the spectre of killings or even genocide, the UN sanctioned the intervention on the basis of the 'responsibility to protect' (R2P), which empowers the international community to protect civilians because of the failure of local government to do so. That the subtext can be regime change in some contexts is borne out by the recent cases of Ivory Coast and Libya.

Alive to this dynamic and to the possibility of even recalcitrant members ELECAM being flies in its electoral ointment, the Cameroon regime stacked the deck in its favor by naming mostly CPDM stalwarts to this body. The European Union decried the partisan nature of this membership while UN High Commissioner indicated its reticence to support it until it could prove to be independent. Piqued by these reactions, Cameroon's Foreign Minister Henri Eyebe Ayissi cautioned foreign partners to "...exert self-discipline and refrain from discrediting national institutions" because they do not conform to dominant political or cultural models, which he saw as a metaphor for "a new form of the civilizing mission".[42] Arguably, the regime could put up its thumb at the international community because it had not reached what Choi Jung-jin, the UN Chief of Mission in Ivory Coast, described as the 'breaking point'.[43]

It was against this backdrop that President Biya convened the Presidential election in October 2011, in which he and twenty-two other candidates, notably Fru Ndi, participated. Unable to adopt an ecumenical approach, the opposition

---

40 See http//www.camer.be/index1.php?art=15788\&rub=6:1.

41 Adam Nossiter, "Many in Ivory Coast may be left out from the vote, *New York Times*, 7 February 2010.

42 Janet Garvey, US Ambassador to Cameroon, in "Cameroon's minister criticizes diplomats on ELECAM", 09Yaounde175, at http://wikileaks.org/cable/2009/09Yaounde175.html.

43 "Ivory Coast: The UN intervention to break the impasse", at http://www.guardian.co.uk/world/2011/apr/05/ivory-coast-un-intervention.

could not designate a single candidate that provided the prospect for alternation in power, as had at least been the case in 1992. As added value, this strategy would have contributed to 'liberalizing electoral outomes' (Howard & Roessler 2006: 375-376). The people questioned the motives of this election because of its ambivalence, specifically citing a lack of integrity of the electoral process, and because the SDF initially asking people to boycott registration. That the state promised 30 million FCFA to every candidate participating in this election only helped to entrench popular skepticism. Capturing this, a cigarette vendor in Kondengui, a neighborhood in Yaounde noted: "We are hungry. This campaign does not interest us. They (candidates) are all thieves".[44]

Ironically, some of the opposition parties participating in the election saw a rationale for synergistic action only after the vote when seven candidates, including Fru Ndi (SDF) and Adamou Ndam Njoya (Cameroon Democratic Union), issued the Yaounde Declaration, a jeremiad against ELECAM, and asked for the elections to be annulled. But by some convoluted logic, the regime blanketed the airwaves with claims that the opposition 'had declared war'. It was not fortuitous that at this moment press reports also emerged that a container belonging to an Anglophone businesswoman in Bamenda had been discovered at the Douala Port. In Cameroon the Anglophone/Francophone binary is imposed on all other cleavages and prompts a reconfiguration of political coalitions. Undeterred, the opposition petitioned the CCfor a cancellation of the elections, even though to no avail. Overall, all of these maneuvers showed that elections had become a safety valve for regulating societal discontent and confining the opposition (Brownlee 2009: 519). This provided the political decor for the proclamation of the results. Biya garnered 77.9% of the votes, with his closest challenger Fru Ndi getting only 10.7%.

This was a remarkable performance for 'the most invisible President in Africa, who does not govern at all rather than badly'. Attributing this to a shortfall in the popularity capital/credit of the opposition though correct will not be conclusive. Smarting from the redound effect following the period of contestation, Cameroon like Mozambique became a 'low-information democracy', arguably peopled by 'uncritical citizens' (Manning 2010: 162). And the state was committed to promoting this. Not surprisingly therefore, drawing lessons from the Egyptian twitter revolution, the Minister of Communication banned twitter in February 2011 and threatened to block all other social networking devices. Censorship was ramped

44 See: http://www.cameroon-info.net/stories/0,29961,@,cameroun-indifference-et-scepticime-pour-la-presidentielle.html.

up when a broadcaster on Cameroon Radio and Television was suspended for playing a song '50 years in power', by Longue Longue, a Cameroonian musician. In the lyrics, he refers to this as 'the African disease' before noting that 'they rule African people as if they are beasts/they lead the people as if they are blind/they don't respect people/we don't want them anymore.'

Even the alternative press was muzzled as indicated by the closing of Equinoxe, one of the thirty private radio and television stations in the country for broadcasting illegally. Its crime however was *lèse majesté* because it broadcast an alternative view critical of the regime's Constitutional revision proposal. Closing down these stations is easy because of the nebulous zone in which they operate. Administrative officials grant them 'administrative tolerance' while examining their applications for licenses interminably. Existential threats to this press are further compounded resource shortages. And so rather than deny the state normative control over the definition of meaning, it is now seen as complicit. This was brought into relief during the Presidential election when Belinga Eboutou, the Director of the Civil Cabinet at the Presidency distributed to each of them amounts varying between 10 and 15 million FCFA during the Presidential election. This smacked of an effort to co-opt this press because in Cameroon's political grammar, 'the mouth that is eating does not speak'. Revealingly also, they received this funding while that promised to the candidates for their campaigns had still not been disbursed by the state treasury.

Seemingly, only the Catholic Church that had issued several Episcopal letters in support of transition to democracy was left to confront this state. And people deferred to it because of their penchant to increasingly turn to religious leaders for moral frames even in secular matters in times of uncertainty. Its commitment to this process was unimpeachable because CENC also belonged to the group of African Church leaders who made recommendations following a 2009 study on challenges confronting the continent such as conflict, poverty and corruption. Signing this Catholic Church pledge for Africa during a visit to Benin in November 2011, Pope Benedict XVI also exhorted African leaders not to "cut off people from their future by mutilating the present".[45] But increasingly Cameroonians doubted whether the Bishops were still champions of political reform. That these doubts surfaced after the Bishops issued the pastoral letter of 22 July 2011 in which they recommended that "half of all (ELECAM) members come from civil society and that its functioning be flawless for a smooth electoral process"

45 http://www.voanews.com/english/news/africa/Pope-Urges-Benin-Leaders-to-Respect-Hopes-of-the-People-134171358.html.

is enigmatic if not paradoxical. So why was it that Cameroonian Bishops while perceptibly still in the same house as their African counterparts were seen to be in a different room?

Fostering this perception of an imbrication of church and regime was the former's "cacophonic incoherence in the public realm."[46] Notable was the appointment of Bishop Joseph Ateba of Kribi as Chairman of the National Communications Council and of Bishop Dieudonné Watio of Bafoussam as a member of ELECAM, institutions that were seen as staving off liberal electoral outcomes. Because of this, an intellectual elite noted, even if facetiously, that "the Episcopal Council had become the nth section of the CPDM."[47] It was redeemed to a certain extent by its deployment of electoral observers in the October election and the declaration of a Bishop over RFI that on the basis of their report the election was a mascaraed. But this redemption was short-lived because Bishop Joseph Atanga (also a Jesuit) as President of the CENC urged Cameroonians to accept "the outcome of the ballot boxes (as) the expression of our choices and convictions", thereby invoking Jesus' exhortation "Peace be with you" and implored "Let us preserve peace in our country and say no to all violence"[48]

In popular consciousness, its decision to hold an ecumenical service at the Yaounde Cathedral following Biya's inauguration was further evidence of the CENC's deleveraging from the democratic process. Its policy switch caused people to look inside this black box. Arguably, some bishops from the Center and South Regions who are Beti like Biya had taken CENC hostage. And determined to wean the Church from its critical position taking, they caused Bishop Atanga, a Beti, to be elected as its President in lieu of the Vice President Bishop Kleda as was standard practice. Emphasis on 'ethno-Catholicism' led to a disregard of process. Decrying this switch which challenged conventional practice of CENC where the Vice President automatically succeeded the President, Cameroon's iconoclastic Christian Cardinal Tumi noted: "I can understand that people in the public service or private enterprise fight for posts, but not that Bishops play the same game".[49] Seemingly, seeing the Church as a monolithic whole, Tumi overlooked its location in the superstructural realm where "the complex, contradictory

[46] See Open Letter to Cameroonian Bishops, by Rev. Fr. Ludovic Lado, Jesuit priest, 20 November 2011.

[47] Cited in *ibid.*

[48] Cited in Tazoacha Asonganyi, http://www.icicemac.com/actualite/11625/episcopal-council-cameroon-abandons-moral-high-ground.

[49] Cited in *ibid.*

and discordant *ensemble* of the superstructure is the reflection of the *ensemble* of social relations of production" (Gramsci, 1971: 336).

The co-optation, if not the capture of CENC and the alternative press that were instrumental in furthering another knowing helped to exacerbate the redound effect among Cameroonians. Exacerbating this is the crucial role of these institutions as triggers of the 'international boomerang effect'. That is, they turn the gaze of the international community, which has leverage on this state, on abuses by government (Levitsky & Way 2009: 295). It was against this backdrop that the vote incentive was eroded and replaced by what Anthony Downs referred to as the 'rationality crisis' (1957: 139).

Table 2. Voter turnout & Voting age population

Parliamentary

Year	Voter turn-out	Total vote	Registration	Voting age population (VAP)	VAP turnout
2007			5,000,000	8,982,601	
2002	65.66%	2,882,164	4,389,572	7,813,588	36.89%
1997	75.60%	2.906,156	3,844,330	6,222,978	46.70%
1992	60.59%	2,435,443	4,019,562	5,482,800	67.03%

Presidential

Year	Voter turn-out	Total vote	Registration	Voting age popula-tion(VAP)	VAP turnout
2004	79.52%	3,738,759	4,701,953	8,256,564	45.28%
1997	87.00%	3,377,833	3,882,725	6,293,250	53.67%
1992	71.87%	3,015,440	4,195,687	5,482,800	55.00%

Source: International Institute for Democracy & Electoral Assistance.

Table 2 above shows that most Cameroonians in the voting age brackets are opting for exit. Explaining this cynicism, S. K. notes: "…the majority does not care. It is the same President that will be there. We do not want to know anymore"[50] But popular participation, Amartya Sen cautioned, is not just sanctimonious rubbish (Sen 1999: 247), thus the need for voice. Voice can be recovered only granting administrative reforms that have been compared to perfecting how balls, strikes and base-running are called in baseball that guarantee electoral security: "Accurate balls are critical, but they are not likely to fill the stands with

[50] Cited in http://www.cameroon-info.net/stories/0,29961,@,cameroun-indifference-et-scepticime-pour-la-presidentielle.html.

fans. People can watch a game to see their team win or because of interest in an important game. Perfect scoring is meaningless if only one team takes the field, and attendance will suffer if two teams are playing that on one can cheer for" (Donovan 2007: 685).

French support for electoral authoritarianism in Cameroon

Leverage of Western governments over democratic reform in Africa, it has been posited, is determined by the intensity of their linkage to the various countries and/or their leaders as well as the vulnerability of the nominal African state. And seemingly, their commitment to promoting democratic governance in Africa was unambiguous. Good governance became a metaphor for sound development management (World Bank 1992), especially as the Wapenhans report noted the negative effects of a de-emphasis of political and institutional factors implementing World Bank loans. This aligned with the EU Council of Ministers Resolution of November 1991 on Human Rights, Democracy and Development that made the promotion of human rights and democracy a conditionality for development cooperation, reiterated in the Article 11 of the Maastricht Treaty where the EU restated its commitment to "develop and consolidate democracy and the rule of law, and respect for human rights and fundamental freedoms". Because of the regime's failure of this litmus, Germany reduced its bilateral aid from $50 million in 1992 to circa $30 million in 1993 and the European Parliament requested the European Commission to investigate human rights abuses following the 1992 Presidential elections Notable, however, is a French loan of 600 mln French francs in 1993 that was used to pay the country's overdue payment on its World Bank debt (Pigeaud 2011: 235-236). Thus, despite a rhetoric criticizing the slow pace of economic and political reforms in Cameroon, the regime "... can count on the last moment international, support" (Konings 2004: 15).

Geo-strategic concerns have been used to justify continuous French support to date. With most countries in the Central African region embroiled in conflict – the crisis in Congo, instability in the Central African Republic and revolts in Tchad – fear loomed large that even 'islands of peace' such as the regime (re)presenting Cameroon could suffer from the 'neighborhood effect'. This was underlined in a 1997 Report by a French Senate team that included the former senator Xavier de Villepin and President Mitterand's former Africa advisor Guy Penne. Noting that Cameroon, despite its membership in the Commonwealth, appeared isolated most of the time, Villepin *et al.* posited that French friendship and support to *it* (my emphasis) – a 'precious gift' – would be critical when circumstances so required

(1998: 15). The pronoun *it* is ambiguous in this context: is the aid for the regime which presented itself as a guardian of peace in a troubled region, or the country itself. Chirac's congratulatory message to Paul Biya, even *before* the official results of the 2004 October presidential election were declared, was interpreted as a clear sign of French support for the regime, even of a flawed one. "Promoting democracy in such contexts poses fundamental policy dilemmas and analytical challenges, as these regimes often represent significant improvements over their predecessors or appear to provide a measure of stability that is welcomed in troubled regions." (Ottaway 2003: 5)

French motivational exuberance was also driven by preferential treatment accorded to French investments in Cameroon by the regime. There were 110 subsidiaries of French companies and over 200 enterprises owned by French nationals and many of these enjoy monopoly rights, guaranteed in some cases by corrupting Cameroonian officials (Pigeaud 2011: 239). Notable is the case of Lafarge that has a monopoly in the production of cement. A project initiated in 2008 by the South Korean Afko Cement Corporation to build another dement plant in Ngueme in the South West Region has stalled, especially as the regime has reneged on its commitment to building the Limbe Port that is integral to this project.[51] The regime's reticence to promote competition which should help get the price of cement right gives the semblance of a regime that is accountable to the French rather than the Cameroonian electorate. Arguably, the regime's tendency to act as a Trojan horse for the French underwrites the latter's acceptance of the thesis, a stated by one of its diplomats in Yaounde thus: "Cameroonians are not ready for a Bamileke (writ large to include Anglophones) president" (Pigeaud 2011: 237). Initially by Joseph Owona, a CPDM Minister, it was recently reiterated by Ahmadou Ali, the Minister of Justice who argues that because of the pathological distrust of Cameroonians in Anglo-Bamilekes, northerners cannot support a Presidential candidate from this group.[52]

In Cameroonian popular opinion, people like Yves Omnes, a former French ambassador to Cameroon, was named as an advisor to Paul Biya at the end of this tour of duty have also been instrumental in advocating for the regime. Determining Omnes influence over the articulation of French policy or in the Biya presidency is difficult to anyone not privy to its internal dynamics. But Oumar Konaré,

51 Hervé Edong, "Matériaux de construction: L'État abandonne le projet de cimentière de Limbe", *La Nouvelle Expression*, 15 November 2011.

52 Janet Garvey in AMEMBASSY Yaounde, "Cameroon's Justice Minister says North will support Biya but not another Beti or Bami", R 121639Z Mar 09, at http://wikileaks.org/cable/2009/03/09YAOUNDE256.html.

a former President of the African Union (AU), labeled people of the Omnes ilk as 'mercenaries in white overalls' (*my translation*) who manipulate African constitutions, embedding anti-democratic dispositions in them (*icicemac,* 22 October 2005). Though Konaré's remarks were prompted by Charles Debbasch's infamous role in Togo's succession crisis, the French Ministry of Foreign Affairs rebutted this by distinguishing between these advisors and French 'technical' advisors. This distinction is moot in so far as these *messieurs de l'Afrique* were also consulted by Quai d'Orsai as experts, and still maintain considerable access to the decision-making instances. Arguably, France would not disregard the recommendations of Omnes, even if reinvented as a lobbyist, whose centrality in formulating France's Cameroon policy for decades was uncontested. Though their reinvention may be pecuniary-driven,[53] its collateral benefits – access – for its African purveyors are considerable. This imbrication problematizes Jean-Francois Bayart's denial of the *paradigm of yoke* (1979) – the tendency to blame the French for all that is wrong in Francophone Africa. Admittedly, there is plenty of blame to go around.

Against this backdrop, it is not surprising that French diplomats in Yaounde succeeded in pre-empting an EU declaration following the appointment of its members who were CPDM stalwarts. Brussels had to intervene for it to be adopted (Pigeaud 2011: 237). Seemingly, the regime believes that absent the international boomerang effect, there will not be a French policy switch. And so to seduce French public opinion, Biya recruited François de la Brosse, who was also Nicolas Sarkozy's Communication advisor in charge of his Internet strategy, to build his campaign website. He also paid *Le Monde* 468,832 euros ($628,000) for a two-page communiqué that was basically an infomercial lauding the democratic process in Cameroon following the elections. This was evidence that *Le Monde's* publishers belonged to the syndicate dubbed 'White sorcerers' who, ostensibly preoccupied with the development of Africa, organize campaigns to confer international legitimacy to African autocrats.[54] However, this infomercial unsettled members of *la Société des Rédacteurs du Monde* (SRM) who pointed out that re-

[53] Bernard Rideau, an advisor to President Abdoulaye Wade of Senegal, even if it be "à titre amicale", admitted that the primary motivation is financial: "Where you would earn 100, in Africa you are going to earn 300 or 400. Africans are very generous. It is very attractive and few can resist it". In the same breath, he accepted their utility function by pointing out that he worked for Gnassingbe Eyadema in Togo "selling him to the Germans who were mistaking him for Amin Dada"! (*icicemac*, 22 Octobre 2005).

[54] See Julie Owono, "Gulf of Guinea leaders buy their credibility", at http:www.aljazeera.com/indepth/opinion/2011/11/20111123123046796894.html.

ports published during the election had concluded that it was neither free nor fair. Consequently, this infomercial was a very serious drift, unworthy of the paper.[55]

Electoral authoritarianism in Cameroon: the K Street Project and the Obama administration

Adopting a static approach, Konings has argued that United States policy toward Cameroon, despite it emphasis on "good governance ... has actually displayed a rather ambivalent attitude toward the regime, often justified in terms of *realpolitik*" (2004: 15). Yet a dynamic perspective also reveals the role of personal greed among and within the power blocs dealing with African regimes. African leaders have exploited this greed to further their own agendas. Evidence of this was Gabon's former president Omar Bongo's willingness to pay US political lobbyist and convicted felon Jack Abramoff $10 million to enable him get a photo-op with President George Bush at the White House.[56] Cameroon's vote in support of the United States resolution in the UN Security Council for the invasion of Iraq earned Biya the privilege of visiting Bush on 20 March 2003, the day of the invasion by the Coalition of the Willing (*Washington Post*, July 27, 2005, p. A19). For Biya, this audience represented, and was presented to Cameroonians, evidence of his legitimacy.

President G.W. Bush in his second inaugural speech noted the willingness of the US "...to seek the support and growth of democratic movements and institutions in every nation and culture, with the ultimate goal of ending tyranny in our world" and by helping 'others find their own voice'. Misconstruing this as his continued commitment to regime change caused several Third World autocratic regimes to seek American certification of their elections. To this end, Biya turned to K Street, issuing an invitation to a delegation of the Association of Former Lawmakers,[57] chartered by the US Congress in 1970 to educate the public on 'the

55 *La Lettre du Contient*, No 624, November 2011.

56 The case was brought into the public domain as part of the investigation into the dealing of Jack Abramoff. Contacts between Abramoff and Bongo were facilitated by David Safavian, a former registered agent for Gabon and at that time a White House Budget official. To secure Bongo a meeting with George Bush, Jack Abramoff asked for US $10 million in a draft agreement prepared on August 7, 2003. Abramoff was ready to travel to Gabon to discuss this contract in "a private aircraft, which bears a substantial cost unfortunately". See *The New York Times* (electronic edition), November 10, 2005.

57 The six-man delegation that comprised former Representatives Michael Forbes (D-NY), Webb Franklin (R-Miss), Andrew Maguire (D-NJ), Richard Schulze (R-PA) Joe Wyatt (D-Texas) and Ronnie Shows (D-Miss).

crucial importance of representative democracy' at home and abroad. Flaunting its credentials, a spokesperson of the Association noted: "... we have a unique pool of experienced legislators (and) "if asked, we can lend our knowledge and be extremely helpful to emerging democracies" (*Los Angeles Times,* February 14, 2005). Skeptics doubted their commitment to these standards, because most of these former law makers had moved to K Street in search of 'sky-high lobbying salaries', according to Congressional Watch.[58] The above-mentioned trip cost the Cameroonian state US $80,000.

The delegation arrived in Cameroon three days before the 2004 elections and was chaperoned throughout their stay by the MINAT. It was the first observer group to patronizingly proclaim that the electoral process was free: "This is what democracy is about" (cited in *Los Angeles Times*, 14 February 2005)! Some international organizations had already specified elements of a comprehensive set of standards for election monitoring.[59] Included in these measures were, *inter alia*, voter registration, access to the media, and enforcement of the electoral law. Observation should focus not on the constitutive aspects of the process (law), but on its performative dimension. Cameroonians doubted that this delegation adhered to these protocols. For example, Cardinal Christian Tumi, a top Church leader in the country, denounced the opacity of the process. But seemingly ascribing an ontological superiority to the Americans, Fame Ndongo, the Minister of Communication, used their approval to rebut Cardinal Tumi who had been referred to by the *Radio France Internationale* as an 'eminent moral personality'. The *Cameroon Tribune* headlined its lead story 'Voting Conduct Impresses Americans', although its truth claims were challenged.

The smoking gun was provided by US Federal Lobby Disclosure records showing that the Biya regime had contracted the services of the Washington DC lobbying firm Patton Boggs in July 2004 for US $40,000, to "help improve ties between the US and Cameroon, including on *'issues relating'* to the October election" (my emphasis). Former Congressman Greg Laughlin, born again as a Wash-

---

58 According to the Congress Watch division of Public Citizen, because of the party slant of control of the institutions in Washington DC, 62% of the Republicans who left Congress in 2000 registered as lobbyists as compared to 52% former Democratic lawmakers in 1998 when the institutions had more of a Democratic coloration. They can easily valorize their unrestricted access to the floors of the Congress, its gym and other off bound areas of the Capital by brokering deals on behalf of their clients. Senator Russell Feingold, a sponsor of the McCain-Feingold campaign law has proposed legislation to curb this access (for details see *Washington Post*, July 27, 2005: A19).

59 See: International Institute for Democracy and Electoral Assistance, 2002, OSCE/ODHIR, 2003.

ington lobbyist for Boggs, contacted the Association to send the delegation to Cameroon. According to him, government officials wanted Americans to monitor the election to showcase the progress they had made. Evidence of a conflict of interest surfaced shortly after the election, when the Biya regime signed Rep. Schulze as a lobbyist, a member of the delegation now reincarnated as an employee of Valis Associates, another lobbying firm. To "maximize the impact of Cameroon's political and economic reforms on agencies and departments of the US government", he and other two lobbyists accepted an initial retainer fee of US $149,972 (*Los Angeles Times*, February 14, 2005). The need to redeem the regime's image was prompted by the repudiation of the certification given to the elections by some of members of the delegation. Maguire, for example, granted an interview to New Jersey's *Star Ledger* condemning Biya as a 'dictator (masquerading) as a democrat' (*Los Angeles Times*, February 14, 2005).

In engaging the services of Schulze, Biya was probably conscious of the operational principle of the beltway that Republican control of the institutions gave the views of the members of this party, such as Schulze, a competitive advantage over those of the liberal fringe represented by Maguire. Further contributing to the buy-in of Schulze's position was the willingness of an 'overstretched' United States to accommodate authoritarian regimes in so far as they served as a firewall against the spread of crisis (Ndegwa 2001: 7). Biya had proved his credentials by supporting the US at the Security Council and allowed the Tchad oil pipeline, touted as the example of cooperation between to private sector and international finance to pass through Cameroon's eminent domain. Repeated condemnations of the regime in the State Department's Human Rights annual reports were perfunctory.

Arguably, Biya's attempts to use lobbyists to gain a democracy complaint status for his regime did not produce the expected pay-off. Notable was his exclusion from the list of African leaders invited to the White House on 14 July 2005. Bush lauded his invitees as leaders of countries that had organized peaceful elections, and pledged that the United States would work "harder and faster to certify (them) for the Millennium Challenge Account" (*Washington Post*, July 14, 2005: A04). That the then United State Ambassador signed the Joint Statement, describing the 2007 elections as a "missed opportunity to continue building public confidence in the democratic process as Cameroon looks ahead to its next elections", also shows that the lobbyists indeed did not succeed in getting a democracy complaint status for the regime. Despite the foregoing, Cameroon has not been declared a pariah, reminiscent of 1992. But neither is regime change in Cameroon on the table – as evidenced by the October 2011 presidential elections, again returning Paul Biya to power.

Even prior to polling, CPDM apparatchiks piled on the US Embassy for organizing a Civil Society Forum for Democracy in September 2011. To Issa Tchiroma, the government's spokesperson, this was interfering in Cameroon's internal affairs. And unlike Alexis de Tocqueville, who attributed the vibrancy of democracy in America to a thick civil society, he saw this as an attempt to destabilize the country.[60] Given that the government had welcomed US involvement in promoting electoral governance, this smacked of dissembling. Despite this, the Embassy organized a roundtable following the election on 'the lessons learned'. Noting the high levels of cynicism among the Cameroonian electorate, the US Ambassador Robert Jackson emphasized the urgency of "finding ways to promote transparency and good governance" to reverse this trend. Among his prescriptions were calls for the ruling party to cease and desist from using government resources to tilt the playing field as well as "refrain from fear mongering by suggesting that voting for the opposition will lead to instability and chaos".[61] Rather than see these as an attempt to redeem Cameroon's democratic process, they evoked well-rehearsed responses from CPDM apparatchiks. Gregoire Owona, the Assistant Secretary General of the CPDM denounced the Ambassador's patronizing attitude while the Minister of External Relations claimed that the October polling was in conformity Cameroon's constitution and laws in force and complied with international norms.[62]

Conclusion

Though not convinced of the normative superiority of democracy as a mode of governance, the Biya regime managed to script Cameroon's transition process. The outcome so far is an electoral authoritarian regime which has institutionalized multiparty elections while the chances of democratization have receded. Laws have been adopted and institutions created. Whereas the regime touts their Cameroonian provenance, MINAT's almost total control of the electoral process has been informed by French cultural narratives. The adaptation of foreign models rather than copying models *per se* is problematic in this context. Notable is

60 http://cameroonpolls.com/index.php?option=com_content\&view=article\&id=78:camercivil\&catid=1:latest-news\&Itemid=50.

61 See transcript of digital video conference on "Democracy and the Role of Civil Society", 22 October 2011.

62 Cited in: http://thecameroonnews.com/index.php?itemid=602.

the fact that Cameroonian functionaries unlike their French counterparts are not a 'universal class' functioning without an acceptable code of conduct that would help revamp the normative terrain to create a level playing field. More concerned with advancing their own upward mobility, they have enabled a 'menu of manipulations' to obtain pre-scripted results that favor the ruling party in elections. Significant was the watershed 2007 parliamentary elections in which the CPDM-regime won more than 80% of the seats.

Its 'landslide victory' only engendered another struggle over the meanings to be recovered from it. Seen through the prism of this party, it was evidence that Cameroonians had given it the '*strong and homogeneous majority*' that Biya had sought, with a view to furthering 'democratic consolidation' and boosting the economy. But in the dissenting view, it was an attempt to foster "the weak demand for vertical accountability that is common of Africa's unclaimed democracies" (Bratton & Logan 2006) and its corollary horizontal accountability. Not surprising therefore, the priority of this homogeneous majority was the revision of the Constitution at the behest of Biya, allowing for unlimited Presidential mandates because term limits were undemocratic.[63] Remarkably however, this revised Constitution was ratified by the Parliament rather than by popular referendum. Opting for this path, as opposed to tacit consent (*de gré à gré*), constituted the use of force. The 16th-century political philosopher Jean Bodin already cautioned us that any sovereign magistrate that contrives to prolong the power entrusted to him through the use of force is a tyrant (2006: 6). The relevance of the French saying *plus ça change, plus ça ne va plus* is undiminished.

It is against this backdrop that Biya won a fourth Presidential term in 2011, 'beating' his main opponent with a margin of 61%. Though this margin was attributable to the failure of ELECAM as an impartial arbiter, it did not absolve the opposition of 'vicarious liability'. Having initially decided to boycott the election, its decision to participate caused a political whiplash in the electorate that attributed this to instrumentalism. Its inability to unite behind a single candidate only lent credence to this charge and caused a dwindling of its popularity credit. This unsettling of relations between civil society and the opposition detracted from the latter's mobilizational capacity, reinforcing voters' cynicism of change through elections in the context of a vulnerable regime. Exacerbating this was

63 Elphie Galland (2008), "Tailored for the President – the Constitution of Cameroon", *Commonwealth Human Rights Initiative* (15)1, Summer.

the use of the politics of information management[64] to enable a low information democracy.

Oppositional politics was further problematized by the contention of Cameroonian 'radical' scholars like Achille Mbembe that change will not come through the ballot box.[65] Plausibly to redeem democracy, the American Embassy organized a Civil Society Forum for Democracy. Any optimism underlying this rescue attempt is attributable to the seduction of democracy among Africans who put a premium on its intrinsic value and the political goods that it promises.[66] According to conventional logic, the leverage of Western states over Cameroon endows them with the capability, if not power, to cause the Biya regime to reverse its course of electoral authoritarianism. In other words, external rather than vertical or horizontal accountability can guarantee oversight of the regime. This fed the public's obsession with the messages of congratulations, or lack thereof, from Nicolas Sarkozy and Barack Obama. Decrying this certification, a group of distinguished African scholars in 2000 cautioned against the "patronizing interventions by intellectuals and powerful governments from the West, whose previous commitment to democracy and human rights was highly questionable" (cited in Chege 2005: 269). French policy in Cameroon that has been captured by 'white sorcerers' and was brought into relief its decision to congratulate Biya in the 2004 Presidential election even before the results were declared lends credence to this critique. Its relevance is problematized in the case of US where attempts to have the US endorse Cameroon's democratic reforms and practice have largely been unsuccessful, especially from the Obama Administration. To this end, Robert Jackson noted "the only way to preserve Cameroon's peace and stability for future generations is by giving Cameroonians a greater stake in their country's future, greater opportunity and a greater voice in their own destiny".[67]

References

Alence, R., 2004. Political institutions and developmental governance in sub-Saharan Africa. *Journal of Modern African Studies* 42(2): 163-187.

64 Erving Goffmann defines the politics of information management as a group's effort to maintain, in the face of possible challenges, its desired definition of the situation (in B. Gregg 2003, *Thick Moralities, Thin Politics*, Durham: Duke University Press, p. 63).

65 See http://africasacountry.com/2011/10/09/cameroon-and-the-president/.

66 Michael Bratton & Robert Mattes (2000), "Support from Democracy in Africa: Intrinsic or Instrumental", *Afrobarometer* Paper No. 1, Cape Town, South Africa IDASA POS.

67 See transcript of digital video conference on "Democracy and the Role of Civil Society", 22 October 2011.

Appadurai, A., 2003. Grassroots mobilization and research imagination, in: A. Appadurai, ed., *Globalization*. Durham, NC: Duke University Press.

Bayart, J-F., 1979. *L'État au Cameroun*. Paris: Presses de la Fondation Nationale des Sciences Politiques.

Bayart, J-F., 1993. *L'État en Afrique: la Politique du Ventre*. Paris: Fayard.

Benjamin, G., 2003. *Thick Moralities, Thin Politics*. Durham, NC: Duke University Press.

Bodin, J., 2006 [1576]. *On Sovereignty*, ed. and trans. by Judith H. Franklin. Cambridge: Cambridge University Press.

Bratton, M. & C. Logan, 2006. Voters but not yet citizens: the weak demand for vertical accountability in Africa's unclaimed democracies. *Afrobarometer Working Papers,* no. 63, September.

Bratton, M. & N. van de Walle, 1997. *Democratic Experiments in Africa: Regime Transitions in Comparative Perspective.* Cambridge: Cambridge University Press.

Brownlee, J., 2009. Portents of pluralism: how hybrid regimes affect democratic transitions. *American Journal of Political Science* 53(3): 515-532.

Castells, M., 2004. *The Power of Identity*, Oxford – Malden, MA: Blackwell.

Commonwealth Secretariat, 2004. Cameroon presidential election, 11 October 2004: Report of the Commonwealth Observer Group'. London: Commonwealth Secretariat.

Commission Nationale Anti-Corruption, (2010), *Stratégie de Lutte contre la Corruption, 2010-2015*. Yaounde: République du Cameroun.

Coppedge, M., 2002. 'Theory Building and Hypothesis Testing: Large vs. Small Research on Democratization', paper prepared for presentation at the Annual Midwest Political Science Association, Chicago, Illinois, April 25-27.

DiPalma, G., 1990. *To Craft Democracies: An Essay on Democratic Transitions.* Berkeley – Los Angeles: University of California Press.

Donovan, T., 2007. A goal for reform: make elections worth stealing. *Political Science and Politics* 40(4): 681-686.

Downs, A., 1957. *An Economic Theory of Democracy*. New York: Harper and Row.

Eboussi, B., 1997. *La Démocratie de Transit du Cameroun*. Paris: L'Harmattan.

Gifford, A., 1998. *African Christianity: Its Public Role*. Bloomington – London: Indiana University Press.

Gramsci, A., 1971. *Selections from the Prison Notebooks,* translated and edited by Q. Hoare & G.N. Smith. New York: International Publishers.

Gramsci, A., 1977. *Quaderni del Carcere*. Edited by V. Gerratana. Turin: Einaudi.

Gyimah-Boadi, E., 2009. Another step forward for Ghana. *Journal of Democracy* 20(2): 139-152.

Halpern, D., 2005. *Social Capital*. Cambridge – Malden, MA: Polity Press.

Hamilton, A., J. Madison & J. Jay, 1961. *The Federalist Papers*. New York: Mentor Books.

Hartlyn, J. & J. McCoy, 2006. Observer paradoxes: how to assess manipulation, in: Schedler, A., ed., *Electoral Authoritarianism: The Dynamics of Unfree Competition*. Bloomington -London: Indiana University Press.

Hirschman, A.O., 1965. Models in reform mongering, in: A.O. Hirschman, ed., *Journey Toward Progress: Studies in Economic Policy Making in Latin America*. Garden City, NY: Doubleday.

Howard, M.J. & P.G. Roessler. 2006. Liberalizing electoral outcomes in competitive authoritarian regimes. *American Journal of Political Science* 50(2): 365-381.

Jua, N. 2001. Democracy and the construction of allogeny/autochtony. *African Issues* 19(1-2): 37-42.

Konings, P.J.J., 2004. Opposition and social-democratic change in Africa: the Social Democratic Front in Cameroon. *Commonwealth & Comparative Politics* 42(3): 1-23.

Konings, P.J.J., 2011. *The Politics of Neoliberal Reform in Africa: State and Civil Society in Cameroon*. Bamenda: Langaa Publishers.

Levitsky, S. & L.A. Way 2006. Linkage and leverage: how do international factors change domestic balances of power? in: A. Schelder, ed., *Electoral Authoritarianism: The Dynamics of Unfree Competition*. Boulder, Co.: Lynne Rienner.

Levitsky, S. & L.A. Way, 2009. International linkage and democratization, in L. Diamond & M.F. Plattner, eds, *Democracy: A Reader*. Baltimore: The Johns Hopkins University Press.

Levitsky, S., & L.A. Way, 2010. *Competitive Authoritarianism: Hybrid Regimes after the Cold War.* Cambridge: Cambridge University Press.

Lindberg, S.I., 2006. *Democracy and Elections in Africa*. Baltimore: Johns Hopkins University Press.

Lindberg, S.I., 2009. A mixed record. *Journal of Democracy* 20(3): 86-92.

Linz, J., 1978. *The Breakdown of Democratic Regimes: Crisis, Breakdown and Reequilibration*. Baltimore: Johns Hopkins University Press.

Machiavelli, N., 1961 [1537]. *The Prince*, trans. G. Bull. Harmondsworth – New York: Penguin Books.

Manning, C. 2010. Mozambique's slide into one-party rule. *Journal of Democracy* 21(2): 151-165.

Mbembe, A., 2001. *On the Postcolony.* Berkeley – Los Angeles – London: University of California Press.

Ottaway, M., 2003. *Democracy Challenged: the Rise of Semi-Authoritarian Regimes.* Washington, DC: Carnegie Endowment for International Peace.

Pigeaud, F., 2011. *Au Cameroun de Paul Biya.* Paris: Karthala.

Przeworski, A., 1991. *Democracy and the Market: Political and Economic Reforms in Eastern Europe and Latin America.* Cambridge: Cambridge University Press.

Przeworski, A., M.E. Alvarez, J.A. Cheibub & F. Limongi 2000. *Democracy and Development: Political Institutions and Well-Being in the World, 1950-1990.* Cambridge: Cambridge University Press.

Rawls, J., 1971. *A Theory of Justice.* Cambridge, MA: Harvard University Press.

Ramsbotham, O., T. Woodhouse & H. Miall, 2005. *Contemporary Conflict Resolution.* Oxford – Malden, MA: Polity Press.

Rakner, L. & N. van de Walle, 2009. Opposition weakness in Africa. *Journal of Democracy* 20(3): 108-121.

Santiso, C. & A. Loada, 2003. Explaining the unexpected: electoral reform and democratic governance in Burkina Faso. *Journal of Modern African Studies* 41(3): 395-419.

Schedler A., 2006. The logic of electoral authoritarianism, in Schedler, A., ed., *Electoral Authoritarianism: The Dynamics of Unfree Competition.* Boulder, Co.: Lynne Rienner.

Schedler, A. 2002. Elections without democracy: the menu of manipulation. *Journal of Democracy* 13(2): 36-50.

Schedler, A. ed., 2006. *Electoral Authoritarianism: the Dynamics of Unfree Competition.* Boulder – London: Lynne Rienner.

Sen, A., 1999. *Development as Freedom.* New York: Anchor Books.

Takougang, J., 2003. The 2002 legislative election in Cameroon: a retrospective on Cameroon's stalled democracy movement. *Journal of Modern African Studies* 41(3): 421-435.

Takougang, J. & M. Krieger, 1998. *African State and Society in the 1990s: Cameroon's Political Crossroads.* Boulder, Co.: Westview Press.

Thompson, J. B., 2000. *Political Scandal: Power and Visibility in the Media Age.* Cambridge: Polity Press.

Van de Walle, N., 2006. Tipping games: when do opposition parties coalesce? in: A. Schedler, ed., *Electoral Authoritarianism: The Dynamics of Unfree Competition.* Boulder, Co.: Lynne Rienner.

Villalón L.A. & P. Von Doepp, eds, 2005. *The Fate of Africa's Democratic Experiments*. Bloomington – London: Indiana University Press.
World Bank, 1992. *Governance and Development*. Washington, DC: World Bank.

Multipartyism and 'big man' democracy in Cameroon, 1990-2011

Ibrahim Mouiche

With the restoration of multipartyism at the end of 1990, Cameroon as from 1991 entered an era of political turbulence in the form of so-called 'ghost town' and 'civil disobedience' campaigns that almost brought down President Paul Biya's regime. Having continuously rejected the idea of a 'National Sovereign Conference' ('Conférence nationale souveraine') persistently called for by the opposition forces but considered as useless ('sans objet'), the President finally accepted the 'Tripartite formula' (a 'deal' between government, opposition and civil society), which calmed down the political atmosphere. This implied a package deal that paved the way for eventual democratic alternation in Cameroon, if only by the acceptance by all parties of the formula of limiting the presidential mandate to two terms. Since then, eleven rounds of elections have been held in Cameroon. In each of these elections the Cameroon Peoples' Democratic Movement (CPDM), the former single party, has always been the winner. This series of repetitive victories has brought many people to conclude that this is 'big man democracy', resulting from the consistent pattern of 'manoeuvring' in favour of the dominant party and its president. In 2008 the CPDM regime even banned the constitutional clause of the limitation of presidential mandates, thus taking away all the chances of political alternation in Cameroon and thereby, for many Cameroonians, putting the country indefinitely on hold due to processes characteristic of 'anocracy', a political constellation whereby power is spread among (often ethnic-based) elite groups who are constantly competing with each other for power.

Introduction

The wave of political liberalisation and pressures for democracy in Africa starting in 1990 also reached Cameroon and led the country to a process of formal restoration of multipartyism. As of 1991, the country entered a zone of political turbulence in the form of 'ghost town' and 'civil disobedience' campaigns, which nearly brought down President Paul Biya's regime, which had been in power since 1982.[1] Having rejected a 'National Sovereign Conference' (*Conférence Nationale Souveraine*), similar to those held in many African countries at the time and persistently demanded by the opposition, the President finally accepted the so-called 'tripartite' formula (Government-opposition-civil society), which took place in November of the same year to calm down the political climate and dampen social unrest. This led to a package deal that also paved the way for eventual democratic power alternation in Cameroon, even if only in the form of the acceptance by all parties of the limiting the presidential mandate to two terms (of 7 years). This was to be confirmed later on by the new constitution, adopted in January 1996. Since then, eleven rounds of elections were held: four presidential in 1992, 1997, 2004 and 2011; four legislatives in 1992, 1997, 2002 and 2007 and three municipals, held in 1996, 2002 and 2007 respectively. In each of these elections, the Cameroon People's Democratic Movement (CPDM[2]), the former single party, always won. This repeated victory led many to the conclusion that we have to do with a form of political development variously called 'authoritarian democratization' (see Schraeder 1994: 69-90; 1995: 12-13; also Kamto 1993: 209-238), a 'cosmetic democracy' (Nyamnjoh 2002: 5-8) 'illiberal democracy' (Konings 2004: 20-21; Van de Walle 2001: 243-245)[3], a 'big man democracy' (Takougang 2003: 433; Gabriel 1999: 173-174)[4], giving evidence of highly manipulated political operations favouring the ruling CPDM (See Gros & Mentan 2003: 131-163; Mouiche 2011a: 90-93).

This chapter offers reflections on the political pluralism in Cameroon said to exist in the past twenty-one years. In this country, voting is correlated to a large extent with ethno-regional expression. The strength of political parties is

1 By the 'ghost town' and 'civil disobedience' campaigns, the population notably in urban areas was called upon to remain quietly in their houses, to withdraw from their civil and fiscal obligations so as to isolate and asphyxiate the state, and consequently provoke the fall of the Biya regime.

2 Its name in French: Rassemblement Démocratique du Peuple Camerounais (RDPC).

3 On the concept of 'illiberal democracies', see F. Zakaria (1997: 22–43); L. Diamond (1996: 20-37); and N. van de Walle (2001: 243-244).

4 Joseph Takougang borrows this concept of 'big man' democracy from Michael Bratton & Nicolas Van de Walle 1997: 233), a form of democracy '... in which the formal trappings of democracy coexist with neopatrimonial political practices. In other words, despite the semblance of democracy, the old one-party system in which one party and one individual were in charge still reigns'.

significantly determined by the territorial distribution of votes and reflects community mobilisation. The choice of the voters is thus often based on candidates with whom they share regional and ethnic affinities (cf. Menthong (1998: 41-42).[5] However, we have to note that there is no absolute correlation between community belonging and voting preference: the voters, also in Africa, are not inevitably determined by 'primordialist' motivations. 'Utilitarian', interest-based and trans-local considerations can also bring people to change their political orientation and prefer a candidate or party different from their group of reference (cf. Otayek 1998: 10; Carbone 2008: 26–27). Many political parties have been created and are supported by people from different ethno-cultural backgrounds. These parties at times take the form of trans-ethnic organisations – what Diamond and Gunther call a 'congressist party', characterised by the will to promote the bringing together and integration of voters or of parties formed from such different communities (Diamond & Gunther 2001).

These identity referents explain why Cameroonian politics is less based on the candidates' projects than on personalities. It is this strong instrumentalisation of the personal variable in Cameroon's politics and in its process of democratisation that has led me to the concept of 'political *bigmanism*'. This term brings out the tendency towards harnessing and sometimes strengthening neopatrimonial practices of the personalisation of power, clientelism and corruption, continued under the system of multipartyism. To quote Jean Pascal Daloz (1999: 13-31), given the very superficial institutionalisation of power and the exceptionally particularistic character of political relations in Subsaharan Africa, an analysis of the modalities of leadership seems more crucial than abstract discussions around uncertain political principles and presumed structures. Understanding the logic of representation prevailing between the 'big men' at the top and their respective followers is key to the interpretation of contemporary constructions of politics in Africa and going beyond certain imported stereotypes. Interpreting elections in Africa in this respect must therefore take in to account the strategic paradigm: the games actors play, particularly the modern elites, electoral competition, partisan rivalries, the political rhetoric in speeches, etc. (cf. Otayek 1998: 8; Mappa 1998: 169). Yet, the emphasis have very often been laid only on the 'top elites', the number 1 and number 2 (see Quantin 1995), to the detriment of other political power holders. This type of studies on upper elites needs to be complemented by attention to the

5 See also Nchoji Nkwi & Socpa 1997: 138–149; Geschiere & Nyamnjoh 2000: 423–452; Nyamjoh & Rowlands 1998: 320–337; Mouiche 2011b: 81-85.

'lower elites' so as to better understand the local political arenas (see Mouiche 2004: 401-432; Mouiche 2005).

For two fundamental reasons, our attention in this chapter is more focused on the ruling party CPDM and its elites, and less on the opposition. On the one hand, from the elite perspective or even in the perspective of the quest for 'big man' status,[6] the opposition remains poorly represented in urban elite recruitment. The CPDM is hegemonic in the coalitions with elites in Cameroon (cf. Mouiche 2005).[7] On the other hand, qualitative research carried out on the political parties of the opposition also certified their own forms of implication in neo-patrimonialist practices, a fact which tends to consolidate the 'big man' traits of the Cameroonian political process, as evident from Piet Konings' paper on the SDF (2004), Krieger's book (2008) on the same political party, and the work edited by Sindjoun on the opposition groups (cf. Sindjoun 2004). In what follows, I specifically address two issues: a) the 'routinisation' of elections and the self-reproducing hegemony of the CPDM, and b) the consolidation of 'big man democracy' in the country by this party.

The routinisation of elections and the hegemony of the CPDM

In recognizing a plurality of political parties at the end of 1990 (i.e., going back to a system that existed in the immediate post-independence period in the 1960s), Cameroon opted for integral 'multipartyism'. Since then, more than 200 political parties have been created, although many have only a nominal existence. Only five to seven parties are effectively present in the electoral processes on the national political level, e.g., in the guise of MPs or municipal counsellors. In this political environment, the CPDM occupies a very dominant if not hegemonic position.

The legislative elections of 1 March 1992 in Cameroon, with 32 competing political parties, constituted the first test of representativeness of these different political forces.[8] They led to the emergence of 'electoral strongholds'. These strongholds have not remained intangible and their configurations evolved according to the voting process, showing the specific historicity of Cameroon politics. As such, to the classical political tensions, mythologised since forty years

[6] The expression the quest for 'big man' borrowed from Jean Pascal Daloz consists of the '...obsession to rise as a dominant and undisputed figure, surpassing all challenges by virtue of the superior capacity of redistribution' (Daloz 2002: 107).

[7] Also see Fred Eboko, Les élites politiques au Cameroun. Le renouvellement sans renouveau? In Jean-Pascal Daloz, *op. cit.*: 99-133.

[8] For a report, see: Collectif Changer le Cameroun 1993.

between different geopolitical poles of Cameroon (Anglophones-Francophones, North-South), has been added the deployment of a new ethno-political dynamics (Beti – Anglo – Bamilekes; allogenes – autochthons; Islamo-Fulani – 'Kirdi', etc.).[9] The two sets of factors – linguistic-geographical and the newly emerging ethno-political – have led to the two groups of political parties emerging in Cameroon and extending their hold over the population: those credited primarily at the national level and those with a regionally rooted base.

Parties with a national posture: the CPDM, the SDF and the UNDP

As will become evident below, the CPDM is the most established and better organised party in Cameroon. Until January 1991 it was the only authorised party. Still in power today and led by President Paul Biya, it has the tendency to overlap with the government of the republic. This party finds its adherents among high-ranking-civil servants, traditional rulers, business operators, big farmers and land owners, and diverse feudal lords, i.e., all those with a large economic stake in the prevailing socio-political order (cf. Faure & Médard 1995). At the ethnic level, it recruits first and foremost among the Beti-Bulu people of the Centre, South and East regions, the ethnic conglomerate from where the president originates. In the Northern regions, the CPDM has also succeeded to instrumentalise secular rivalries between the Islamic Fulani and the Kirdi, so as to cast its net among the latter group. In the course of the various electoral rounds, the CPDM has become the ultra-dominant party in Cameroon, making all the other parties satellites in their respective strongholds. Notwithstanding this dominant national posture, the CPDM remains an 'administrative' party without serious social or community roots; in fact, the problem of its survival as a political force will inevitably arise the day its leaders will lose power and control over the country's administration.

The largest Cameroonian opposition party is the Social Democratic Front (SDF), dominated by the charismatic figure of John Fru Ndi (an Anglophone of the North West and a former book seller). Its role magnified after the legendary challenge that its founder posed to the CPDM party in May 1990.[10] This party gets its essential electorate from the Anglophones and the Bamileke (in the North West,

9 'Kirdi' is a term from the Arabic dialect of the Ouadai and the Banguirmi, which means 'unbelievers' (designating non-Muslims). It is used by the Fulani (*Kaado* or *Habe*) to designate the 'pagan ethnic groups' of the Northern Cameroon. But this this ancient label is no more exact, since many *Kirdi* converted to Christianity and Islam.

10 On 26 May 1990, John Fru Ndi launched the Social Democratic Front in Bamenda, resulting in clashes with the security forces opening fire, killing six young civilians. Perceived locally as 'martyrs', their death created the first surge of national popular outrage. The until then obscure Fru Ndi became the resistance leader, 'Ni John'.

the South West, the Western and the Littoral regions). This constituency basis led to the term 'Anglo-Bami' at the beginning of 1990, designating the so-called opposition ethnic groups, the Anglophones and the Bamileke. But hampered since the mid-1990s by factional and hegemonic fights (the Anglophones against the Bamileke; the Anglophones of the North West against those of the South West regions, the stranglehold of the *founding fathers* gathered around chairman John Fru Ndi), and surreptitiously engaged for years in the 'politics of the belly',[11] today the SDF has lost its position as a national party and became more and more thrown back on its traditional stronghold in the North West, with some additional support in the town of Douala in the Littoral and in the Mifi division in the West.

Another opposition party, the UNDP (Union Nationale pour la Démocratie et le Progrès), has as president the Fulani Bello Bouba Maigari (a former minister under President Ahmadou Ahidjo and a former prime minister under President Paul Biya); it recruits in majority from the three northern regions (Adamaoua, North and Far North), notably amongst the Islamo-Fulani in opposition to the *Kirdi*. This party claims the heritage of the republic's first president Ahidjo, but following the struggle of positioning among its different leaders and after its repeated compromising with the CPDM regime,[12] among other factors, the UNDP has now become only a shadow of its former self. From 68 deputies in the 1992[13] legislative, this score has passed respectively to 13, 1 and 6 deputies in 1992, 2002 and 2007, acquired exclusively from the North Region. Like the SDF, the national representativity of the UNDP is thus today a standard formula.

Parties with a regional basis

Three other parties render the situation more complex in Cameroon with their regional, not to say ethnic, character: the UDC (Union Démocratique du Cameroon), the MDR (Mouvement pour la Défense de la République) and the UPC (Union des Populations du Cameroun). The UDC has as leader Adamou Ndam Njoya, a Bamun and a former Minister under Ahidjo. Its followers or members are from the Noun division (i.e. the Bamun kingdom), from where its president originates (see Mouiche 2005, Ch. 6). The leader of the MDR is Dakolle Daïssala, a *Kirdi* from the Toupouri ethnic group in the Far North Region, and a former political prisoner of Biya's.[14] This party gets its electorate from the Toupouri zones of the Mayo-

11 John Fru Ndi is accused by many Cameroonians and media to have received money from the CPDM regime, with the objective to destabilise the opposition.

12 On this compromise, read Socpa 2000: 103; Moukoko Priso 1994: 90-92.

13 The UNDP profited in fact, from a transfer of votes in the South of the country due to boycott in the said elections by the opposition considered 'radical' notably the SDF.

14 After the abortive *coup d'Etat* against Paul Biya in April 1984, the MDR leader Dakolle, at the

Kani and the Mayo-Danay divisions. Unlike the UNDP the MDR is today, among other factors, the victim of a 'compromise' between its leaders and the CPDM regime, as shall be seen below. From six deputies in 1992 in its traditional fief, the score moved down to three in 1997, then to one in 2002 and zero in 2007. But the MDR is today still in control of five Municipal Offices.

What about the UPC? As Mehler has said (1997: 118): 'To write on the historic party the UPC is a particularly difficult task. It is not possible to stick to one version of fact, for the party is divided into two main camps as well as in many personalised segments.' However, its basis is in the Bassa ethnic group, which benefited notably the late Augustin Frederic Kodock, a Bassa and Secretary General of the most representative faction of this political group.

The MDR, the UPC and the UNDP have since 1992 remained very conciliatory towards the Biya regime so as to participate in a 'large union' government in the framework of '*démocratie apaisée*' which the regime propagated. It is only since 2007, following their disgraceful defeat in the legislative elections that the UPC and the MDR were expelled from the government. It has to be recalled that after the legislative elections of March 1992 it was thanks to the coalition with MDR that the CPDM, a minority in the parliament although dominating, succeeded to form a government. This precedent was emulated in the ranks of the UNDP and UPC, as just after the presidential elections that same year these two parties also entered the government. Since then, the UNDP has sat in the government without interruption. On their part, the SDF and the UDC remain in the parliamentary opposition. This is the reason why Moukoko Priso has qualified the MDR, the UPC-K (the Kodock faction) and the UNDP as part of the 'conservative camp' and the SDF and UDC as the 'democratic opposition' (see Moukoko Priso 1994: 89 and ss.). Apart from these six parties, no other party was able to continue its presence in Cameroon politics. Despite the five surviving parties mentioned, the CPDM's dominance was reproduced in every election to date.

The 'ultra-dominance' of the CPDM

Most analyses of the African political party systems are about the dominance of parties. In spite of reforms adopted since 1990 many African political regimes are dominated by parties that achieve a large majority in two, three or even four successive elections. The singularity of Africa lies then in the high frequency of this type of phenomenon; in many cases the party that won the 'transitional' or

---

time general manager of SOTUC (Société des Transports Urbains du Cameroun), was arrested and incarcerated for seven years without being tried. This happened to many other personalities from the North.

'founding' elections – be it a former single party or a newly formed party of the opposition (as in Zambia and Malawi) – has succeeded to stay in power during all subsequent elections. These episodes of prolonged power have evoked critical studies on the reasons for the 'dominance' of such parties. Questions relative to this phenomenon are: when does a party become dominant? Is there a difference between dominance and hegemony? What are the causes of dominance and what are its consequences? (cf. Carbone 2008: 32)

Using the perspective of Lester (1965: 18), certain questions can be raised so as to give an account of the influence of political parties in Cameroon on the population. How many and which political parties solicited the ballots of the population since the first multiparty elections of 1992? What were the results in terms of deputies' seats, municipal counsellors or mayor's positions? To answer these questions, not all the elections shall be taken into consideration, but only the municipal and parliamentary elections (The presidential elections are excluded since they mobilise less parties and candidates). In the parliamentary elections one notes an unequal representation of Cameroonian political parties: in fact, in spite of their large number less than 50 political parties actually solicit the popular vote during elections. And only a small fraction of them is able to reach any convincing results. For instance, during the double polls in 2007, 45 parties were in contending for the legislative and 27 for the municipal seats (see *Cameroon Tribune* no. 8860/5059 of 1 June 2007). In the end, only six political parties won for the municipal seats (314 for CPDM against 18 for the SDF, with UNDP 13, UDC 8, MDR 5 and UPC 2). Five parties won in the legislative elections: 153 seats for CPDM, with SDF 16, UNDP 6, UDC 4 and 1 for the MP. It should be noted that only the CPDM is able to present candidates in all the electoral constituencies; followed in descending order by the UNDP and the SDF meanwhile the UPC, UDC and MDR are contented with the smallest share. Apart from these parties, many formations invest their candidates in only one or two constituencies generally where their respective leaders originate.

This inequality of political participation can be observed at the local level as well. Let us take the 1996 municipals in the Western region: twelve political parties there solicited the vote of the population. In the end only the SDF, the CPDM, the UDC and the UFDC[15] were able to win seats in 17, 14, 9 and 2 communes (or municipalities) respectively, and the ANDP[16] had two seats of municipal counsel-

15 The UFDC has as its leader Victorin Hameni Bieuleu, a Bamileke of the Upper-Nkam Division.

16 ANDP (Alliance Nationale pour la Démocratie et le Progrès) was created by Minister Hamadou Moustapha, a Fulani from the Far North, following his expulsion from the UNDP after the legislative elections of 1992. Hamadou Moustapha in fact had negotiated and obtained his entry

lors (see Mouiche 2005: 30). In 2002 there was a reverse in the tendency in favour of the CPDM in this same region, as well as the disappearance of the UFDC from the commune stage: 29 were for CPDM, 8 for UDC and 4 for SDF (see Mouiche 2005: 221). An overview of the four legislatives elections since 1992 is given in Table 1 below.

Table 1: Parliamentary representation and party identification in Cameroon since 1992

	Election Years			
Political parties	1992	1997	2002	2007
CPDM	88	116	148	153
SDF	Boycott	43	23	16
UNDP	68	13	1	6
UDC	Boycott	5	5	4
UPC	18	1	3	0
MDR	6	1	0	0
MLDC	Boycott	1	0	0
MP	Boycott	0	0	1
Total	180	180	180	180

As can be seen from this table, the distribution of votes confirms the movement in favour of the CPDM from one election to the other, thus reinforcing the hegemony of this party. One can note a tendency of toward a '*cpdmicisation*' of national political life following every election. The CPDM since the double elections of 2007 has the control of 314 *communes* out of the total of 360 in Cameroon. Another salient fact is that only seven political parties were able until now to send deputies to the National Assembly.

Since the return to multipartyism in Cameroon, only the CPDM, SDF, UNDP, UDC, MDR, UPC and UFDC have been able to get involved in the management of municipal constituencies by obtaining the relative or absolute majority in elections. In the same vein, two or three parties succeeded to gain some seats in municipal councils. Lastly, while in 1992 the CPDM had the majority only in four

into the government without the support of the UNDP hierarchy. Without any electoral weight of his party, the ANDP leader continues until today (December 2011) to be in the government. The ANDP has even become an extension of the CPDM and supports presidential candidate Paul Biya since 1997.

regions out of the ten in the country, it was otherwise in 1997, when it became dominant in seven regions. Since 2002 the CPDM controls nine regions: only the North West, stronghold of the SDF, escaped the electoral machine of this party. It is no exaggeration to say that in the actual context of multipartyism in Cameroon the CPDM fulfils a function of 'national integration' similar to the former African single parties, as noted by Enoh Meyomesse:

> Truly speaking, the New Deal Regime[17] instead of thinking about the future has rather turned to the past, digging it up with force and exuberance to end up with the same results: the taming of multipartyism and democracy in general. The New Deal Regime has not invented anything at all; it has quite simply been inspired by that of the 'national unity' of Ahmadou Ahidjo, simply with lesser imprisonments and political assassinations (Enoh Meyomesse 2009: 22-23).

In contemporary global political discourse, democracy has become a 'moral good', not to say an 'imperative' (Diamond & Morlino 2005: x). In most of the world the question of democratisation occupies a central position. It calls for interpretations which aim at explaining how and why certain political regimes have become democracies and to evaluate the quality of that alleged or real democracy. Yet, in the case of political mutations in Cameroon nearly all the authors agree that we have to do with 'political liberalisation' rather than with 'democratisation'. There has been some measure of opening up of political space, but power at the centre is retained by the same elite, and alternation is not in the books. How then does the CPDM consolidate this 'big man' democracy?

The CPDM hegemony and consolidation of 'big man' democracy

One of the problems brought up by the frequent use of the concept of 'dominance' to qualify African political parties is the fact that it covers different cases. Certain parties are aptly qualified as 'dominant parties', but others are in fact 'hegemonic parties' (*i.e.*, monopolizing, authoritarian dominant parties, see Satori 1976: 230). In the first case there exists a certain degree of competition (even minimal), whereas in the second case the system is non-competitive, despite appearances and rhetoric. In other words, a *dominant* party is that which wins a series of consecutive mandates (at least three according to Sartori) in the framework of real elections; that is, elections exempted from major frauds. In this case, opposition parties simply fail to modify the choices of the electorate and to oust the party in

[17] New Deal Regime: in French 'régime du Renouveau', an expression claimed since 1982 by President Biya to designate and distinguish his regime.

power. In the case of *hegemonic* parties, elections are organised but equally their results (through electoral frauds or other means): '...other parties have the right to exist, but (...) the possibility of power rotation is not in any case envisaged' (Sartori 1976: 230-231; see also Carbone 2008: 32). In the case that concerns us, as in Burkina Faso with the CDP party of President B. Compaoré (cf. Loada 1998: 64), many factors seem to be at the origin of the CPDM hegemony, among them the organisation of the party, its human and material resources, its capacity of invasion, the public financing of parties, its dominance over the means of coercion and repression – army, police – and its entrenched business interests.

A strong electoral machine and a conservative hegemonic coalition

Political parties are intermediary institutions between state and society. Their common goal is to look for ways to influence collective action and decision-making. This process can be analysed through the concept of 'linkage', forged by Kay Lawson, which means '...interactive connections between the orientations of elites and the population's preferences'. Political parties are at the centre of these processes, for they are '...the agents which forge links between citizens and decision makers. Their *raison d'être* is to create connections between those in power and the governed' (Lawson 1980: 3). In this perspective, research on political parties in Africa seems to be in agreement on the idea that 'connection through rewards' is rampant. Many authors affirm that in imperfect democracies that have emerged from transitional processes relations between patrons and clients are crucial in the lives and functions of parties. Political competition brings about a more acute rivalry between elite members over state control, which remains the principal venue to resources in the African political economy. Political carriers are attractive, for they give access to the state, the central place of accumulation. In this context, political parties are less the expression of social cleavages or ideological orientations than 'the instrument of factional mobilisation' that permits clientelistic redistribution. In other words, African parties today '... don't help to aggregate interest – they rather assure a function of representation in a clientelist context' (see Osei 2008: 40).

In Cameroon, the CPDM, facing an opposition weakened notably by internal divisions, disposes of a powerful electoral machine. The ruling party in fact has coopted the essential administrative, economic and social elites of the country. As rightly underlined by Frederic Farverjon, a French researcher and eye witness of the 1996 municipal elections in the West of Cameroon, Cameroonian politics is very little based on ideology:

> ... it is precisely the politics of assembling behind a person on which one depends. Polit-

ical parties place at the top of theirs lists candidates with a certain aura who have demonstrated this through their actions in the village. These elites rally voters basing more on who they are, rather than on their political programs. Typically, the CPDM candidate in the Nde division in the legislative elections were Niat in 91 (the director-general of SONEL- Société Nationale d'électricité du Cameroun) and Tchouta Moussa in 97 (the director-general of the ONPC, the Office National des Ports du Cameroun). The electorate voted for these elite members more because of their generosity towards their brothers than for the CPDM, disgraced by the population and of which their assessment is less gratifying.[18]

The bad score of the ruling party in a locality is interpreted as a rejection of elites by the population and constitutes a reason likely to cause the disgrace of the said political leaders. In response, the latter generally resort to numerous techniques of fraud so as to assure CPDM electoral victory. These techniques go from intimidation to the creation of fictitious polling stations through ballot box jams, unequal distribution of seats, selective registration of electoral lists, displacement of polling stations on election day, and the organisation of 'electoral charters' or 'international electors'[19] (see Socpa 2000: 105-106; Gros & Mentang 2003: 131-165).[20] Enoh Meyomesse thus talks of such elites as 'guard dogs of the regime' (see Meyomesse 2000: 23-24). To this author, such elites are 'true militants of the CPDM'. For a very good reason, it is in the best interest of these 'civil servants' and 'business men', 'winners of procurement contracts', that the regime remains in power. That is why during electoral periods all flow into the towns and villages,

---

18 See Frédéric Faverjon, on http://membres.lycos.fr/rdefap/faverjon/politique.html?,p5.

19 The experience of 'international voters' is observed in frontier districts of Cameroon, principally in the northern part; it consists of bringing in people from Chad and Nigeria to vote in Cameroonian territory. This practice of 'Charters of Voters' and ínternational voters' explains the sudden increase in population in certain localities on election day; it also justifies why electoral lists are denied publication at least one week before election day, in conformity with the electoral code.

20 People with the age to vote (20 years and above) have increased about 16% between 1992 and 1997. The second is based on the fact that the proportions of those who register in regard to the eligible population have decreased during the same period. It has passed from 78.54% during the 1992 presidential (78.80% in the legislatives of the same year) to 67.98% in the municipal elections of 1996, four years later, to 60.16% in the legislative elections of 17 May 1997 and 66.11% for the presidential election of 12 October 1997. Opposition parties, NGOs and local civil organizations as well as international observers condemned the selective and repeated purges of electoral lists, arbitrary and discriminatory strategies of selective inscription on electoral lists and the distribution of voters' cards that in 1997 deprived about two million Cameroonians (well aimed to the ethnic and linguistic plan) of their voting rights (see Bakery 1998: 10-11). These fraudulent maneuvers made the SDF, UDC and UNDP to boycott this election.

proceed to intimidate the population and to blackmail by presenting an apocalyptic vision of their Division or even ethnic constituency '... if they commit the monumental error of not voting 100% the CPDM, and naturally they systematically fill ballot boxes'. As Meyomesse continues: 'After having realised this 'patriotic' work, supposedly to the benefit of the tribe or District, they hurry to Yaoundé to present their electoral 'victory' to the CPDM Central Committee which they trade to the government for posts', given that they substituted themselves to true candidates of the party, having fought on their behalf transforming the latter in a simple foil and political walk-on. Throughout the period of electoral campaigns, they deserted their offices and went around in the local administration's vehicles, consuming state fuel for private use.' Truly, this author says, '... they have purely and simply embezzled public funds' (Enoh Meyomesse 2009: 29-30).

In the general report of the National Office of Elections (NEO)[21] on the unfolding of the electoral operations during the legislative and municipal elections of 2002[22] it is clearly mentioned that certain 'careerist civil servants are convinced that their salvation passes through the manipulation of results in their constituencies'. According to NEO, the obstinacy of 'elites' in general and of the high ranking of the public service in particular to influence the local population in a way so as to corrupt the electoral process greatly preoccupies all political parties and administrative authorities: Administrative authorities find it very difficult to resist the influence and the pressure from the urban elites whose interest-based interference in the village affairs is more and more discredited and harmful to the orderly procedure of the elections' (*ibid.*). As the report continued: 'The elites impose their own registrations to the administrative authorities, as well as those of persons residing in the village, but did not care to present themselves to the commission in charge of revising the electoral lists' (*ibid.*) Such type of late registrations done without any verification have detrimental consequences for the control of the electoral process and are chiefly manifested in the phenomenon of multiple registrations. Given these serious infringements NEO recommended that the management of the electoral file be withdrawn from the administrative authorities and confined to an independent organ. Besides, the report recommends a restructuring of existing commissions so as to free them from the control of the administrative authorities, or the combination of the two propositions. The neutral

21 The NEO (ONEL) was replaced in December 2006 by the ELECAM (Elections Cameroon), an organ with far more extended powers but still under the dominion of the CPDM.

22 Observatoire National des Élections, *Rapport général sur le déroulement des opérations électorales des élections législatives et municipales 2002*, Yaoundé, SOPECAM, 2003.

organ to be created would be in charge of the management of electoral register from the beginning right to the delivery of the voters' cards.[23]

Since the 1990s the CPDM has enlarged its political class mainly with Cameroonian business men; and in the Bamileke area many of these patrons have become mayors in their localities (see Mouiche 2005). The thesis of Bratton and Van de Walle (1997: 167) according to which it was very 'natural' for many Bamileke entrepreneurs in the 1990s to be active in the opposition seems problematic. According to J.M. Gabriel (1999) these two authors are right only if they refer to small entrepreneurs; if on the contrary, they mean the barons and principal business men they would be wrong (Gabriel 1999: 191). Moreover, the CPDM has worked for a political division of the territory, leaning on the old structures of the former single party in the regions, divisions, communes, villages and quarters. As such, of the 58 sections fitting the contours of Divisions, just before 1992, this party in 1993 has multiplied almost by two the number of the said political units. In 1996 the CPDM gained 53 new sections, reaching 111. In 2006 it reached control over 168 sections (see Tchejip Kaptchouang 2006: 72-73).[24]

Another 'innovative trait' that characterises the CPDM resides in primaries, a method of democratic selection of the candidates, as in vogue in the United States. First of all, not only do these primaries are said to permit the democratic and impartial management of exponential demands of candidates, fuelled by the party's eagerness for elective posts, but also to better divert the inevitable frustrations that come as a result. In reality the game has not always been democratic or sincere in certain electoral constituencies. Just before the January 1996 municipal elections there was call to order by the Secretary General of the CPDM Central

---

[23] Long before the NEO's report, bishops of Cameroon met in a National Episcopal Conference on 4 July 2002, where they pointed out grave and multiple infringements on the freedom to vote of citizens and who had already blacklisted the elites; 'We had pointed out these irregularities that put to question the electoral results to the competent authorities before the 30th of June'. 'These shortcomings were again noticed on the polling day. They were perpetrated here and there by elites, traditional heads, local authorities of the territorial administration and members of political parties in competition' (see *Cameroon Tribune*, 8 July 2002, pp. 6-7). But notwithstanding these practices detrimental to democratic development, one can agree with Patrick Quantin that disloyal practices and weaknesses of electoral discipline are not 'African anomalies'. If an idea does not tie with the comparison it is that by which non occidental societies in general and Africans in particular would be carriers of an exceptional inclination to electoral fraud and reluctance in regard to rational legal procedures. It suffices to look at France and Great Britain in the 19th century to see the degree to which electoral democracy was born in the absence of norms (Quantin 1998: 21).

[24] To which one might add six others from outside the national territory: France (two), Great Britain, Germany, Benelux countries and the USA (one respectively).

Committee (the central authority of electoral nominations) to those who were inclined to force their nomination at the level of this structure: 'That our friends who have come to solicit the 'confirmation' of their nomination at the Central Committee understand that things have changed since 30 November. Nominations are no longer done by the summit but by the base' (*L'Action*, 5 January 1996, p. 6). But this official intervention is still not put into practice: the popularity tests of candidates are often falsified through the publication of candidates' lists as rendered public by the Central Committee of the party. It is not then fortuitous if the official speech of the CPDM makes use of circumlocutions to describe the technique of the primaries. This technique, however, has proved to be profitable to the presidential party, since not only does it permit the selection in general of the most representative (i.e., locally powerful) candidates, which thus maximises the chances of winning of the CPDM in elections. It equally gives some 'democratic lessons' to the opposition party.

Lastly, by many of its practices, the CPDM has given the impression that they do not value the equality of chances presumed in the definition of a regime of rational financing of political parties and electoral campaigns. For long it was content with a 'legal silence' that prevailed until the promulgation of the law on the financing of political parties of 19 December 2000. Moreover, the two legal provisions as established in France, for instance, the legislative recognition of public financing of electoral activities and also establishing a ceiling of this expenditure – the Cameroonian legislators seem to have voluntarily kept away from the second part. At the same time it condoned party financing to the dominant party CPDM – a party which draws an advantage from hidden financing. In the same way, by opting to base the distribution of the money allocated to parties on criteria of the number of seats obtained during the last legislative elections and on the obtaining of at least 5% in the electoral constituencies, the CPDM in a strategic way placed itself in a pole position in the sharing. This legislation does not address the *de facto* inequality of power between the CPDM and other political parties.

The 'alimentary logic' and the territorial logic valorising political clientelism

According to Gero Erdmann and Ulf Engel (2007) there exist two types of exchange around the purchase of votes: clientelism and patronage. Patronage refers to the political distribution of favours in the form of (promises of access to) collective goods. Employment in the public sector or in development projects, for instance, is geared toward certain groups, at times via the use of state resources.

Clientelism on its part is based on favouring others on the basis of interpersonal relations, often between two individuals. Deputies and candidates intervene in the private affairs of voters: they pay funerals, school fees or other bills, provide jobs, or give out small sums of money (Erdmann & Engel 2007: 95-119). The current literature admits that receivers of these 'gifts' are characterised primarily by their ethnic origin and it is true that parties are very often active in a specific region or within of an ethnic group. The effect of clientelism and patronage should however not be exaggerated. In fact, very often, material benefits are collected by only a few elite members or a close circle of party leaders. This does not prevent citizens from having the feeling that their interest will better be served if members of their ethnic group are in power. It means that this '*chop money*' alone does not guarantee the vote but has to be combined with mobilisation strategies and appeals to the ethno-political identities of voters. The secrecy of the ballot in fact forbids parties from controlling the effectiveness of their vote purchase (Osei 2008: 41)

This said, just after the independence of Cameroon, state participation in the economic activity was more advanced than today. This participation was justified by the necessity to put in place a modern economic system in the absence of economic agents capable of procuring sufficient investment. As a result it was the state that inspired and orientated most economic activities. Hence, the interventionist state which was forged by first president Ahmadou Ahidjo in the shadow of the single party owed its solidity to a certain efficiency in the allocation of prebends. The state could control ethnic and regional tensions by resorting to the creation of jobs in the civil service or through the economy of indebtedness, of commercialisation or of distribution (investments, allocation of land titles and bank loans, granting of procurement contracts and public works, regulation of commerce import-export, subvention system, attribution of salaries, advantages and bonuses, allocation of equipments and infrastructure). It is also on this basis that the regime was able to constitute its clientele and to consolidate its network of patronage. This political management helped to sustain a very complex system of transfers of revenue, from formal and official circuits to parallel circuits, from urban households to rural households, from the richest (or most wealthy) to the poorest through the bias of family assistance, for expenses and for diverse prestations such as payment of school fees, health expenses, funeral expenses and participation in customary ceremonies. All these devices were managed according to the principal of 'regional balance' (Mbembe 1993: 367-368).

The 'New Deal' advocated by President Paul Biya, who took over power in 1982, did not constitute a break with this heritage. Moreover, the economic crisis that Cameroon witnessed from 1986 and multipartyism aroused 'alimentary expectations' of the electorate instead. Conscious of these expectations, the CPDM turned even more to the clientelist distribution of resources (money, food products, loincloths, tee-shirts, gadgets, etc.), since due to its control over the state apparatus the party had no difficulty to extract the necessary resources for its electoral campaigns and exercise its power over the electoral process. With the governmental monopoly of the allocation of state resources, it was also very common to see certain CPDM big shots able to influence the territorial allocation of state investments or disposing of the latest information on investment projects, claiming achievement or merit for them, thus greatly reinforcing favourable publicity. It is scarcely surprising in this perspective that the number of inaugurations of public works spectacularly increases at the eve of elections. At this level, it is good to distinguish this 'alimentary pressure' from the ethnic type of pressure, even if the two are complementary.[25]

'Ethnic pressures' are based on what is called the 'the logic of the soil' ('la logique du terroir', Mouiche 2005). In fact, in Africa, where career assessment of a higher official is often brought down to the question what real advantages he brought to his people (e.g., in terms of the most envied social positions, credit facilities, the obtainment of procurement contracts, recruitment in great schools, employment in para-public corporations, scholarships, or the realisation of development infrastructure), these 'ethnic pressures' consist of asking voters directly to cast their vote for their 'brothers' or for their 'godfathers'. As for the 'alimentary pressure' or those of manducation (see Bayart 1989), it is based on offering things to eat or drink to one's voters or to promise the nomination of a son of the locality to an important post in the higher echelons of the state so as to obtain their votes. In all, 'ethnic pressure' refers to patronage using the strategy of moral corruption, while 'alimentary pressure' deploys the weapon of material corruption (Socpa 2000: 92-93).

This clientelist logic and manducation led Frédéric Faverjon to say that the CPDM is more of 'a conglomerate of opportunists than a political party'.[26] To Faverjon, the tactic of the party in power consists of becoming inescapable to who so ever wishes to have a portion of power in the country. Just as in the good old times of the single party in Cameroon, it is almost a necessity to pay allegiance to the CPDM if one wants to carry out businesses undisturbed or to remain in a responsible position in the administration:

[25] To better understand the alimentary and clientelist logics in the Cameroon political game, see Socpa 2000: 91-108.

[26] See Frédéric Faverjon, http://membres.lycos.fr/rdefap/faverjon/politique.html?, p. 5.

> I believe I don't know any CPDM militant having adhered to the party by conviction. In fact, this party assembles opportunists who wish to occupy posts so as to test the crumbs from the feast, elites who want to preserve their places in the administration or in para-public corporations, merchants wishing to carry out their commerce without impediments. Intimidations and arbitrary appointments are still legion for all those who are disobedient; this is meant to make cringe civil servants who dare take any initiative, without being covered by their hierarchy. To adhere to the party for most militants is a means to have something to eat or to have job security.

In the absence of a developed civil society, to accede to the state is to accede to riches. Taking into account the thinness of the cake to be shared and the principle of the authoritarian management of the state, it is convenient to stand behind a well-placed relative who has a better position so as to pretend having the crumbs of the feast. Due to the extended African family and to the weight of community obligations, requests sent to those who have access to money are many. Therefore a highly placed civil servant will at the same time look for ways to redistribute the booty to his relatives in order to be assured of their support and to reinforce his position and hinder other family and ethnic networks from acceding to the few riches available. He then creates a relationship of reciprocal dependence between those at the top and those at the bottom. This overlapping of mutual aid networks permits that the state be undermined without this appearing to be 'morally reprehensible'. (Faverjon, *ibid.*)

It should nevertheless be said that, contrary to the above and to the illusions evoked until now by the universal claims of the European nation-state model, we have here the operating mode of politics in Africa. After all, there exists no social security in a poor and crisis-ridden Africa. Better still, the coherence of the African conception of politics lies in a 'functional logic' where it is the job to get things done that determines the degree of organisation. As Le Roy has said:

> 'This pragmatic conception of social organisation goes back to the problem of legitimacy. It is less the beauty of the institutional design than the practical advantages drawn from an organisational system that legitimate, in the eyes of actors, the interest or not of envisaged forms' (Le Roy 1996: 99).

Such is also the hypothesis of Richard Banégas in his studies of the moral economy of electoral corruption in Benin. While avoiding the trap of culturalism, he demonstrates that there is meaning with regard to the native moral code 'of riches, of the belly, of kinship' and 'the social logic of negotiation, of brokerage, of '*cadeautage*' and of the redistributive accumulation' before boldly advancing that may be it is in 'merchandising' votes that the real processes of the formation and consolidation of democracy south of the Sahara are being carried out (Banégas 1998: 75-87). For truly, before coming in contact with the West, African societies had elaborated their proper conception and practices of political power, even if these were not always explicit everywhere. They were founded on imaginary significations as regards the place of the individual in the group, of his insertion in the world, his relation to others to the natural and the supernatural, to death, etc. that propped up the entire power instituted: that of the lineage, of the village, of the clan, of the tribe, and even – of present – the royal powers. Changes which came up with colonialism are inscribed in this traditional dynamics; firstly, the putting in place of the colonial state and of independence thereafter were not been a rupture in relation to tradition, as is often thought. The state apparatus inherited by colonialism had been clothed by perceptions and practices of power which local society recognized and confirmed (cf. Mappa 1998: 11-12; Mbembe 2000: 66; Sandbrook 1987: 23-24).

Three elements are therefore combined and crystallised in one set: power without neither check and balance nor accountability; a confusion of the public and private properties, and social pressure valuing ostentation and redistribution and playing on prestige rivalries (cf. Olivier de Sardan 1998: 108). In this respect, it is needless to recall that since many years Cameroon figures among the world's top spots concerning corruption and the embezzlement of public funds (according to the rankings of *Transparency International*).[27] In 1999, and especially in 2006, after a presidential 'anti-corruption initiative' called *Opération Épervier*, and under pressure of the international community, some corrupt officials, ministers, and general managers of para-statal enterprises and their accomplices, recruited essentially from the ranks of the CPDM, have been sued, tried and thrown in jail. But this initiative of President Biya remains very limited and selective. Many oligarchs who got rich illegally continue to live peacefully, displaying their exuberance and scoffing at the population and the private press which denounced their acts of misappropriation. Many compromising cases are still without result, waiting for the president to give the green light for prosecution. He continues to stigmatise 'evil' in his speeches, everything that contrasts his legendary reserve.

To conclude, it should be pointed out also that 'gifts' also play an essential role in the formation and volatility of political alliances in Cameroon. Corruption of certain political leaders is the subject of frequent debate and it is commonly said that these leaders receive sums of money in order to merge their political

[27] In 2011 Cameroon was in place 134 of the TI Corruption Perceptions Index (on a total of 182 countries).

parties with the ruling party or to destabilise a well established political party in a region with an important electoral stake. This seems to very often be confirmed through certain spectacular changes in the behaviour and public declarations of political leaders. It is common that individuals from time to time change their political party in the course of one year, and especially on the eve of election day. This 'political transhumance' leaves one perplexed and gives reason to think that in the absence of a valid political motive, opinion leaders or politicians of opposition parties often seem to be in urgent need of resources and will therefore do any politics just to satisfy their immediate material/financial needs. The political alliance between the MDR and the CPDM a day after the legislative elections of 1992, that permitted Paul Biya to constitute a governmental majority, seems to be explained by this prevalence of primary needs over the interests of the MDR militants and those of the entire Cameroonian opposition. For example, it is known that its leader Dakole Daïssala, Biya's prisoner, who had been arrested on the day after the abortive *coup d'état* of 6 April 1984 and was in prison for seven years without being tried, was only liberated due to popular pressure in the years 1989-1990, with other political prisoners. But he entered into an alliance in 1992 with President Biya. Without prejudice to the fact that each political party is free to ally with one or more other parties of its choice, this alliance seems to be quite surprising: not based on any common ideological platform but rather on a clientelist scaffolding that recalls the 'politics of the belly' (Socpa 2000: 103). At the time, a parliamentary coalition of MDR-UPC-UNDP would have created a cataclysm in the national political arena and might have precipitated the departure of President Biya. It did not happen. That is why, according to Moukoko Priso, writing in 1994, MDR leader Dakole Daïssala seemed '... to be essentially driven by a set of personal considerations, either revenge or *ventrique*':

> Until now he enjoys playing upon the secular disputes of the non-Moslem population of the Northern regions (notably the Far North) with their Fulbe neighbours. For the moment, his desire for revenge against the latter and his will to 'eat his own share' seem to have made him forget the misery which certain extremist clans around Biya made him undergo not long ago, including time in prison and various humiliations (Moukoko Priso 1994: 93-94).[28]

[28] The same author qualifies the UPC-Kodock group (discussed above) as 'a union for commerce'. This is again to emphasize the 'politics of the belly', as illustrated by the late Augustin Frédéric Kodock when he entered into the coalition government with the CPDM.

Conclusion: the improbability of democratic alternation in Cameroon

In this chapter we have aimed to give an account of the subversion of multipartyism and democratisation in Cameroon, produced by the omnipresence and hegemony of the incumbent CPDM and its president. As Mwalimu George Nwane noted (2004), in the 1990s the quest for democracy was based on desires for greater participation in decision-making, more delegation of authority to the regions, a better consideration of the Anglophone problem, more power and autonomy of the population over local natural resources, greater economic responsibility, and more opportunities for each Cameroonian to present himself and to obtain elective positions. Unfortunately, like in many other African countries, multipartyism in Cameroon has not resulted in democracy and social equity but rather to the reverse of the situation: to the rule of an ultra-dominant party, the CPDM, and a situation of sharing the sources of prebends and power between the coalition of parties around CPDM. The chief responsibility for this impasse in the country lies with the incumbent political elite personalities (cf. Ngwane 2004: 23-24; Nyamnjoh 2002: 5-8). The renewal of political elites in Cameroon, allowing new representative candidates to emerge from below, is doubtful if not impossible. Indeed, analysed at the alder of a logic of pluralist and representative democracy of the elector's choice, the Cameroonian political scene distinguishes itself by the hegemonic position of the party in power, with the conciliating participation of certain opposition parties. The monopolisation of power and the political game by President Biya and his CPDM prevented a pluralist and representative democracy reflecting voters' choices, and predictably brought about the end of a 'trusteeship liberal transition', to quote Fred Eboko.[29] This seems to have sealed the return of the former single party as a *de facto* dominant party.

The omnipresence and hegemony of the CPDM assured the improbability of democratic alternation, even if there would be a possibility of transparent and fair elections in Cameroon. On the one hand, with a one round presidential poll, Cameroon is renowned for the absence of an 'alternative coalition government', an expression borrowed from Goran Hyden and Michael Bratton who by this term meant a 'powerful and coherent opposition' that is 'indispensable to progress toward good governance' (Hyden & Bratton 1992: 71, Mghanga 2006: 6-9, Göranson 2007: 3). Certainly, alliances which have a large base, like those which mark the political life of most Western democratic countries, do not really exist in sub-Saharan Africa, where political participation has long been limited to a small minority. In a representative democracy, broader alliances would be part of the

[29] Cf. Fred Eboko, cited in Daloz 1999: 100.

normal political game, reflecting pragmatism and not being aimed at a forced unanimity, which characterized the one-party systems (cf. Bourgi 2003). In addition, in Cameroon, the moderate material means of which the opposition parties dispose is lamentable, and in combination with internal dividedness, clientelism, and inability to unite they are largely tamed by the CPDM. The economic logic of Cameroonian politics – based on the idea that those who have power have the material resources and the power to 'distribute' them according to their preferences and strategic interests – has thus worked against political democratization.

On the other hand, faithful to his *big man* posture, the CPDM in 2008, at the cost of many deaths perpetrated by the security forces firing at protesters, scrapped the constitutional clause limiting the presidential mandate, thereby opening the possibility to simply perpetuate President Biya in power. At the same time, the electoral system was bolted: ELECAM, the organisation in charge of organization and supervision of the elections, created in December 2006 and functional since 2008, underwent two amendments even before having managed any election. The first amendment brings again administrative authorities in the electoral process, although formerly discredited; the second amendment, taking into account the recent crisis in Ivory Coast, took away from ELECAM the possibility of publishing electoral results, giving this possibility to the Constitutional Council (which is in fact non-existent). Besides, ELECAM officials, its director general, and the electoral council are appointed by the president of the republic alone. In addition, the Electoral Council counts 12 CPDM activists amongst its 18 members. All this puts into question its impartiality, even if these ones formally 'resigned' from the CPDM. After much national and international pressure, the regime raised the initial number of 12 members in the Electoral Council to 18, and amended the law for this. President Biya added six other members, belonging to 'civil society' organisations, but if fact being hand-picked supporter of him and his party. The CPDM in power thus holds on to the wheel. It is no surprise that the rupture of public trust with the electoral system or in a larger sense with the political system is significant.[30] Governmental measures to persuade the electorate to register for elections (e.g., handing out a free national identity card before the 2011 presidential elections), remained in vain. It is not surprising that President Biya nevertheless won this election – for the sixth time.

Apart from the growing general feeling of the uselessness of elections and the necessity to be politically *dis*engaged, the greatest and most pressing danger of

[30] Since many years voters are reluctant to register on the electoral lists. A joint survey of *Cretes* and of the journal *Le Messager* done in January 2008 just confirmed this public disaffection with politics in Cameroon. See *Le Messager* of 23 January 2008.

the stagnation of the democratic process is that of 'doing politics through other means' (Bakary 1998). These means have been viewed by many in a heroic or revolutionary vision of political change even in the Leninist and Sorelian manner of defending violence. This view has seen many adherents in Africa, e.g. in armed insurgent movements in the post-colonial era, and can yield disastrous results, especially in view of underlying ethnic tensions.

In Cameroon it is asserted that 'big man' democracy is accompanied by heavy corruption and 'state tribalism' largely to the benefit of the *Beti*, the ethnic group of President Biya. This iniquitous disturbance of the ethno-regional equilibrium – maintaining it was the positive point of the Ahidjo regime – has placed Cameroon on a volcano. As the question today is no more when the President will leave but what to do after that day has come, it is of paramount importance to prevent Biya's departure from leading the country into a conflagration. Already on the eve of the 2011 presidential elections, in which the President's 'victory' was not doubted, many people predicted doom and gloom. Cameroon might be said to shows more and more characteristics of an *anocracy*, a 'system' where power is not vested in accepted chosen leaders and solid public institutions, but spread among elite groups who are constantly competing with each other for power and whereby ethnic or kinship bonds and personal allegiances to leaders play a key role.[31] 'Anocracies' present many further characteristics which can be summarised thus: concentration of power and the absence of the separation of the three branches of power, endemic corruption, exacerbated clientelism, the vacuity of political programs, anaemia of the administrative apparatus, repeated electoral frauds, weak legitimacy of institutions, persistent ethno-regional tension and social injustice. Cameroon seems to be a perfect example of this: a hybrid between military dictatorship and a façade democracy,[32] lacking proper governance, marked by pervasive corruption, and thus subverting the rights and influence of the citizens and turning politics into shadow theatre. This underlines the limits of the democratic transition that began in Africa in the 1990s.

References

Abbink, Jon, 1999. Introduction: rethinking democratisation and election observation, in: J. Abbink & G. Hesseling, eds, *Election Observation and Democratisation in Africa*. Basingstoke – London: Macmillan Press, pp. 1-17.

31 See: http://africanhistory.about.com/od/glossarya2/g/def-Anocracy.htm.

32 See also Pérouse de Montclos 2010: 11 ff.

Bakary, Tessy, 1998. La démocratie en Afrique: l'ère post-électorale, paper presented at the Colloquium of the 9th General Assembly of CODESRIA, Dakar, 14-18 December 1998.

Banégas, Richard, 1998. Marchandisation du vote, citoyenneté et consolidation démocratique au Bénin. *Politique Africaine* 69: 75-87.

Bourgi, Albert & Casteran, Christian, 1991. *Le Printemps de l'Afrique*. Paris: Hachette.

Bratton, Michael & Nicholas van de Walle, 1997. *Democratic Experiments in Africa. Regime Transitions in Comparative Perspective*. Cambridge: Cambridge University Press.

Carbone, Giovanni M., 2008. Comprendre les partis et les systèmes de partis africains. *Politique Africaine* 104: 18-37.

Collectif Changer le Cameroun, 1993. *Le 11 Octobre 1992. Autopsie d'une Élection Présidentielle Controversée*. Yaoundé: Editions C3.

Daloz, Jean-Pascal, 2002. *Elites et Représentations Politiques. La Culture de l'Échange Inégal au Nigéria*. Pessac: Presses Universitaires de Bordeaux.

——, 1998. Les approches élitaires comme nécessaire antidote. *Politique Africaine* 69: 13-31.

Daloz, Jean-Pascal & Patrick Quantin, eds, 1997. *Transitions Démocratiques Africaines*. Paris: Karthala.

Daloz, Jean-Pascal, ed., 1999. *Le (Non-)Renouvellement des Élites en Afrique Subsaharienne*, Talence: CEAN.

Diamond, Larry, 1999. *Developing Democracy. Toward Consolidation*. Baltimore – London: Johns Hopkins University Press.

Diamond, Larry & Gunther, Richard, eds, 2001. *Political Parties and Democracy*. Baltimore – London: Johns Hopkins University Press.

Enoh Meyomesse, 2009. *Le Retard de la Démocratie en Afrique Centrale. Le Cas du Cameroun*. Yaoundé: Les Éditions du Kamerun.

Erdmann, Gero & Ulf Engel, 2007. Neopatrimonialism reconsidered – critical review and elaboration of an elusive concept. *Journal of Commonwealth and Comparative Studies* 45(1): 95-119.

Faure, Yves-A. & Jean-François Médard, 1995. L'État business et les politiciens entrepreneurs. Néopatrimonialisme et *big men*: économie et politique, in: S. Ellis & Y-A. Faure, eds, *Entreprises et Entrepreneurs Africains*. Paris: Karthala/ORSTOM, pp. 289-309.

Gabriel, Jürg M., 1999. Cameroon's neopatrimonial dilemma. *Journal of Contemporary African Studies* 17(2): 173-196.

Geschiere, Peter & Piet Konings, 1993. *Itinéraires d'Accumulation au Cameroun / Pathways to Accumulation in Cameroon*. Paris – Leiden: Karthala – ASC.

Geschiere, Peter & Francis B. Nyamnjoh, 2000. Capitalism and autochthony: the seesaw of mobility and belonging. *Public Culture* 12(2): 423–452.

Göranson, Bo, 2007. Democracy needs parties, not only democrats. And more women! *News from the Nordic Africa Institute* 1/2007: 2-4.

Gros, Jean-Germain & Tatah Mentan, 2003. Elections and democratization in Cameroon: problems and prospects, in J-G. Gros, ed., *Cameroon. Politics and Society in Critical Perspectives*. Lanham – Boulder – New York – Toronto – Oxford: University Press of America, pp. 131-165.

Hyden, Goran & Michael Bratton, eds, 1992, *Gouverner l'Afrique. Vers un Partage des Rôles*. Paris: Nouveaux Horizons.

Kamto, M. 1993. Quelques réflexions sur la transition vers le pluralisme politique au Cameroun, in: G. Conac, ed., *L'Afrique en Transition vers le Pluralisme*. Paris: Economica, pp. 209-238.

——, 1993. *L'Urgence de la Pensée. Réflexions sur une Précondition du Développement en Afrique*. Yaoundé: Édition Mandara, SD.

Konings, Piet, 2004. Opposition and social-democratic change in Africa: the Social Democratic Front in Cameroon. *Commonwealth & Comparative Politics* 42(3): 1–23.

——, 2005. Assessing the power of newly created teachers' organisations during Cameroon's political liberalisation. *Journal of Higher Education in Africa* (JHEA/RESA) 3(2): 129-152.

Krieger, Milton, 1994. Cameroon's democratic crossroads, 1990-4. *Journal of Modern African Studies* 32(4): 605-628.

——, 2008. *Cameroon's Social Democratic Front: Its History and Prospects as an Opposition Political Party*. Bamenda: Langaa-RPCIG Publications.

Lawson, Kay, 1980. *Political Parties and Linkage: A Comparative Perspective*. New Haven: Yale University Press.

Le Roy, Etienne, Gouvernance et décentralisation ou le dilemme de la légitimité dans la réforme de l'Etat africain de la fin du XXe siècle. *Cahiers du GEMDEV* no. 24, L'Etat en Afrique, indigénisations et modernités, juin 1996, pp. 97-99.

Loada, Augustin Marie-Gervais, 1998. Les élections législatives burkinabé du 11 mai 1997: des 'élections pas comme les autres? *Politique Africaine* 69: 62-74.

Mappa, Sophia, 1988. *Pouvoirs Traditionnels et Pouvoir d'Etat en Afrique. L'Illusion Universaliste*, Paris: Karthala.

Mbembe, Achille, 1993. Crise de légitimité, restauration autoritaire et déliquescence de l'Etat, in: P. Geschiere & P. Konings, eds, *Itinéraires d'Accumulation au Cameroun / Pathways to Accumulation in Cameroon*. Paris – Leiden: Karthala – ASC, pp. 345-373.

Mehler, Andreas, 1998. Cameroon and the politics of patronage, in D. Birmingham & P. Martin, eds, *History of Central Africa: The Contemporary Years*. New York: Longman Press, pp. 43–65.

——, 1997. Cameroun: une transition qui n'a pas eu lieu, in: J-P. Daloz & P. Quantin, eds, *Transitions Démocratiques Africaines*. Paris: Karthala.

Médard, Jean-François, 1991. L'Etat néopatrimonial en Afrique noire, in: Médard, J-F., ed., *Etats d'Afrique Noire. Formations, Mécanismes et Crise*. Paris: Karthala, pp. 323-353.

Menthong, Hélène-Laure, 1998. Vote et communautarisme au Cameroun: un vote de cœur, de sang et de raison. *Politique Africaine* 69: 40-51.

Mghanga, Mwandawiro, 2006. Political parties and the challenge for democracy in Kenya. *News from the Nordic Africa Institute*, 2/2006: 6-9.

Moukoko Priso, 1994. *Cameroun/Kamerun. La Transition dans l'Impasse*. Paris: L'Harmattan.

Mouiche, Ibrahim, 2000. Ethnicité et multipartyisme au Nord-Cameroun. *Revue Africaine de Science Politique – African Journal of Political Science* 5(1): 46-91.

——, 2004. Processus électoraux et rotation locale des élites au Cameroun. *Law and Politics in Africa, Asia and Latin America* 4: 401-432.

——, 2005. *Autorités Traditionnelles et Démocratisation au Cameroun. Entre Logique du Terroir et de l'Etat*. Münster: Lit Verlag (Modernity & Belonging Series, vol. 5).

——, 2011a. Autochtonie, libéralisation politique et construction d'une sphère publique locale au Cameroun. *African Studies Review* 54(3): 71–99.

——, 2011b. Democratisation and political participation of Mbororo in Western Cameroon. *Africa Spectrum* 46(2): 71-97.

Mwalimu George Ngwane, 2004. Processus démocratique au Cameroun: une vision pour 2020. *Bulletin du CODESRIA* 3-4: 23-29.

Nchoji Nkwi, Paul & Antoine Socpa, 1997. Ethnicity and Party Politics in Cameroon: the politics of divide and Rule, in P.N. Nkwi & F.B. Nyamnjoh, eds, *Regional Balance and National Integration in Cameroon. Lessons Learned and Uncertain Future / Equilibre Régional et Intégration Nationale au Cameroun. Leçons du Passé et Perspectives d'Avenir*. Leiden – Yaoundé: ASC – ICASSRT, pp. 138-149.

Nyamnjoh, Francis B., 2002. Cameroon: over twelve years of cosmetic democracy. *News from the Nordic Africa Institute* 3/2002: 5-8.

Nyamnjoh, Francis & Michael Rowlands, 1998. Elite associations and the politics of belonging in Cameroon. *Africa* 68(3): 320-337.

Osei, Anja, 2008. La connexion entre les partis et les électeurs en Afrique: le cas du Ghana. *Politique Africaine* 104: 38-60.

Otayek, René, 1998. Les élections en Afrique sont-elles un objet scientifique pertinent? *Politique Africaine* 69: 3-11.

Pérouse de Montclos, Marc-Antoine, 2010. *Vers un nouveau régime en Afrique subsaharienne? Des transitions dans l'impasse.* Paris – Bruxelles: Les Études IFRI.

Quantin, Patrick, 1995. 'Les élites démocratiques face aux transitions démocratiques', in: Centre d'Étude d'Afrique Noire, *L'Afrique Politique 1995. Le Meilleur, le Pire et l'Incertain.* Paris: Karthala, pp. 277-285.

Quantin, Patrick, 1998. Pour une analyse comparative des élections. *Politique Africaine* 69: 12-28.

Quantin, Patrick, 2000. La difficile consolidation des transitions démocratiques africaines des années 1990, in: Chr. Jaffrelot, ed., *Démocraties d'Ailleurs. Démocraties et Démocratisations hors d'Occident.* Paris: Karthala, pp. 479-507.

Sandbrook, Richard, 1987. Personnalisation du pouvoir et stagnation capitaliste. *Politique Africaine* 26: 15-37.

Sartori, Giovanni, 1976. *Party and Party Systems. A Framework for Analysis*, Cambridge: Cambridge University Press.

Schraeder, Peter J. 1994. Elites as facilitators or impediments to political development? Some lessons from the 'third wave' of democratization in Africa. *Journal of Developing Areas* 29: 69-90.

Sindjoun, Luc, 1994. La cour suprême, la compétition électorale et la continuité politique au Cameroun. *Afrique et Développement* 19(2): 21-69.

Sindjoun, Luc, ed., 2004. *Comment Peut-on Être Opposant au Cameroun. Politique Parlementaire et Politique Autoritaire.* Dakar: CODESRIA.

Socpa, Antoine, 2000. Les dons dans le jeu électoral au Cameroun. *Cahiers d'Études Africaines*, 40(1), no. 157: 91-108.

Takougang, Joseph, 2003. The 2002 legislative election in Cameroon: a retrospective on Cameroon's stalled democracy movement. *Journal of Modern African Studies* 41(3): 421–435.

Tchejip Kaptchouang, Célestin, 2006. *Partis Politiques et Démocratie Locale au*

Cameroun: une Analyse de la Compétition Politique Locale. Yaoundé: Université de Yaoundé II (Thèse de doctorat en science politique).

Zakaria, Fareed, 1997. The rise of illiberal democracies. *Foreign Affairs* 76: 22-43.

Notes on the contributors

Jon Abbink is a senior researcher at the African Studies Centre, Leiden, where he headed the research group 'Social Movements & Political Culture in Africa' until December 2011. He is also a research professor of African Studies at VU University, Amsterdam since 2000. He carried out historical-anthropological field research chiefly in Ethiopia, and his interests are ethnicity, land use and identity issues, political anthropology, and culture and religion in the Horn of Africa. Among his recent publications are papers in *Africa Spectrum*, *African Affairs*, and *Social Anthropology*. His recent books are *The Anthropology of Elites* (edited with T. Salverda, New York 2012, in press), *Land, Law and Politics in Africa: Mediating Conflict and Reshaping the State* (edited with M. de Bruijn, Leiden-Boston 2011), a *Bibliography of Ethiopian-Eritrean Studies in Society and History, 1995-2010* (Addis Ababa – Leiden 2010). He also co-edited a recent special issue of the *Journal of Eastern African Studies* (2011), about Ethiopian politics and society.

Robert M. Akoko is holder of a PhD in Anthropology from the University of Leiden, based on his thesis *"Ask and you shall be given": Pentecostalism and the economic crisis in Cameroon* (Leiden 2007). He currently heads the Department of Sociology and Anthropology, University of Buea, Cameroon. In addition, he is the current president of the Pan African Anthropological Association (PAAA). He has published extensively in the areas of religion in Cameroon, with special focus on church and politics and Pentecostalism. In addition, he wrote on various aspects of politics in the country since the introduction of multi-party politics in the early 1990s. Some of his recent papers appeared in the *Journal of Contemporary African Studies*, *Africa Today* and the *Journal for the Study of Religion*.

Deborah Fahy Bryceson is a Reader in the Geographical and Earth Sciences School at the University of Glasgow. She has published on the theme of African deagrarianization and livelihood diversification, including the edited volumes *Farewell to Farms: De-Agrarianization and Employment in Africa* (Ashbury, 1997), *Disappearing Peasantries: Rural Labour in Africa, Asia and Latin America* (Intermediate Technology Publications, 2000), *African Urban Economies* (Palgrave Macmillan, 2006), and *How Africa Works: Occupational Change, Identity and Morality in Africa* (Practical Action Publishing, 2010). She currently coordinates the Urbanization and Poverty in Mining Africa research programme funded by the United Kingdom's Department for International Development (DfID) and the Economic and Social Science Research Council (ESRC). During the last five years her work has concentrated on documenting the world of East African artisanal mining. She was a Senior Research Fellow at the Afrika-Studiecentrum, Leiden, from 1992 to 2005.

Peter L. Geschiere is Professor of African Anthropology at the University of Amsterdam, and has previously taught at Leiden University and VU University in Amsterdam. Since 1971 he has undertaken historical-anthropological fieldwork in various parts of Cameroon (e.g., on Maka society) and elsewhere in West Africa. His research interests are ideology and witchcraft in Africa, comparative studies on 'modernity', autochthony and citizenship debates in Africa, and historical anthropology. His many publications include *The Modernity of Witchcraft: Politics and the Occult in Post-colonial Africa* (Virginia UP, 1997) and *Perils of Belonging: Autochthony, Citizenship and Exclusion in Africa and Europe* (Chicago UP, 2009). Currently he is working on a book on *Witchcraft, Intimacy and Trust: Africa in Comparison.*

Benedict Nantang Jua joined the Faculty of South Carolina State University in Orangeburg, USA, in 2005. Currently, he is Associate Professor of Political Science and Chair of the Department of Social Sciences. Prior to this, he worked in Cameroon as a 'Maitre de Recherche' at Cameroon's Ministry of Scientific and Technical Research and also taught at the University of Buea between 1993 and 1999. He has been a Visiting Research Fellow at the African Studies Center in Leiden in 2002. His research interests are in state construction, democratization and social transformations in Africa, and he published widely on these subjects in *African Studies Review, Africa Insight, Democracy and Development, Cahiers d'Études Africaines, Africa,* and other journals as well as several edited books.

Ineke van Kessel is a senior researcher with the African Studies Centre in Leiden, the Netherlands. Trained as a historian, she has also worked as a journalist. Her main research interests focus on social and political movements in contemporary South Africa and on the historical relations between the Netherlands and the Gold Coast (present-day Ghana). Her publications include: *Beyond our Wildest Dreams': the United Democratic Front and the Transformation of South Africa* (Charlottesville and London: University Press of Virginia, 2000), *Zwarte*

Hollanders: Afrikaanse Soldaten in Nederlands Indië (Amsterdam: KIT Publishers, 2005), and *Nelson Mandela in een Notendop* (Amsterdam: Bert Bakker, 2010); and as editor, *Merchants, Missionaries and Migrants: 300 years of Dutch-Ghanaian Relations* (Amsterdam/Accra: KIT Publishers/Sub-Saharan Publishers, 2002) and with S. Ellis, *Movers and Shakers: Social Movements in Africa* (Leiden: Brill, 2009).

Ibrahim Mouiche is a political scientist, specializing in political anthropology and political sociology studies and works as an associate professor in the Department of Political Science at the University of Yaoundé II. He earned his doctoral degrees at the University of Yaoundé (1994) and Leiden University (2005). His main research interests are: ethnicity and ethnic minorities; traditional chiefs and democratization; gender; and Islam and politics in Cameroon. His major publications include: *Autorités Traditionnelles et Démocratisation au Cameroun. Entre Centralité de l'Etat et Logique de Terroir* (Münster, Lit Verlag, 2005) and *Minorités Ethniques et Démocratisation au Cameroun. Entre Dogmatisme du Principe Majoritaire et Centralité des Partis Politiques* (2012, Dakar, CODESRIA). He is currently (2012) a fellow at the Netherlands Institute for Advanced Study (NIAS), Wassenaar.

Paul Nchoji Nkwi is Professor of Anthropology at the Catholic University of Cameroon, Bamenda, where he is also serving as the Deputy Vice Chancellor for Academic Affairs. He taught anthropology at the University of Yaoundé I for more than 30 years until he retired there in 2006. He did research and published widely on African (Cameroonian) history and society, e.g., *The German Presence in the Western Grassfield, 1891-1913: A German Colonial Account* (1989), and (co-)edited various books on anthropology in Africa, on field research methodology in Africa, and on managing biodiversity in Africa. His last book, edited with F.B. Nyamnjoh, is *Regional Balance and National Integration in Cameroon: Lessons Learned and the Uncertain Future* (Bamenda, 2011). In the 1980s he was engaged in promoting football in Cameroon at the grassroots level when he with other elite members from the rural village of Njinikom created the club *Njinikom Sportif*, which rose to second division but later melted into oblivion for lack of sustained financial resources. Using a technical school that he established in 1989, he began to teach and promote football among the students of this institution. He has published several articles on the subject.

Francis B. Nyamnjoh holds an MA (1985) from the University of Yaounde, Cameroon, and a PhD (1990) from the University of Leicester, UK. He joined the University of Cape Town in August 2009 as Professor of Social Anthropology from the Council for the Development of Social Science Research in Africa (CODESRIA), where he served as Head of Publications from July 2003 to July 2009. He has taught sociology, anthropology and communication studies at universities in Cameroon and Botswana, and has researched and written extensively on Cameroon and Botswana, where he was awarded the 'Senior Arts Researcher of the Year' prize for 2003. He is a 2010 B2 rated Professor and Researcher by the South African National Research Foundation (NRF), and a Fellow of the Cameroon Academy of Science since August 2011. Recent scholarly books include *Negotiating an Anglophone Identity* (Brill, 2003), *Rights and the Politics of Recognition in Africa* (Zed Books, 2004), *Africa's Media, Democracy and the Politics of Belonging* (Zed Books, 2005), *Insiders and Outsiders: Citizenship and Xenophobia in Contemporary Southern Africa* (2006), *Mobile Phones: The New Talking Drums of Everyday Africa* (2009). Dr Nyamnjoh has published widely on globalisation, citizenship, media and the politics of identity in Africa. He has also published seven ethnographic novels, *Mind Searching* (1991), *The Disillusioned African* (1995), *A Nose for Money* (2006), *Souls Forgotten* (2008), *The Travail of Dieudonné* (2008), *Married but Available* (2009), *Intimate Strangers* (2010), and *Homeless Waters* (2011), a play *The Convert* (2003), a collection of short stories, *Stories from Abakwa* (2007), and a collection of poems, *Predicaments* (2011).

Bibliography of Dr. Piet J.J. Konings (May 2012)

Academic books

2011 *The Politics of Neoliberal Reforms in Africa. State and Civil Society in Cameroon*. Bamenda, Cameroon: Langaa Publishers & Leiden: African Studies Centre.

2010 *Crisis and Neoliberal Reforms in Africa: Civil Society and Agro-Industry in Anglophone Cameroons Plantation Economy*. Bamenda, Cameroon: Langaa Publishers & Leiden: African Studies Centre.

2009 *Neoliberal Bandwagonism: Civil Society and the Politics of Belonging in Anglophone Cameroon*. Bamenda, Cameroon: Langaa Publishers.

1998 *Unilever Estates in Crisis and the Power of Organizations in Cameroon*. Hamburg: Lit Verlag – Leiden: African Studies Centre.

1995 *Gender and Class in the Tea Estates of Cameroon*. Aldershot: Avebury.

1993 *Labour Resistance in Cameroon: Managerial Strategies and Labour Resistance in the Agro-Industrial Plantations of the Cameroon Development Corporation*. Portsmouth, N.H.: Heinemann.

1988 *Trade Unionism and Labour Control in Agro-Industry in Cameroon: the Case of the Cameroon Development Corporation, 1947-1986*. Leiden: African Studies Centre.

1980 *The Political Potential of Ghanaian Miners: a Case Study of the AGC Workers at Obuasi*. Leiden: African Studies Centre (Research Report 9)

1977 *Vakbeweging en Ontwikkelingsstrategie van de Overheid in Ghana, 1874-1976*. Tilburg: Katholieke Hogeschool (PhD dissertation).

Co-authored:

P.J.J. Konings & F.B. Nyamnjoh

2003 *Negotiating an Anglophone Identity: a Study of the Politics of Recognition and Representation in Cameroon*. Leiden – Boston: Brill.

P.J.J. Konings & J.J. Ravell

1986 *The State and Rural Class Formation in Ghana: a Comparative Analysis.* London – Boston: Routledge & Kegan Paul.

Co-edited:

P.J.J. Konings & D.W.J. Foeken, eds
2006 *Crisis and Creativity: Exploring the Wealth of the African Neighbourhood.* Leiden – Boston: Brill (African Dynamics, vol. 5).
P.J.J. Konings, G.S.C.M. Hesseling & W.M.J. van Binsbergen, eds
2000 *Trajectoires de Libération en Afrique Contemporaine: Hommage à Robert Buijtenhuijs.* Paris: Karthala.
P.L. Geschiere & P.J.J. Konings, eds
1993 *Itinéraires d'Accumulation au Cameroun / Pathways to Accumulation in Cameroon.* Paris: Karthala.

Academic papers and chapters

2011 Settling border conflicts in Africa peacefully: lessons learned from the Bakassi dispute between Cameroon and Nigeria. In: J. Abbink & M. de Bruijn, eds, *Land, Law and Politics in Africa: Mediating Conflict and Reshaping the State,* Leiden: Brill, pp. 191-210.
2011 Foreword. In: M. Atanga, *The Anglophone Cameroon Predicament*, Bamenda: Langaa, pp. xi-xv.
2010 Occupational change, structural adjustment and trade union identity in Africa: The case of Cameroonian plantation workers. In: D.F. Bryceson, ed., *How Africa Works: Occupational Change, Identity and Morality,* London: Practical Action Publishing, pp. 229-244.
2009 University crisis and student strikes in Africa: the case of the University of Buea (Cameroon). *Journal of Higher Education in Africa* 7(1-2): 211-233.
2009 The history of trade unionism in Cameroon. In: C. Phelan, ed., *Trade Unionism since 1945: Towards a Global History,* vol. 1, *Western Europe, Eastern Europe, Africa and the Middle East*, Oxford – Bern: Peter Lang, pp. 315-341.
2008 Autochthony and ethnic cleansing in Cameroon: the 1966 Tombel disturbances. *International Journal of African Historical Studies* 41(2): 203-222.
2008 Cameroon. In: H. Melber & K.van Walraven A. Mehler, eds, *Africa Yearbook: Politics, Economy and Society South of the Sahara in 2007*, Leiden – Boston: Brill, pp. 205-214.

2008 Church-state relations in Cameroon's postcolony: the case of the Roman Catholic Church. *Journal for the Study of Religion* 20(2): 45-64.

2008 De Engelstalige minderheid en federalisme in Kameroen. In: J. Abbink & A. van Dokkum, eds, *Verdeeld Afrika: Etniciteit, Conflict en de Grenzen van de Staat*, Diemen (NL): AMB, pp. 75-97.

2008 Neo-liberalism and capital accumulation in Cameroon. In: A.E. Fernández-Jilberto & B. Hogenboom, eds, *Big Business and Economic Development* (Second, revised, paperback edition), London – New York, pp. 251-273.

2008 Privatisation and labour militancy: the case of Cameroons tea estates. *Journal of Contemporary African Studies* 26(1): 51-70.

2008 Revival religioso nella chiesa cattolica romana e il conflitto autoctonia-alloctonia in Camerun. *Afriche e Orienti* 9(3-4): 57-69.

2008 The history of trade unionism in Cameroon. In: C. Phelan, ed., *Trade Unionism since 1945: Towards a Global History:* Oxford – Bern: Peter Lang, pp. 203-230.

2007 Cameroon. In: H. Melber & K. van Walraven & A. Mehler, eds, *Africa Yearbook 2007: Politics, Economy and Society South of the Sahara in 2006*, Leiden – Boston: Brill Academic Publishers, 2007, pp. 197-206.

2007 China and Africa in the era of neo-liberal globalization. *CODESRIA Bulletin* 1-2: 17-22.

2007 China and Africa: building a strategic partnership. *Journal of Developing Societies* 23(3): 341-367.

2007 Trade unionism in Cameroon: from crisis to revitalisation? In: C. Phelan, ed., *Trade Union Revitalisation: Trends and Prospects in 34 Countries*, Oxford – Bern: Peter Lang, pp. 431-443.

2006 "Bendskin" drivers in Douala's New Bell neighbourhood: masters of the road and the city. In: D.W.J. Foeken & P.J.J. Konings, eds, *Crisis and Creativity. Exploring the Wealth of the African Neighbourhood*, Leiden: Brill, pp. 46-65.

2006 Assessing the role of autonomous teachers' trade unions in anglophone Cameroon, 1959-1972. *Journal of African History* 47(3): 415-436.

2006 Cameroon. In: A. Mehler, H. Melber & K. van Walraven, eds, *Africa Yearbook: Politics, Economy and Society South of the Sahara in 2005*, Leiden: Brill, pp. 187-196.

2006 Solving transportation problems in African cities: innovative responses by the youth in Douala, Cameroon. *Africa Today* 53(1): 35-50.

2006 with D.W.J. Foeken & R.A. van Dijk
The African neighbourhood: an introduction. In: D.W.J. Foeken, R.A. van

Dijk & P.J.J Konings, eds., *Crisis and Creativity: Exploring the Wealth of the African Neighbourhood*, Leiden: Brill, pp. 1-21.

2006 The neoliberalising African state and private capital accumulation: the case of Cameroon. In: A.E. Fernández Jilberto & B. Hogenboom, eds, *Big Business and Economic Development: Conglomerates and Economic Groups in Developing Countries and Transition Economies under Globalisation*, New York – London: Routledge, pp. 175-208.

2005 African trade unions and the challenge of globalisation: a comparative study of Ghana and Cameroon. In: C.L. Phelan, ed., *The Future of Organized Labour: Global Perspectives*, London – New York: Peter Lang, pp. 1-35.

2005 Anglophone university students and anglophone nationalist struggles in Cameroon. In: J. Abbink & I. van Kessel, eds, *Vanguard or Vandals: Youth, Politics and Conflict in Africa*, Leiden – Boston: Brill, pp. 161-188, 2005.

2005 Assessing the power of newly created teachers' organizations during Cameroons political liberalization. *Journal of Higher Education in Africa* 3(1): 129-152.

2005 Cameroon. In: A. Mehler, H. Melber & K. van Walraven, eds, *Africa Yearbook 2004*, Leiden – Boston: Brill, pp. 185-189.

2005 Féderalisme et sécession au Cameroun anglophone. *La Nouvelle Expression*, 2005, pp. 3-6.

2005 The Anglophone Cameroon-Nigeria boundary: opportunities and conflicts. *African Affairs* 104(415): 275-301.

2004 Good governance, privatisation and ethno-regional conflict in Cameroon. In: J. Demmers; A.E. Fernandez Jilberto & B. Hogenboom, eds, *Good Governance in the Era of Global Neoliberalism: Conflict and Depolitization in Latin America, Eastern Europe, Asia and Africa*, London – New York: Routledge, pp. 306-330.

2004 with Ben Nantang Jua
Occupation of public space: anglophone nationalism in Cameroon. *Cahiers d'Études Africaines* 44(175): 609-633.

2004 Opposition and social-democratic change in Africa: the Social Democratic Front in Cameroon. *Journal of Commonwealth & Comparative Politics* 42(3): 1-23.

2004 with Francis B. Nyamnjoh
President Biya and the "'Anglophone problem"' in Cameroon. In: J.M. Mbaku & J. Takougang, eds, *The Leadership Challenge in Africa: Cameroon under Paul Biya*, Trenton, NJ: Africa World Press, pp. 191-234.

2004 Trade union activism among university teachers during Cameroon's political liberalization. *Nordic Journal of African Studies* 13(3): 289-301.

2003 Privatisation and ethno-regional protest in Cameroon. *Afrika Spektrum* 38(1): 5-26.

2003 Religious revival in the Roman Catholic Church and the autochthony-allochthony conflict in Cameroon. *Africa* 73(1): 31-56.

2003 Chieftaincy and privatisation in Anglophone Cameroon. In: W. van Binsbergen, ed., *The Dynamics of Power and the Rule of Law: Essays on Africa and Beyond, in Honour of Emile Adriaan B. van Rouveroy van Nieuwaal*, Leiden – Münster: African Studies Centre – Lit-Verlag, pp. 79-99.

2003 Organised labour and neo-liberal economic and political reforms in West and Central Africa. *Journal of Contemporary African Studies* 21(3): 447-471.

2002 Structural adjustment and trade unions in Africa: the case of Ghana. In: A.E. Fernández Jilberto & M. Riethof, eds, *Labour Relations in Development*, London – New York: Routledge, pp. 311-336.

2002 University students revolt, ethnic militia, and violence during political liberalization in Cameroon. *African Studies Review* 45(2): 179-204.

2002 with Francis B. Nyamnjoh
Anglophones or autochtones? In: P.N. Nkwi, ed., *The Anthropology of Africa: Challenges for the 21st Century*, Yaoundé: ICASSRT.

2001 Mobility and exclusion: conflicts between autochthons and allochthons during political liberalization in Cameroon. In: M. de Bruijn, R. van Dijk and D. Foeken, eds, *Mobile Africa: Changing Patterns of Movement in Africa and Beyond*, Leiden – Boston: Brill, pp. 169-194.

2001 with Francis B. Nyamnjoh
President Biya and the Anglophone problem. In: J. Takougang and J.M. Mbaku, eds, *The Leadership Challenge in Africa: Cameroon under Paul Biya*, Aldershot: Ashgate, pp. 69-95.

2001 Mobility and exclusion: conflicts between autochthons and allochthons during political liberalisation in Cameroon. In: M. de Bruijn, R. van Dijk & D. Foeken, eds, *Mobile Africa: Changing Patterns of Movement in Africa and Beyond*, Leiden – Boston, pp. 169-194.

2000 with Francis B. Nyamnjoh
Construction and deconstruction: anglophones or autochtones? *The African Anthropologist* 7(1): 5-32.

2000 Ghana: een modelland voor democratisering in Sub-Sahara Afrika. In: N. Tellegen, ed., *Afrika-Expertbijeenkomst: Ghana, Mali, Mozambique, Sierra*

Leone, Congo, Rwanda: 9 en 10 oktober 2000, Den Haag – Leiden: Directie Afrika, Ministerie van Buitenlandse Zaken / Afrika-Studiecentrum, pp. 5-12.

2000 with W.M.J. van Binsbergen and G.S.C.M. Hesseling
Introduction: l'étendue des travaux de Robert Buijtenhuijs. In: P. Konings, W.M.J. van Binsbergen and G. Hesseling, eds, *Trajectoires de Libération en Afrique Contemporaine: Hommage à Robert Buijtenhuijs*. Paris: Karthala, pp. 7-15.

2000 with W.M.J. van Binsbergen and G.S.C.M. Hesseling
Introduction: the scope of Robert Buijtenhuis's work. In: P. Konings, W.M.J. van Binsbergen & G.S.C.M. Hesseling, eds, *Trajectoires de Libération en Afrique Contemporaine: Hommage à Robert Buijtenhuijs*. Paris: Karthala (Hommes et sociétés), pp. 17-25.

2000 Trade unions and democratisation in Africa. In: P. Konings, W.M.J. van Binsbergen & G.S.C.M. Hesseling, eds, *Trajectoires de Libération en Afrique Contemporaine: Hommage à Robert Buijtenhuijs*, Paris: Karthala (Hommes et Sociétés), pp. 167-183.

1999 The anglophone problem and chieftaincy in anglophone Cameroon. In: E.A.B.van Rouveroy van Nieuwaal & R.van Dijk, eds, *African Chieftaincy in a New Socio-Political Landscape*, Hamburg: Lit Verlag, pp. 181-206.

1999 The Anglophone struggle for federalism in Cameroon. In: L.R. Basta-Fleiner & J. Ibrahim, eds, *Federalism and Decentralization in Africa: the Multicultural Challenge*. Fribourg: Institut du Fédéralisme, pp. 289-325.

1998, with Henk Meilink
Regional economic integration in sub-Saharan Africa. In: A.E. Fernández Jilberto & A. Mommen, eds, Regionalization and Globalization in the Modern World Economy: Perspectives on the Third World and Transitional Economies, London –New York: Routledge, pp. 143-145.

1998 Unilever, contract farmers and co-operatives in Cameroon: crisis and response. *Journal of Peasant Studies* 26(1): 112-128.

1998 Women plantation workers and economic crisis in Cameroon. In: S. Jain & R. Reddock, eds, *Women Plantation Workers: International Experiences*, Oxford – New York: Berg, pp. 151-165.

1997 Agro-industry and regionalism in the South West Province of Cameroon during the national economic and political crisis. In: P.N. Nkwi & F.B. Nyamnjoh, eds, *Regional Balance and National Integration in Cameroon: Lessons Learnt and the Future*, Yaoundé: ASC/ICASSRT, pp. 289-306.

1997 with Francis B. Nyamnjoh

The Anglophone problem in Cameroon. *Journal of Modern African Studies* 35(2): 207-229.
1996 Chieftaincy, labour control and capitalist development in Cameroon. *Journal of Legal Pluralism and Unofficial Law* 37-38: 329-346.
1996 Le problème anglophone au Cameroun dans les années 1990. *Politique africaine* 62: 25-34.
1996 Privatisation of agro-industrial parastatals and anglophone opposition in Cameroon. *Journal of Commonwealth & Comparative Politics* 34(3): 199-217.
1996 The post-colonial state and economic and political reforms in Cameroon. In: A.E. Fernández Jilberto & A. Mommen, eds, *Liberalization in the Developing World: Institutional and Economic Changes in Latin America, Africa and Asia,* London – New York: Routledge.
1995 Chieftaincy, labour control and capitalist development in Cameroon. In: E.A.B. Rouveroy van Nieuwaal, ed., Proceedings of the Conference on the Contribution of Traditional Authority to Development, Human Rights and Environmental Protection: Strategies for Africa. Leiden: African Studies Centre, pp. 261-276.
1995 with Peter Geschiere
Empirical studies and conceptual dilemmas: a reply to Janet Roitman. *Cahiers d'Études Africaines* 140(45): 927-928.
1995 Plantation labour and economic crisis in Cameroon. *Development and Change* 26(3): 525-549.
1994 De geschiedenis van Kameroen. In: M. Douma, ed., *Kameroen op Zoek naar Nieuwe Verhoudingen.* Kampen: Kok, pp. 10-21.
1993 Contract farming and capital accumulation in Cameroon: the case of the CDC smallholder schemes. In: P. Geschiere & P. Konings, eds, *Itinéraires d'Accumulation au Cameroun / Pathways to Accumulation in Cameroon,* Paris: Karthala, pp. 217-239.
1993 with P. Geschiere
Introduction. In: P. Geschiere & P. Konings, eds, *Itinéraires d'Accumulation au Cameroun / Pathways to Accumulation in Cameroon.* Paris: Karthala, pp. 9-31.
1993 Vakbonden, structurele aanpassing en democratisering in Afrika. *Internationale Spectator* 47(2): 113-117.
1989 La liquidation des plantations Unilever et les conflits intra-élite dans le Cameroun anglophone. *Politique africaine* 35: 132-137.
1989 Trade unionism and labour control in agro-industry in Cameroon: the case

of the Cameroon Development Corporation, 1947-1986. In: P. Konings & P. Geschiere, eds, *Conference on the Political Economy of Cameroon, Historical Perspectives / Colloque sur l'Économie Politique du Cameroun, Perspectives Historiques: Proceedings/Contributions*, Leiden: African Studies Centre, pp. 25-56.

1987 Préface. In: V. Ombé Ndzana, ed., *Agriculture, Pétrole et Politique au Cameroun*. Paris: L'Harmattan, pp. 11-14.

1986 L'État, l'agro-industrie et la paysannerie au Cameroun. *Politique africaine* 22: 120-137.

1986 The state and the defence committees in the Ghanaian revolution. In: G. Hesseling, L.R. Bastia & F. Reijntjens, eds., 'State and Local Community in Africa'. *Cahiers du CEDAF* 2-3-4: 261-285.

1984 Capitalist rice farming and land allocation in Northern Ghana. *Journal of Legal Pluralism* 22: 1-28.

1984 Rawlings en de revolutie in Ghana. In: W. van Binsbergen & Gerti Hesseling, eds, *Aspecten van Staat en Maatschappij in Afrika – Recent Dutch and Belgian Research on the African State*. Leiden: African Studies Centre, pp. 345-366.

1983 Riziculteurs capitalistes et petits paysans: la naissance d'un conflict de classe au Ghana. *Politique africaine* 11: 77-94.

1979 Politiek bewustzijn en aktie van mijnwerkers in Ghana. *Sociologische Gids* 26(2-3): 209-223.

1979 The importance of trade unions: a contribution to the debate on the labouring poor and urban class formation in Africa. *Manpower and Unemployment Research* 11(1): 77-94.

1978 Political consciousness and political action of industrial workers in Ghana: a case study of VALCO workers at Tema. *African Perspectives* (Leiden) 2: 69-82.

Book reviews: many dozens; no record kept.

Reports, consultancies, working papers, popular press and magazine articles

2002 *National Populism, Social Democracy and Labour in Africa.* Amsterdam: University of Amsterdam, Department of International Relations, Working Paper.

2000 National Populism and Social Democracy in Africa: Feasible Alternatives to the Current Neoliberal Hegemonic Project? Amsterdam: University of Amsterdam, Department of International Relations, Working Paper.

1995 with I.S.A. Baud
Rapport de mission: evaluation intermédiaire, projet des travailleurs Mali et Tanzanie. The Hague: DGIS / DPO / IO.

1991 Evaluatierapport van de Panafrikaanse Instituten in Afrika. Den Haag: Ministerie van Ontwikkelingssamenwerking.

1988 The Ghanaian developmental state and the International Monetary Fund. Amsterdam: Universiteit van Amsterdam.

1986 *The role of the defence committees in the Ghanaian revolution.* Ibadan: s.n. (Revolutionary Monographs on Culture and Society of Africa).

1984 Arbeiders en arbeidersbeweging in de Ghanese Revolutie: de vakbonden. *Ghana Nieuwsbrief*, no. 10, pp. 5-16.

1984 Arbeiders en arbeidersbeweging in de Ghanese revolutie: de arbeiderverdedigingscomités. *Ghana Nieuwsbrief*, no. 9, pp. 5-14.

1984 The state of food and land: a close look at Oyarefa in Southern Ghana. Legon: University of Ghana, Research Report 4.

1983 Dutch aid and the rural dairy project in Zambia. The Hague: Institute of Social Studies.

1983 Crisis in de Ghanese economie en emigratie. *Ghana Nieuwsbrief*, no. 3, pp. 4-13.

1983 Het revolutionaire proces in Ghana. *Derde Wereld*, no. 4, pp. 46-67, 1983.

1982 Rawlings zit de vakbonden niet dwars. *De Bondgenoot* (FNV Kaderblad), p. 1-3, 1982.

1982 FNV dolk in de rug van het Ghanese bewind. *Ghana Nieuwsbrief*, no. 1, pp. 14-18, 1982.

1982 De Rawlings coup en Nederlandse ontwikkelingshulp aan Ghana. Rapport voor de Tweede Kamercommissie voor Ontwikkelingssamenwerking en CEBEMO. Den Haag: s.n., 1982.

1981 Aspects of commercialisation among the Tonga of the Southern Province of Zambia. Den Haag: Inspectie Ontwikkelingssamenwerking te Velde.

1981 Peasantry and state in Ghana: the example of the Vea irrigation project in the upper region of Ghana. Leiden: Afrika-Studiecentrum, Working paper no. 5.

1981 The co-operative movement in Zambia: the example of the Chikuni Fruit and Vegetable Producers Co-operative. Den Haag: Inspectie Ontwikkelingssamenwerking te Velde, Missierapport.

1981 Traditional cattle in Zambia. Den Haag: Inspectie Ontwikkelingssamenwerking te Velde.

1977 Trade unionism and government development strategy in Ghana, 1874-1976. Tilburg: Catholic University of Brabant.

1974 De vakbeweging in West-Afrika: een literatuurverkenning. Tilburg: Katholieke Hogeschool, Werkdocument no. 4.

1974 Industrial relations in Ghana. The Hague: Institute of Social Studies

1974 Werkloosheid onder schoolverlaters in Ghana. Tilburg: Katholieke Universiteit van Brabant.

1972 Church leaders and their attitudes towards their church: a survey in an urban community, Winneba (Ghana). Legon: University of Ghana, Department of Sociology.

Josephat Obi Oguejiofor, Tobias Wendl (Eds.)

EXPLORING THE OCCULT AND PARANORMAL IN WEST AFRICA

LIT

Josephat Obi Oguejiofor; Tobias Wendl (Eds.)

Exploring the Occult and Paranormal in West Africa

The point of departure of this book is a phenomenon which is often referred to as the "return of the religious", a recent but apparently ubiquitous phenomenon which does not fit the modernist axiom of secularisation, neither in the "developed" nor the "developing" worlds. In Africa, the last two decades have witnessed a remarkable and steady increase in the spread and reinforcement of occult and paranormal phenomena. The reports on these developments are not restricted to specific countries or areas; they cover the whole continent and surface in the most diverse images, media, stories and rumours. The credence accorded to them has become an important factor that shapes social relationships in everyday life, economic and political actions, medical decisions and religious adherence.

Bd. 47, 2012, 280 S., 29,90 €, br., ISBN 978-3-643-90183-5

LIT Verlag Berlin – Münster – Wien – Zürich – London

Auslieferung Deutschland / Österreich / Schweiz: siehe Impressumsseite

Mayke Kaag; Maud Saint-Lary (Eds.)
The New Visibility of Religion in the Development Arena. Nouvelles visibilités de la religion dans l'arène du développement
This issue of the APAD-Bulletin approaches the ambiguous relationship between religion and development. The different papers analyse the ways in which religious elites are involved in the elaboration and implementation of 'development'. Insightful case studies from Nigeria, Niger, Burkina Faso and Senegal demonstrate how religious elites may collaborate with other development actors, such as the State, or, on the contrary, present themselves as competitors and alternatives in the development arena.
Bd. 33, 2011, 176 S., 29,90 €, br., ISBN 978-3-643-11342-9

Bea Vidacs

Visions of a Better World

Football in the Cameroonian Social Imagination

LIT

Beata Vidacs
Visions of a Better World
Football in the Cameroonian Social Imagination

Examining the social and political significance of football in Cameroon, Bea Vidacs's anthropological study goes beyond sports. Encompassing the period between 1994 and 2006, the work throws light upon changes in Cameroonians' political attitudes and interpretations of politics and of football as the revolutionary fervor of the early 1990s waned over time and increasingly turned into political disillusionment. Taking the ethos of sport as an ethnographic starting point she addresses such issues as politics, power, powerlessness, identity construction on a local, national and international scale, as well as the meaning of the postcolonial experience both on an individual and national level.

"Rich in ethnographic detail and command of relevant literature, the study demonstrates how, and with what consequences, Cameroonian football impinges upon and is influenced by local, national and global socio-cultural, economic and political realities. This original and highly informative work is pleasantly accessible in style, with a simplicity that is bound to appeal beyond the ivory tower of academia, reaching down to the very heart of ordinary folks with football at heart." (Francis B. Nyamnjoh, Department of Social Anthropology, University of Cape Town, South Africa)

Bea Vidacs is a Senior Research Fellow at the Max Planck Institute for Social Anthropology, Halle, Germany.

Bd. 21, 2010, 232 S., 29,90 €, br., ISBN 978-3-643-10431-1

BEITRÄGE ZUR AFRIKA - FORSCHUNG
Gerd Spittler, Michael Bourdillon (eds.)
African Children at Work
Working and Learning in Growing Up for Life
LIT